THE AMERICAN PRIVATE SCHOOL

THE AMERICAN
PRIVATE SCHOOL

A Cultural History

Lawrence R. Samuel

ROWMAN & LITTLEFIELD
Lanham • Boulder • New York • London

Published by Rowman & Littlefield
An imprint of The Rowman & Littlefield Publishing Group, Inc.
4501 Forbes Boulevard, Suite 200, Lanham, Maryland 20706
www.rowman.com

86-90 Paul Street, London EC2A 4NE

British Library Cataloguing in Publication Information Available

Library of Congress Cataloging-in-Publication Data Available

ISBN: 979-8-8818-0378-0 (cloth)
ISBN: 979-8-8818-0379-7 (ebook)

♾™ The paper used in this publication meets the minimum requirements of American National Standard for Information Sciences—Permanence of Paper for Printed Library Materials, ANSI/NISO Z39.48-1992.

CONTENTS

INTRODUCTION

The American Private School: A Cultural History is, as the title makes clear, a history of private (or independent or preparatory) schools in the United States. Supported by hundreds of articles written over the past century, the book strives to fill a niche in the history of education, sociology, and the United States as a whole. Documenting the fascinating journey of private schools in the United States over the past century adds to our understanding of one of the more interesting and important sites of contemporary society, I believe. Controversy has routinely surrounded prep schools in the United States, making them a fascinating subject to explore in depth. The work is truly interdisciplinary, crossing over into a wide variety of arenas of everyday life.

Told chronologically and divided into ten decades, *The American Private School* sheds new light on the important role that the K–12 independent school has played in this country over the last one hundred years. "Independent" and "nonpublic" complement "private" as a descriptor of the schools, linguistic devices intended to remove some of their exclusive nature. For the sake of convenience, I use the terms private, independent, nonpublic, and preparatory/prep interchangeably, although one could argue there are distinctions in their meanings. The subject is parsed through the voices of educators, intellectuals, and journalists who have weighed in on its many different dimensions from the 1920s right up to today. The private school is a key site of race, class, religion, and gender, and we learn from a survey of its history, revealing some of the tensions embedded in our constructed social divisions.

While telling such a big story is an ambitious undertaking, *The American Private School* represents a significant and timely endeavor. A myriad of issues related to education are in the news every day and deservedly so given the role it places in the lives of our children and the nation as a whole. Locating the subject in a historical context can do much to bring much-needed perspective into what is a passionate, emotionally charged theme in contemporary society. Education has consistently been perceived as being in a state of crisis, with schools often blamed for having caused it. Rather than a straight line, however, the narrative takes many twists and turns, reflecting the social and economic climate of the times.

It's important to note that my analysis includes numerous private schools that are not in the top echelon, and I acknowledge the reality that even in the most prestigious prep schools, students are characterized by low academic performance, chronic misbehavior, lack of motivation, and disdain for teachers and school officials. This has presented a challenge for the school's college advisors in writing reference letters for such students' admission to good colleges, especially given that parents are likely paying a lot of money in tuition and perhaps room and board.

Sources for the work rely more on secondary sources—period articles published in newspapers, educational journals, intellectual magazines, and the mainstream media—versus archival and institutional records. I'm a big believer that journalism truly is the first draft of history and that we can learn much from reporters covering the beat of a particular subject daily. In addition to mainstream newspapers, African American newspapers (the *Atlanta Daily World, Baltimore Afro-American, Chicago Defender, Cleveland Call and Post, Los Angeles Sentinel, Michigan Chronicle, New York Amsterdam News, Norfolk Journal and Guide, Philadelphia Tribune*, and *Pittsburgh Courier*) are also drawn upon. Books relating to private schools and education in general help to provide context and locate this one within the historical literature dedicated to the field.

The principal argument of *The American Private School* is that Americans have had and continue to have a love-hate relationship with private schools; we both admire and disdain them for their apparent elitist ways. Suspicion has often been directed toward "nondemocratic" institutions in this country, as they violate the myth of our being an egalitarian meritocracy. At the same time, however, we long to be part of organizations or experiences that are somehow exclusive, as privacy in all its forms carries major social currency (and is often an avenue of wealth). With this intriguing thesis and its ambitious scope, *The American Private School* aims to be recognized not just as a seminal guide to the history of the American private school but a revelatory portrait of the contradiction that is the United States.

Woven throughout the history of American private schools is condemnation for their purposeful distancing from civic life. Withdrawing from the truly miraculous development that is the nation's public school system has frequently been seen as inconsistent with the noble ideals of the Founding Fathers. Particularly attention-getting have been occasions in which public officials who espouse egalitarian principles send their kids to private schools, a case of saying one thing and doing another. Americans have an obligation to serve the common good, and many reasonably believe that choosing private schools is a selfish act that ultimately undermines society. That the vast majority of independent schools in the United States have historically been based in Catholicism has generated additional apprehensions about nonsecular education.

The decision to opt for a private school has typically been rationalized as doing what was right for one's family—an almost criticism-proof defense—but there has remained the nagging feeling of hypocrisy. Notable private school graduates such as Bill Gates (Lakeside School in Seattle), Ted Kennedy (Milton Academy in Massachusetts), and Jeb Bush (Phillips Academy in Andover, Massachusetts) have gone on to improve public schools in some way and that has further complicated the issue. I contend that institutions of privilege like private schools are disturbing reminders that we are not all middle class, as we often pretend to be, threatening one of our core mythologies. The populist antipathy expressed toward private schools is thus in some way a reflection of our discomfort with the idea of class in general, perhaps complemented by a bit of envy that we are not part of the upper crust.

Hollywood certainly hasn't been very kind to American private schools (or teachers, for that matter), often presenting them as rigid, repressive institutions in which individuality in any form is crushed by authoritarian administrations. Prep schools have been used as convenient foils against which young people can rebel and claim their independence, an ideal plot device to generate conflict and audience empathy. Presenting private schools as benevolent and nurturing institutions shaping young people's minds doesn't fit into the Hollywood formula, after all, meaning the one-sided, stereotypical films are not fair representations. Still, movies have a significant impact on our popular imagination, making a brief survey of a handful of films set in private schools released over the past few decades a worthwhile exercise.

David Resnick certainly captured this idea in his analysis of a few movies about private schools. Writing for the *Journal of Educational Thought*, Resnick considered *Dead Poets Society*, released in 1989 and set in 1959, "the quintessential portrayal of all that is wrong with private schools." In the film, century-old Welton Academy claims it's "the best preparatory school in the United States" and that more than three-fourths of its (all-white, all-male) graduates go on to the Ivy League, but its sins are many (including physical abuse of students by the principal). *School Ties*, released in 1992 and set in 1955, focused on anti-Semitism at the decidedly WASP-ish (relating to upper- or middle-class American white Protestants) and corrupt St. Matthews, which also considered itself "the finest preparatory school in the nation" (and was all-white and all-male).[1]

In the 1992 *Scent of a Woman*, viewers see no teaching or studying going on at the (yet again all-male and all-white) Baird School located somewhere in New England, with the protagonist's only education seemingly taking place during a wild weekend in New York City. This film, like the others mentioned here, features characters who come from wealthy families and were more often than not sent by their parents to an elite private school as a means to extend the privileges of their class and eventually assume their rightful place as leaders of society. The 1998 *Rushmore* is set at Rushmore Academy in Houston, where money and entitlement appear to be the typical students' primary credentials, rather than intelligence or integrity. In the 2000 *Finding Forrester*, a bright African American student is offered a scholarship to Mailor-Callow in Manhattan mostly because it is believed he can improve the school's basketball team's record. In the 2009 *The Blind Side*, the physically impressive but less than scholarly African American protagonist is recruited by Wingate Christian School in Tennessee to play on its football team.

Private schools don't fare much better in the 2002 *The Dangerous Lives of Altar Boys*. Set in the early 1970s at St. Agatha's in Savannah, Georgia, the characters in the movie rebel against the Catholic school's (and particularly Sister Assumpta's) restrictive ways via the usual teenage vices of sex, drugs, and rock and roll, as well as by creating a rather sacrilegious comic book. *The Emperor's Club*, released that same year, takes place at St. Benedict's Academy, a boys' boarding school on the East Coast, and is also situated in the early seventies. An incident involving cheating is ignored by the headmaster, as the offending student's father is a large donor to the school. Finally, things are more sanguine in the hilarious *School of Rock*, released the following year, although the principal of Horace Green (seemingly a riff on Horace Mann in the Bronx) is tight as a drum until loosened up by beer and the voice of Stevie Nicks.

Alongside such criticism of private schools, both on the screen and in real life, has been, paradoxically, a mad rush for a child to be admitted to a top one. Displaying good citizenship was one thing, but elite independents had a phenomenal track record in placing students in Ivy League colleges and their equivalents. Over the past century, Americans have played it both ways, branding private schools as elitist institutions that perpetuate and promote our vast social and economic inequalities yet doing whatever it takes to join the clubs. Are private schools agents of American-style success or one of the most divisive forces one can imagine given the path they lay for children? Private schools have thus served as a most curious phenomenon in American culture, exposing the ambiguities between civic duty and personal advancement.

The American Private School joins an impressive body of literature related to the history of the American private school and, more broadly, the history of education in this country. (Note that I do not address military schools or those that serve special needs in this work, as those are subjects unto themselves.) In his 1944 *Our Independent Schools: The Private School in American Education*, Ernest Barrett Chamberlain showed that Christianity was the foundation of many of the nation's early private schools, although most eventually became nondenominational. Founded by Protestant laymen but headed by ministers, institutions such as St. Paul's in Concord, New Hampshire; the Kent School in Kent, Connecticut; the Cranbrook Schools in Bloomfield Hills, Michigan; the Westminster Choir School in Dayton, Ohio; and the George School in Newtown, Pennsylvania, made an indelible impact on American education in the eighteenth and nineteenth centuries (and continue to do so today). Chamberlain argued that there had been four main periods of the American private school: colonial, antebellum, the late nineteenth century, and the twentieth century, the last of which when country day schools and progressive schools became prevalent.[2]

There has been a loud clamor over vouchers or tax credits for private schools in recent years, but E. G. West's 1976 *Non-Public School Aid: The Law, Economics, and Politics of American Education* showed that the debate goes back at least a half-century. Whether governmental assistance to independent schools was constitutional represented the legal side of it, the other side being that most Americans simply haven't wanted their taxes to go to private education. The separation of church and state has undergirded both sides of the issue, West argued, with both the Supreme Court and ordinary citizens feeling that the federal government has no business supporting any particular religion. Most private schools have been and remain religion-based, making this issue an especially sensitive topic in the history of American education. Even state assistance continues to generate controversy because of Americans' distaste for public money being used for private interests.[3]

In his essay in the *Proceedings of the Academy of Political Science* published two years after West's book, Thomas Vitullo-Martin explained that the issue went back centuries. "Federal aid to private elementary and secondary schools preceded aid to public schools," he noted, the first reported instance of it having taken place in 1810 when Thomas Jefferson had the Departments of Interior and War pay the rent for a Catholic schoolhouse in Detroit.[4] And in his 1999 *Between Church and State: Religion and Education in a Multicultural America*, James W. Fraser discussed how direct government subsidies for private schools, almost all religious in nature, were common in the early nineteenth century. St. Peter's Roman Catholic Parish in New York City began receiving funds from the state in 1806, he noted, but such money for sectarian schools was halted by the 1820s as Protestants gained control over public schools.[5]

Lloyd P. Jorgenson's *The State and the Non-Public School, 1825–1925*, published in 1987, also explored the tenuous relationship between education and religion (referred to as the great "Schools Question" in the nineteenth century). Catholics were successful in driving the teaching of Protestant-based religion in public schools (specifically by removing Bible reading, usually from the King James version), according to Jorgenson, but the cost was the denial of governmental funds for parochial schools.[6] Susan D. Rose's *Keeping Them Out of the Hands of Satan: Evangelical Schooling in America*, published the following year, was an ethnographic study of the contemporary Christian school movement. Rose made the interesting argument that the movement was an attempt by devout Protestants to regain some of the social and political capital they had lost as religion was eliminated from public schools.[7]

Common sense prevailed in Luis Benveniste, Martin Carnoy, and Richard Rothstein's 2003 *All Else Equal: Are Public and Private Schools Different?* After a thorough analysis of sixteen schools, public and private, the authors found no discernible differences between the two kinds of institutions. There was variation between schools in terms of accountability and classroom management, but that was based more on location than anything else. "The social, cultural, and economic backgrounds of the parents and the community in which the school was located seemed to be the main determinant of variation, much more so than a school's public or private character or, within the latter group, whether it was religious or secular," they wrote in the book.[8]

Ruben Gaztambide-Fernandez might have challenged those findings based on his experience as documented in his remarkable 2009 *The Best of the Best: Becoming Elite at an American Boarding School*. Gaztambide-Fernandez was somehow able to have such a school allow him to spend two years on campus and write a book about his time there, although he agreed to fictionalize elements that would otherwise allow readers to identify the school. As a fly-on-the-wall ethnographer at what he called the "Weston School," Gaztambide-Fernandez found that students tended to rationalize their elite status, claiming that they, unlike other students, were there to learn and had not been ordered to go there by their parents.[9]

Particularly interesting were the author's findings related to the earning of status and popularity. Through much of the twentieth century, status at an elite prep school relied on a student doing one thing very well—academics, sports, or the arts, usually—but Gaztambide-Fernandez found that it was the versatility that led to popularity. Getting good grades, playing an instrument, and being captain of an athletic team was "the perfect Westonian," a high bar to clear. The most telling parts of the book were, however, those capturing the experiences of African American and Latino students at the school. Students of color had to endure much emotional pressure and abuse despite Weston's rhetorical commitment to diversity, something that would be documented by African American alumni from such institutions a decade later.[10]

While I discuss Christopher A. Lubienski and Theule Lubienski's *The Public School Advantage: Why Public Schools Outperform Private Schools* in the final chapter, it's worth mentioning here that the book challenged one of the principal assumptions in education—that independents were academically superior to public schools. A market model of education driven by competition did not produce better results, the authors argued based on their research, claiming that demographics (economic status, specifically) represented the most significant factor in academic performance. The findings suggested that the momentum behind voucher programs and charter schools could be slowed, but that didn't appear to be the case.[11]

That book made quite a splash, given its surprising findings, as did Michelle Purdy's 2018 *Transforming the Elite: Black Students and the Desegregation of Private Schools*. Purdy traced the untold story of how seven students became the first African American pupils to attend the Westminster Schools, an elite private school in Atlanta, in 1967. Westminster, like all private schools, was not legally required to admit Black students, as public schools were after *Brown v. Board of Education*, making the institution's decision to do so an area of inquiry for Purdy. The book also explained why those students chose to blaze such a difficult trail given what they assuredly knew would be a climate of blatant, administration-approved racism. Spoiler alert: the annual fundraiser that academic year was inspired by a slave auction, while the Junior-Senior Ball was set in the "Old South" in which students were encouraged to wear Confederate uniforms.[12]

Briefly tracing the history of the private school in America from the birth of the country to the end of World War I helps to put this study in useful context and perspective.[13] The first schools in America were not public ones, as many believe, but private ones, many of them religious in nature which charged fees. (Private tutors were another option for the more affluent.) From the late seventeenth century to the early nineteenth century, these "Latin" or "grammar" schools, as they were often called, taught reading, writing, and arithmetic to boys who could be released from work or trade apprenticeships (much like the monastic schools of medieval Europe). The brightest and usually wealthiest boys had the chance to go to college after graduating, hence the name "preparatory schools" that became attached to them. These included the Collegiate School in New York City; the Hopkins Grammar School in New Haven, Connecticut; the Roxbury Latin School in Roxbury, Massachusetts; Trinity School in New York City; and the William Penn Charter School in Philadelphia.[14]

Prep schools can thus be seen as a by-product of the nation's collegiate system (also lifted from Europe) rather than as a strictly stand-alone form of education. "The type of education developed in the preparatory schools was largely determined by the requirements and educational policies of the Eastern colleges," wrote Donald W. Rogers in the *Journal of Higher Education* in 1944, since those elite institutions "in effect controlled the secondary schools by forcing them to train students to pass college-entrance examinations."[15]

The next generation of WASP-based private schools in the United States were academies, which also tended to have a religious—that is, Protestant—orientation. Bequests from wealthy individuals or families typically served as the founding for boarding schools such as Exeter, Andover, and Deerfield, which also prepared their male pupils for college. Girls could enroll in some of these academies, although their curriculum was designed to teach these future ladies the skills to function effectively in upper-class society. Growing out of the academy movement were what might be called church (usually Episcopal) schools, these too funded by wealthy patrons. Patterned after English "public" schools such as Eton and Harrow and distinctly conservative, these institutions included St. Paul's School in Concord, New Hampshire; St. Mark's School in Southborough, Massachusetts; Groton School in Groton, Massachusetts; and St. George's School in Middletown, Rhode Island.[16]

Despite catering to the cultural elite, life for students at these New England boarding schools was hardly a luxurious affair. American parents had "a tendency to overindulge their children, to want to make life easy for them, a natural result of which is that their children sometimes lack intellectual and moral and physical fibre," remarked Endicott Peabody, Groton's founding rector. There was a solution for this selfishness and softness, however. "At Groton and other schools, the students were provided with a considerable amount of corrective salutary deprivation," as David V. Hicks diplomatically described it in the *American Scholar* in 1996. Sons of the rich were treated to tiny, spartan rooms and cold showers to help produce "high-minded and public-spirited gentlemen," Hicks wrote, with the development of "wise habits" prioritized over producing brilliant scholars.[17]

Although Christianity served as boarding schools' "organizing principle providing ritual, ceremony, and a coherent set of norms," Hicks continued, they were not overtly religious institutions. Games—what we today call athletics or sports—played an equally important role, offering lessons in perseverance, courage, teamwork, and loyalty. Games "stoked the furnace of ambition and fired the will to excel," Hicks posited, so much so that he believed them to likely be "the most enduring legacy of these schools." While hardly inclusive, the schools did serve a valuable role for their time and place. "If the old boarding schools failed to teach their students a wholesome regard for people not of their own race, color, creed, or class," Hicks wrote, "at least they passed on moral, intellectual, and even aesthetic standards that enabled their graduates to discern good from evil, to judge opinions by their reasonableness, and to be discriminating in their choice of friends and amusements."[18]

Finally, there were philanthropic schools, which emerged in the nineteenth century and were more innovative than their predecessors. Over time, institutions such as the McDonogh School in McDonogh, Maryland; Girard College in Philadelphia; and the Mount Hermon School in Mount Hermon, Massachusetts, evolved into places where students received vocational guidance and industrial training. There were sufficient academics to get admitted to and make it through college, but these schools were better equipped to serve those interested in farming and the many trades.[19]

In addition to this set of institutions steeped in white Anglo-Saxon Protestant culture, however, there were those defined by alternative religions and by race. The rise of Roman Catholic schools in the nineteenth century can be seen as a response to pro-Protestantism in both the private academies and in the burgeoning public school system. (Religious zeal stemming from the Second Great Awakening had much to do with that.) Anti-Catholic sentiment was common in textbooks and classrooms, Patricia M. Lines noted in her 1986 essay in *Phi Delta Kappan*, leading Catholics, many of them European immigrants, to create their own schools. While state aid was denied, the number of Catholic schools and students grew rapidly. "From the middle of the 19th century until the mid-1960s, well over 90% of the children in private schools were in Roman Catholic schools," Lines wrote, with many Protestants seeing the institutions as a threat to public schools and even as anti-American.[20]

African American private schools, meanwhile, have had an even longer history, dating back to the 1770s. Many of the schools were founded by missionaries to spread religious thought, while others were started by abolitionists and still others to prepare Blacks to recolonize Africa. Despite slavery, independent schools thrived in the Deep South, situated in private homes due to laws based on fear that an educated African American population would incite uprisings. Black private schools continued to represent a significant component of the nation's educational landscape until the Supreme Court's landmark desegregation decision, *Brown v. Board of Education*, in 1954. Integration into public schools led to a sharp reduction of African American independent schools, although there was a revival of them a generation later.[21]

It's hard to underestimate the role that African American private schools played in the South before 1920. There were more than two hundred "academies," as they were commonly called, and given segregation and the lack of public high schools for Blacks, African Americans relied on them to receive an education at the secondary level. Supported in part by philanthropists such as John D. Rockefeller and Andrew Carnegie, African Americans established their own schools, the initial focus on the kind of "industrial education" that Booker T. Washington advised would be useful for Blacks to apply in the workplace. That changed under the guidance of W. E. Du Bois, who urged African Americans to pursue a classical education as preparation for college. Both kinds of schools could be found in the South, each serving its own purpose.[22] With that thought in mind, we can move on to our main story, which begins soon after World War I.

❶

THE 1920s: DARE TO BE DIFFERENT

"It possesses its own soul which cannot be taken away from it."

—William Thayer, headmaster St. Mark's School, 1928

In 1920, an anonymous writer for the *Christian Science Monitor* offered his or her not-very-flattering portrait of the American private school. The institution was, at its essence, "a business proposition on a small scale, with a rigidly limited ownership and control," he or she proposed, making the private school sound like a tightly run shop around the corner. The administration, meanwhile, was "an autocracy, sometimes becoming a despotism of benevolence," explaining why faculty salaries were typically skimpy but could include an unexpected raise. The students who came forth from such schools were equally unimpressive, at least in terms of their subsequent relationship with their alma mater. "Its body of graduates is too inconsiderable, too scattered, and too lacking in spirit to function effectively in connection with school matters," the piece continued, a rather uninspiring description of the alumni of this academic dictatorship.[1]

Such was some of the more acerbic criticism directed toward the American private school as the 1920s began. Private schools took a wild ride through the Roaring Twenties, both vigorously attacked and enthusiastically praised. Regardless of what was being said or written about them, however, enrollment rose steadily through the decade, creating what can be said to be the modern era of private schools in America. Private schools proliferated in both number and type, meeting the growing demand for an alternative to public education. The story is indeed a curious one, juxtaposing Americans' enduring faith in democracy against our equally powerful drive to reap the rewards of privilege.

REAL AMERICAN CITIZENS

If some had their wish, there would be no private schools in America, at least for children under high school age. In Michigan, a movement called "One Flag, One Language, and One School" was underway, its goal to abolish K–8 private schools via an amendment to the state Constitution. The leader of the movement was James Hamilton, president of the Wayne County Civic Association, who had enlisted hundreds of volunteers to help with his cause. The workers had more than one hundred thousand Michiganers sign a petition, which was then filed with the Secretary of State, at which point the issue would be put on the ballot for a vote. "It is not a religious question," Hamilton stated, "but simply one of Americanism." Religious instruction (Bible classes, typically) as well as daily prayer were included in school curricula based on Roman Catholicism, however, and it was this that Hamilton found objectionable. Only in religion-free public schools could children at an impressionable age receive an education to be "real American citizens," he explained, implying that those of certain faiths (and ethnic backgrounds) did not fit that description.[2]

The situation in Michigan was big news in that state but, in these pre-twenty-four-hour news cycle days, many Americans were not aware of it. Leaders of private schools across the country did learn of the movement, however, and were naturally concerned that it could become a national phenomenon. Frank S. Hackett, headmaster of the Riverdale Country School in the Bronx, was certainly worried that his institution could be going out of business. "By laying down the law as to where and how a child shall be taught, not just what minimum he or she shall accomplish, this proposed statute goes to the very heart of personal and civic freedom," he wrote for the *New York Herald Tribune* in 1920. Hackett had a keen read on the value of private schools, seeing them as entirely in the tradition of the self-made man. "The measure of a private school is not how closely it conforms to the plan of the public schools, but what kind of Americans it helps to develop," he added, thinking that it was the former that was more likely to produce adults willing to blaze new trails.[3]

Hackett dismissed claims that private schools were a breeding ground of superiority of manner and snobbishness, arguing that such people would have those traits regardless of where they had received their education. The headmaster considered Teddy Roosevelt, the ex-president and Franklin Delano Roosevelt, the young fellow who was currently running for vice president, as excellent examples of the kind of people who could have chosen selfish paths but instead had committed themselves to public service. (Teddy had been homeschooled, while FDR had attended Groton, the Episcopal boarding school in Massachusetts.) The fact was that it was rarely questioned whether any successful individual had gone to elementary or secondary school; his or her success spoke for itself, suggesting there was no reason to abolish private schools.[4]

In another piece for the *New York Herald Tribune*, Hackett rejected other popular misconceptions about private schools and their students. One was that such children didn't get along with others in public schools, making private education a kind of haven or refuge for them. In addition to harboring these alleged misfits, there was the notion that private schools were a dumping ground for both lazy and "slow" students, most of whom came from wealthier families. "The fact is that the educational standards of the worthy private school are far higher than those of the average public school," Hackett pointed out. It was, most of all, students of higher intelligence who would suffer most should states eliminate private schools. Such students would get lost in what Hackett termed the "factory plan" of public education characterized by huge classes, enormous buildings, and a pedagogical approach seemingly patterned after Henry Ford's assembly line that was at the time busily churning out Model Ts.[5]

Nonsectarian private schools were of generally two types: the country day school, in which students lived at home, and the boarding school, where students lived in dormitories on campus. Each was at the time heavily restricted to white Protestants, making a person of color or Jew a rare sight. Catholics could of course be found at schools run by dioceses or religious organizations as well as at the many parochial schools, which were typically managed by local parishes. (I make a distinction between Catholic schools and parochial schools in this book.) Boarding schools date back to the early days of the republic in New England, borrowing on the English tradition. Exeter Academy (now Phillips Exeter Academy), founded in 1781 in New Hampshire, and Andover (now Phillips Academy Andover), founded in 1778 in Massachusetts, served as the model for generations of Yankees.[6]

Almost a century and a half later, boarding schools could be found in almost every state in the nation. Beginning in 1914 with the onset of

World War I, boarding schools had reached their zenith in both demand and prestige. Military schools were understandably packed to the gills, and their popularity spilled over to nonmilitary boarding schools. Many fathers had enlisted, the basis for sending a child to a boarding school, and the robust wartime economy allowed a good number of families to afford the not-insignificant tuition. (Exeter charged \$800–\$1,000, which was equal to about \$15,000 in today's dollars.) Boarding schools, now flush with money, invested in new buildings, additions to old ones, and athletic fields. (Many dormitories were made fireproof, taking advantage of new, nonwooden construction technology.) Students came from near and far to attend better boarding schools, with applicants exceeding the number of open spots.[7]

Even though boarding schools were as old as the nation itself, it's fair to say they were not a particularly American idea. Americans held home life as sacred, and the prospect of sending a child away to school, as the English elite did, was not a natural thought. Social forces were making the more well-to-do consider the option, however. Cities were becoming increasingly urbanized, with millions of immigrants still pouring in from Europe. (The Immigration Act of 1924 would change that through quotas.) At the same time, it was becoming increasingly clear that the rural one-room schoolhouse no longer could serve their communities particularly well. Boarding schools were benefiting from these two quite different expressions of modernity, resulting in high enrollment of both city and country folk.[8]

Parents who thought their child would necessarily flourish in a prestigious boarding school were often proved wrong. Distance from home could help but, at the end of the day, a poor student was generally a poor student. The key difference between a boarding school and a country day school had less to do with instruction, and more with the fact that students spent all of their time at the former, save for vacations and summers. Still, there was more instruction at boarding schools than at country day schools; the school week was typically six days, with more hours of instruction on those days. A school day went from early morning to early afternoon and, after a couple of hours of free time, more instruction from late afternoon to early evening.[9]

The common denominator between boarding schools and country day schools was that both really were in the country. Unlike rural schools, however, boarding schools made full use of their environment; athletic fields were big, and participation in sports was strongly encouraged. Coaches in a wide range of sports were typically on staff. Long hikes were a mainstay, and even hunting was sometimes included in a school day. Nature study, forestry, and farming were other opportunities for students to take in the great outdoors.[10]

Parents weighing the choice between boarding school and country day school had to think long and hard about what would better serve their child (and the family). The truth was that in some families, a child didn't play a particularly important role, or the parents didn't have much interest in being parents. In such families, boarding school would likely be a good choice, as such schools were known to help young people develop self-discipline, a sense of duty, and an ethos of public service. Children from even the most close-knit families were known to go to boarding school; however, the principal draw was the close associations they would almost certainly cultivate. Experience and competition among peers—on a team or in a student organization, say—was perceived as more valuable than the guidance even the best parents could provide. For boys, Exeter, Andover, and Mount Hermon (now Northfield Mount Hermon) were the cream of the crop in the early twenties, while for girls it was Abbott (which merged with Phillips Academy in 1973), Westover (still extant), and Northfield (which merged with Mount Hermon in 1971).[11]

ONE OF OUR FUNDAMENTAL AND SUSTAINING INSTITUTIONS

While boarding schools date back to the late eighteenth century, country day schools were a more recent phenomenon. The first one was reportedly the Gilman Country School, founded in 1897 on seventy-five acres in the Roland Park district of Baltimore. The story goes that a group of parents who had missed their sons and their friends while they were away at boarding school for the year sought to create what they saw as the best of both worlds in education. A school for boys during the day in the country (that area was decidedly less urban at the time) would offer all the academic benefits and extracurricular activities of boarding school but without the boarding, a formula that at least seventy-five more institutions across the country would follow over the next couple of decades. New York City alone had four country day schools in 1920—Riverdale, Barnard, Horace Mann, and "Poly Prep"—all for boys. Day schools charged about $275 for the year, which was equal to about $5,000 today.[12]

In his pursuit of "One Flag, One Language, and One School," James Hamilton made no distinction between boarding schools and country day schools. The movement was rooted in the "100 percent Americanism" movement that had swept the country during and immediately following World War I. The Wilson administration had recognized that the entry of the United States into the war could serve not just foreign but domestic objectives, specifically the uniting of an increasingly diverse population. (The metaphor of the nation being a "melting pot" was very much in vogue at the time.) The president thus perceived the Great War not only as a fight for American liberalism but as an opportunity to bring the country's divided factions, many of them ethnic-based, closer together. With broad support of the war, Wilson believed, "nagging social conflicts would be swept away in a wave of patriotic unity," easing the administration's implementation of domestic policies, particularly among the many immigrants.[13]

Overzealous organizations such as the Committee on Public Information and the American Patriotic League, however, pressured many Americans to adopt their ideological stance. The former, led by George Creel, distributed millions of pamphlets proclaiming the virtues of democracy over European-style autocracy and orchestrated the efforts of some 7.5 million public speeches at theaters, clubs, and concerts, preaching "100 percent Americanism." The American Patriotic League, with a membership of 250,000, was a quasi-official federal agency, the largest of various organizations created to promote Wilson's brand of patriotism. Fears of "alien," subversive ideologies, specifically Bolshevism and anarchy, ran rampant, with labor strikes and leftist "radicalism" all part of what has been called "The First Red Scare."[14]

Many of the huge numbers of Americans who had emigrated from Europe had been put under particular pressure to demonstrate public support for the war, as overt signs of ethnicity were considered an indication of potential divided allegiances. Over the twenty-five years preceding the onset of World War I, about eight million immigrants came to the United States, most of them from countries that would be involved in the war. Retaining loyalties to the Old World, the administration believed, was a catalyst for a divided population split along the lines of ethnic background. National origin was officially perceived as the basis for what Wilson called "camps of hostile opinion, hot against each other." For these suspect groups, buying Liberty bonds, singing the national anthem in public, and displaying the American flag became important symbols of national loyalty, as well as measures of avoiding psychological or physical threats. Americans of recent foreign origin and their children were thus effectively forced to show their undivided allegiance to the United States.[15]

Hamilton's effort to apply lingering sentiment toward "100 percent Americanism" was thus directly related to the majority of students, faculty, and staff who populated private and especially parochial schools—Catholics or immigrants. (It was not unusual for nuns in their full habits to serve as teachers.) This was the third attempt to put the issue to a vote; the two previous attempts having been rejected on legal technicalities.[16] It appeared that Hamilton had received enough signatures to get the question on the ballot for a vote in the fall of 1920, however, much to the chagrin of Roman Catholic leaders in the state who were leading a campaign against the proposition.[17] The measure did not pass (it received 36.7 percent of the votes cast), but the indefatigable Hamilton was at it again two years later. "There is no place in a democracy for divided allegiance on the part of any of its citizens toward such an institution as the public school," he said before the 1922 vote, perfectly fine with private school students meeting after the regular school day or on any of the 180 days of the year when there was no public school.[18]

Michigan wasn't the only state considering eliminating private schools between kindergarten and eighth grade. The measure was on the fall 1922 ballot in Oregon, with the additional proposal that English be the only language taught to grammar school-age students. In Oregon, it was the Masons and its Scottish Rite branch that were leading the movement, which received more than enough signatures to get on that state's ballot. In Michigan, legal technicalities obstructed the issue going to a popular vote that year and again in 1923. In Oregon, the measure was passed, although that state's Supreme Court ultimately declared it unconstitutional.[19]

While private schools would not be legally abolished in either state, the criticism directed toward them appeared to encourage defenders to point out what Walter S. Hinchman called their "distinctive merits." Private schools were smaller, had greater financial resources, and spent more money than public schools, he pointed out, all of this resulting in their students receiving more attention from teachers than possible in most public schools. Paradoxically, perhaps, there was also the expectation for private school students to be self-reliant; this is another good quality to nurture. Finally, there was more awareness of the private school as being a community and that each student should serve it in some way, this too something that would later pay dividends not just for the individual but for society.[20]

For Eloise R. Tremain, president of the National Association of the Principals of Schools for Girls, it was the higher academic standards of private schools that facilitated what she called "broad mental training." Even if not overtly religious, many if not most boarding schools also required a morning or evening visit to the chapel, for Tremain an experience that added "a quickening of the spirit." Daily exercise and an awareness of health in general too was typically woven into private school life, contributing to the development of each student's overall character.[21]

M. Mercer Kendig, who served as director of *Red Book Magazine*'s School Department, could not give higher praise to the nation's private schools. "The American private school is one of the greatest factors in the civilization and welfare of the world and today holds its place as one of our fundamental and sustaining institutions," she wrote in 1922 in that magazine. Because private schools were selective, brighter students were not held back by what Kendig diplomatically called "lesser intellects." In short, private schools were designed to produce leaders, something the country could certainly use more of. Kendig unapologetically explained that *Red Book* would each month give a voice to educators who espoused the benefits of private schools as a service to its readers.[22]

One might have thought that Angelo Patri, as the principal of Public School 45 in the Bronx, would pooh-pooh private schools by casting them as elitist institutions for the privileged class. But Patri, who was also the author of *A Schoolmaster in the Great City*, believed that just as with everything else, one got what one paid for in education. Parents ideally placed their child in the school that was best for that child, as education shapes an individual for life. Most public schools simply were no match for private schools, whether determined by physical environment, breadth of study, commitment of teachers, or standard of ethics. Public schools could learn a lot from studying private schools, Patri concluded, thinking the latter was well worth the investment.[23]

HIGHER EDUCATIONAL PRIVILEGES

Such support for private schools was just one side of the story, however. Olive M. Jones, another public school principal in New York City who had recently been elected president of the National Education Association (NEA), saw things entirely differently from her colleague in the Bronx. Jones had heard many graduates of private schools boast that they had "never been inside a public school," an observation that she found not just elitist but misguided. Rather than private schools, it was American public schools that served as an ideal training ground for work (and world citizenship, she added) in that the latter inherently brought together those with opposing viewpoints. Private schools were certainly thorough and had devoted teachers but were "not calculated to build the child's capacity for vision, inspiration, and independent thinking."[24]

Jones's view was consistent with popular opinion that private schools were insular in nature—a function of their selectivity and organizational culture—while public schools were open-minded and egalitarian. Henry N. MacCracken, president of Vassar College in 1923, disagreed with this assessment. Students at his college had attended private and public high schools in roughly equal numbers, allowing him to draw conclusions that he believed were valid. Public high schools were not the democratic institutions many claimed; fraternities and sororities were very much in vogue in such schools at the time, and student bodies were typically divided into numerous cliques in which membership was closely guarded. While there could very well be subcultures within private schools, a collective *esprit de corps* tended to permeate those institutions, making them just as or even more "democratic" than the community public school.[25]

Indeed, because public schools were run by state-appointed officials seeking consistency and efficiency, it was those that could be said to be more uniform and conformist. That was the opinion of S. P. Capen, Chancellor of the University of Buffalo. Every private school, on the other hand, was unique, having its history, traditions, and ways of doing things. There was no private school "system" as there was for public schools; this alone was an indication of how it was the former which was likely to produce citizens who, as Capen put it, "dare to be different."[26]

If daring to be different wasn't enough, there was the simpler fact that private schools saved taxpayer money, in that they drew a certain number of students from the public school system. (More schools, teachers, and materials would be needed if that weren't the case.) In Michigan and elsewhere, a supervision law was in place that required private schools to have the same standards as public schools, whether that be in terms of sanitary conditions, curricula, and quality of teachers. Inspection of such was also legally required, although that, like the standards, was typically ignored by the state. An annual visit to a private high school might be made by someone from the state's board of education to renew certification, but nonpublic elementary schools were entirely left to their own devices.[27]

States were, however, becoming more interested in the general education of young people, suggesting that there would be greater overseeing of private schools in the future. The 1920s were an era in which the principles of scientific management were celebrated, with the feeling that society as a whole could and should be run more like a machine. Private schools resided beyond the control of the government, creating among some an uncomfortable sense of inefficiency and disorder. Fortunately, a large percentage of students at the best colleges graduated from private schools (as did many of their parents), perhaps saving them from extinction. As well, there was research showing that private school students were as a whole intellectually superior to public school students, another good reason to not declare them enemies to the state.[28]

The criticism directed at private schools following World War I was curious because education in America was for most of its history up to that point not public. In the eighteenth century, the mid-Atlantic and southern colonies had little interest in educating children, and even more erudite New England private schools held sway. "It was well into the nineteenth century before it was commonly recognized that the state should provide educational opportunities for all, and it was much later before public opinion was ready to demand compulsory attendance," I. N. Edwards wrote in *Elementary School Journal* in 1925. The state-based public school system developed alongside an increasingly large number of independents ranging from industrial schools for boys to finishing schools for debutantes. The common thread was that the independents cost money—sometimes a little and sometimes a lot—attracting parents who earned relatively high incomes. Professionals—doctors, lawyers, and bankers—were very highly represented, as were parents who owned their own businesses, while manual laborers and farmers were virtually nonexistent.[29]

Governments' increasing interest in the goings-on of private schools was creating a rather new field of educational legislation. One didn't have to be a lawyer to see how all kinds of legal issues could potentially be raised about what these unregulated fiefdoms could and could not do. Legislation varied widely by state but using public money for what was often called "sectarian" purposes was almost always off-limits. Private school students had to attend classes just like public school students, but a host of other issues—instruction in foreign languages, the teaching of religion, absence on holy days, and, importantly, how to tax preparatory schools, to name just a few—were in play. Supporters of private schools argued that their constitutional freedoms were being violated by such legislation or even discussion of such, but states were showing no signs of reversing their direction.[30]

It was easy to see how state laws could conflict with the interests of educational institutions that purposely separated themselves from the public domain. In Massachusetts through the early 1920s, for example, a vigorous debate raged over whether children in that state's private schools had to be vaccinated as public school students did. Christian Scientists did not subscribe to such medical treatment and strongly objected to the state's ruling. Some parents, in fact, were withdrawing their children from public school because of the issue (foreshadowing what would take place a century later when COVID-19 vaccinations became mandatory in many states).[31] The state ultimately decided that private school students did not have to be vaccinated, seeing the issue as more within the realm of public health than education.[32]

While there were many issues at stake, it was the quality of instruction of private schools in which states appeared most interested. Parochial schools spent a lot of time on religion and, with just so many hours in the day, those classes had to come at the expense of other, more practical ones like mathematics or English. There was little hard evidence to suggest that private school students were not being well educated, but that did not stop some school districts from taking action. (Again, anti-Catholic and anti-immigrant attitudes were more likely the basis for such.) In the District of Columbia in 1925, for example, it was mandated that private school instruction be "equivalent" to that delivered in the public schools, although there was considerable subjectivity in making that determination. The superintendent of public schools in Washington, DC, was given the authority to decide whether the curricula of a particular private school and the quality of its teachers corresponded with those of public schools. Instances in which students were tutored (an early form of homeschooling) presented a special challenge, with each case to be treated individually.[33]

As the government at various levels continued to encroach on the independence of private schools, an equally powerful opposing force made itself apparent. Those who had purposely bypassed public education for schools that were perceived as more aligned with their academic objectives or personal values were showing no signs of changing their ways. Stories came forth that illustrated the passion associated with particular private schools, demonstrating that states would have quite a fight on their hands should they attempt to exert greater power over what took place in these self-contained universes of education.

One such story involved the Berkeley Hall School in Los Angeles. (The school—the oldest independent one in that city—still exists today as nonreligious.) The school was founded in 1911 by two Christian Scientist sisters, with the initial twenty students taught in a cottage. Berkeley Hall kept growing, however, having to move to new, larger locations to handle the additional students. By 1926, the school had settled on a large piece of property outside the city limits, so large that parents of students could buy lots on which to build houses. The case of Berkeley Hall proved that there was a demand for specific types of private schools in the educational marketplace and that parents would go to rather extreme measures to get what they thought was best for their children.[34]

Meanwhile, *Red Book Magazine* continued to serve as a leading proponent of the American private school. In a 1926 advertisement for itself,

Red Book turned the tables on the idea that private schools were bastions of foreignness, implying that it was rather public schools that posed a threat to "Americanism." "The idea of responsible parenthood is growing throughout the land," the ad read, stating that "men and women are seeking higher educational privileges for their children." It was within private schools where the freedoms that the Founding Fathers had conceived could be found, M. Mercer Kendig, the director of *Red Book*'s Department of Education proposed, perhaps reasoning that the best defense was a good offense.[35]

Red Book went beyond rhetoric by acting as a clearinghouse for private schools across the United States. Parents or guardians were welcome to send a letter to Kendig's department stating what type of school they were interested in, whether the student was a boy or girl, his or her age and previous education, their religious affiliation, the desired location, and a budget for tuition and boarding. The magazine would reply with the schools or schools that best fit those criteria (stamped, self-addressed return envelope kindly appreciated).[36]

THE EDUCATION OF THE MODERN BOY

By 1927, private schools had progressed so far that a new magazine wholly dedicated to them was founded. In the first issue of *Independent Education*, F. M. Garver offered three reasons why private schools were needed despite the unarguable fact that they could not be legitimately called democratic. First, as a whole they provided good education, something that could not be said for many public schools strained by inadequate resources; second, because there was no board of education to have to report to, they were better equipped (in theory, at least) to employ innovative pedagogical methods; and third, in the case of boarding schools, they offered an alternative educational experience for children whose home life was for some reason not satisfactory.[37]

While Garver was obviously a supporter of private schools, he felt it was reasonable to attach a few conditions to amplify their democratic standing. Meeting the educational standards of the state's public schools was a must, he felt, and private schools should not be founded or managed as a for-profit business. As well, some kind of social service should be built into the philosophy or mission of each private school, a means of integrating them into their community and capitalizing on their usually privileged status. "Both can seek to train for efficient participation in a democratic society,"

Garver wrote in the premier issue of the magazine, seeing private and public schools as two sides of the same coin.[38]

More support for private schools came from data showing that they were increasing in number at a faster rate than public schools, and that enrollment at the former was increasing at a higher rate than at the latter. The economy had much to do with that, as the Roaring Twenties kicked in, as did the sharp slowdown in immigration. There were many other reasons why both boarding and day schools were thriving, however, and some of them were rather odd. Many urban parents with the means chose day schools for their children not because of their superior education but because a fair number of the schools had started bus services for the students. A bus picking up students at home in the morning and dropping them off in the afternoon was seen not just as more convenient than a parent taking on the task but safer than their having to walk or use public transportation.[39]

A lesser documented but very influential factor in parents' willingness to pay for school when it could be free was the belief that children would make a "better" group of friends. The truth was that the vast majority of private school students at the time came from wealthier families, an attractive thing for more status-oriented parents wanting their children to mix with the right sort of people. Not just social class but race and ethnicity were obviously built into this equation, as (nonsegregated) public schools were far more diverse than private schools. Such thinking was not limited to childhood friendships; parents saw relationships forged early in life paying off dividends later through business connections and perhaps even marriage. School administrators were not reluctant to dangle this carrot in their promotional efforts.[40]

Thankfully, there were more substantive reasons to invest in private school. More than anything else, perhaps, teachers at private schools were willing to personalize instruction for their students; it was this that many believed truly justified the expense. Such teachers were not necessarily better trained than those at public schools; rather, they were selected for their ability to treat each student as an individual who possessed a unique set of strengths and weaknesses. "The child must be carefully studied, and the effect of each method closely observed and checked before we can know with confidence how to help, not hinder the pupil in his growth," Mary Yost of Stanford University stated in her endorsement of private schools.[41] (The field of child psychology was advancing rapidly these years, helping to drive such thinking.) In some cases, the value of this could not be overestimated. Students deemed "eccentric" could very well have a tough time in the public school factory, while in a good private school, their unconventional ways could be recognized and even appreciated.[42]

Many parents didn't even consider private school as an option, whether for financial reasons, the fact that their district had adequate or better public schools, or the belief that independents were not a good fit for their child. Again, it was those children who could benefit from more attention who were deemed good candidates for private schools. Private schools were also seen as conducive to the nurturing of special talents or for getting extra help in subjects in which students were weak. It may have been too soon to know, but whether or not the child planned to go to college was a key consideration. (Preparatory schools were by definition designed to have students meet college entrance requirements.) All kinds of factors—size and location of a school, academic rigor, tuition and fees, and many more—went into the decision, with a school visit and meeting with the director or principal highly recommended.[43]

The most complex things about private schools likely had to do with money. Salaries for teachers (often called "masters" in boarding schools) ranged widely; in some cases, they far surpassed those for public school teachers while in other cases they were far below. (Each state had laws prescribing annual salaries for public school teachers, although African Americans were routinely paid less than whites.) A 1929 survey of seventy private schools revealed that the highest-paid teachers had an average annual salary of $3,869 while that of the lowest was $1,390. (About $70,000 and $25,000 respectively today.) As with public schools, private schools in the South consistently offered lower salaries than those in the Northeast. (An unnamed school for girls in Manhattan topped the list.) Interestingly, teacher salaries at elite private schools approached those for professors at the country's top universities and colleges, including Princeton, Yale, Chicago, Columbia, and Williams. Room and board were, however, often included as extras for boarding school teachers, quite a valuable perk.[44]

While it might have been considered a bad form for private schools to be conceived as for-profit businesses, as F. M. Garver had argued, the reality was that many heads of them had undeniably become rich from them. (Tuition at the most expensive boarding schools had risen to a whopping $4,000 by 1928—more than $70,000 in today's money.) It was perhaps distasteful to think of private schools as commercial enterprises, but that was what most were, much like a private college or university.[45]

Also distasteful was contemplating the slippery slope that elite private schools were located on because of their almost aristocratic position in society. In a rather remarkable 1928 book called *The Education of the Modern*

Boy: A Symposium by Six Private School Masters, a half-dozen leaders in the field were given the opportunity to offer their thoughts on the present and future of the American private school. Boys were more likely to attend such schools in preparation for college and then careers, hence the title of the book.[46]

In his essay, William Thayer, the headmaster of St. Mark's School in Southborough, Massachusetts, hit the nail on the head in terms of the two fundamental, very different directions prep schools could take. Private schools could leverage its most precious asset—its freedom from governmental intervention—by fully embracing their unique capacity to develop the intellectual abilities of young people who could then be well equipped to steer the country in a positive direction. The alternative path would be for the schools to "degenerate into a pleasant association of the materially favored classes, where athletics, good manners and social isolation are its only assets or liabilities," Thayer wrote, urging that his esteemed colleagues navigate their own institutions toward the former course.[47]

Such advice was useful given the criticism that was being directed to private schools as the 1920s wound down. In his 1929 essay in *School Review*, George A. Boyce posed the question, "Is the private school fulfilling its function?," concluding that the answer was no. Boyce of Western Reserve Academy in Hudson, Ohio, conceded that private schools did a generally good job of preparing students for college but, he noted, what that offered was "certainly not the best training in the more apparent matter of preparing for life." For Boyce, private schools were too stuck in the past, their curricula not having changed much over the past century or even longer. "Caesar's wars and Cicero's speeches in Latin, the binomial theorem in algebra, innumerable dates of military campaigns in history—for what do these a boy?" he asked. Private schools were not doing nearly enough in pushing scholarship forward by introducing new subjects more in synch with modern times, according to Boyce, and not taking advantage of their smaller size, low student-to-teacher ratio, freedom from regulations, and, as he put it, "brighter group of pupils."[48]

The most scathing attack on private schools to date arrived in a 1929 article in the *North American Review*, however. The essay, titled "John's Adventures in Education," was written anonymously by the mother of a fourteen-year-old boy who had been sent to one of the "best and most famous" preparatory schools in New England. Although John had long attended private school (in England), he lasted just a week at this new one at which point his mother whisked him away. Rather than being the best and brightest, readers learned, John's classmates spent as much time as possible reading pulp magazines, listening to jazz, and talking about cars and money. It wasn't surprising that the boys enjoyed discussing money and what it could buy; some of them had a dozen expensive suits hanging in the closets of their dorm rooms. (Seven percent of American children attended private school at the time, almost all of them coming from upper-middle or upper-class families.[49]) Criticism of private schools was about to get more intense, however, as much harder times swept across America.

2

THE 1930s: THE SELECTED
SEED OF THE NATION

"Is there anything that quite takes the place of one's Old School?"

—Millicent Taylor, 1939

In 1930, a war of sorts was taking place between Phillips Academy and Teachers College at Columbia University. Officials at the latter, which was widely recognized as the premier teachers college in the United States, had gone on the record stating that private schools did nothing but turn out snobs and that they had outlived their usefulness. Alfred Stearns, principal of Phillips Academy, responded by saying that Teachers College taught only subjects that were "worthless and dangerous without character." The back-story was that the Andover, Massachusetts–based school, which was one of if not the most elite of its kind, did not hire graduates of Teachers College for the reasons Stearns had made clear. "We don't like their product and won't use them in our schools," he said.[1]

The spat between the two leading institutions symbolized the larger conflict that was heating up between supporters of the nation's public schools and proponents of private schools. The former claimed that private schools exploited and widened the social and economic gap between Americans, and subscribed to a class-based model of education that should have been left in the Old World. Supporters of private schools, meanwhile, held that many of the nation's problems sprang from character-less, religion-free public education. Americans' love of materialism and pursuit of pleasure were the direct result of a system designed to produce automatons trained to memorize facts rather than use reason, they argued, the battle lines clearly drawn.

Private and public schools had always had an uneasy relationship, but the stock market crash in October 1929 and the onset of what would be called the Great Depression had added considerable fuel to the fire. The Depression would prove to be disastrous for privately funded institutions, as it became hard to justify the expense of independent education. Enrollments fell, and simply keeping the doors open became a major challenge for most private schools. By the late thirties, however, the national economy improved, and private schools would make a strong comeback, making them more of a presence in American culture than ever before.

A COMPLETE PLAN

The clash between public and private schools was grounded in Americans' uneasy feelings toward social class. It was no secret as to which side Porter Sargent, whose annually published *Private Schools and Summer Camps* had served as a kind of underground guide to those fields among educators for many years, was on. (The book's "Who's Who" section was especially popular.) In his 1930 spinoff, *A Handbook for Private School Teachers*, Sargent did not hold back in his praise for private schools and disdain for public ones. Those attending the latter were "shackled to the wheel of the state" and were "scholastically communized," he wrote, summing up mass education as "crass and crude."[2]

Porter was unapologetically elitist, not disguising the fact that the majority of private school pupils came from families with incomes of $10,000 or more, of which there were only two hundred thousand with children in the United States. (That amount translated to a minimum of $184,000 today.) While money and intelligence may or may not be directly correlated, financial success in our capitalist system was clear evidence of outstanding ability, Porter suggested. "This is the selected seed of the nation," he mused, obviously enjoying his position to stir up the pot.[3]

Henry Suzzallo, director of the National Advisory Committee on Education, took a more diplomatic approach to the growing conflict between public and private schools. For Suzzallo, the two were "supplements in the American educational system" which together offered "a complete plan" for parents trying to decide what was best for their child. While the numbers showed that public schools were for the majority and private ones for

the minority, the two were complementary in nature rather than opposi-
tional foes. Suzzallo believed there was a kind of romantic quality to private
schools, however; their willingness to distance themselves from the norm
was an attractive thing to many young people seeking their own individuality among peers.[4]

By late 1930, however, it appeared that the egg that Wall Street had laid
a year back was going to be bigger, potentially taking some of the romance
of what could be seen as an expensive luxury item. As part of its research,
N.W. Ayer & Sons, a major advertising agency, decided to survey preparatory schools to learn if and how they were being affected by the economic
Depression. The research showed that while some schools had experienced
a decline in enrollment for the 1930–1931 school year, most were doing just
fine, at least for now. Enrollment at vocational schools, especially those to
train nurses and secretaries, had risen, not too surprisingly given the bleak
employment situation.[5]

One may assume that George Boyce was disappointed to learn that
private schools remained a popular educational choice among wealthier
families. Boyce, who had expressed his thoughts on the matter the previous
year in his essay in *School Review*, had moved over to Teachers College at
Columbia, an out-and-out enemy of private schools. Boyce had done new
research that indicated that American private schools were inferior to public schools and were not preparing young people for the harsh realities of
modern life. The primary mission of private schools—to prepare students
for college—was misguided within the context of a broader, more relevant
view of education, Boyce argued. Private schools emphasized subjects that
college admission officers liked to see—analytical geometry and astronomy,
for example—at the expense of those that would be more useful in getting a
job—that is, the arts and sciences. Most private schools did not offer classes
in biology, physiology, drawing, and music, Boyce's survey showed, leaving
a big hole in the knowledge of the next generation of adults.[6]

At least one private school, however, was exposing its students to the real
world. The Scudder School, one of the top schools for girls in New York
City, offered a program in which students taking classes in sociology and
political economics took the job of a "wage earner" for at least a week. The
school had tested the program in 1930 and, having determined it successful,
was planning to repeat it in 1931. More reason to offer it again was that,
given the way things were going in the economy, the privileged girls might
have to enter the actual labor market after graduating.[7]

The innovative Scudder program was mostly about community service
and what was called social welfare, however. Studying such subjects was

one thing but going out into the field, even for as little as a week, was seen as a practical means to learn how to help those in need. Scudder had an impressive history of civic service and saw this latest effort as a way to extend it. During the Great War, Scudder girls, like those at many other private schools across the country, had volunteered for the Red Cross and other humanitarian organizations. Now they were reading textbooks about and discussing topics such as child welfare, housing, labor problems, immigration, unemployment, and working conditions in factories. Following that, girls worked in factories in which unskilled labor was required and kept daily dairies of their experiences. The girls found the work dull and monotonous, not surprisingly, and, as their final assignment, suggested ways to make the jobs more interesting.[8]

Such programs inspired by aristocratic *noblesse oblige* did little to ease the antagonism between supporters of public and those of private schools, however. As the enmity intensified, Margaret E. Wells, director of the Riverside School in New York City, called for a truce. A compromise should be reached between those who labeled private schools as highbrow institutions more interested in frills than fundamentals and those who saw those same institutions as responsible for their success in life. America was a big place, Wells pointed out, big enough to accommodate all kinds of approaches to and methods of learning. As well, any arena consisted of the good, the bad, and the mediocre, she added, making it not fair to generalize about either kind of school.[9]

However, a handful of schools were trying to bridge the gap between private and public schools. Beaver Country Day School in Chestnut Hill, Massachusetts, was one of them, calling itself a "public private school." While privately financed, the school recognized its responsibility to the public, an unusual position to take. Beaver Country Day was conceived and founded by a group of parents in and around Boston, an interesting thing in itself given the number of private schools within a hundred-mile radius of that city. As Eugene Randolph Smith, headmaster of the school described it, Beaver Country focused on "the whole child, educating him physically, mentally, emotionally, morally, and socially, instead of simply teaching him a few facts of subjects," words that could be found in the mission statement of many of today's private schools.[10]

A PALL OF UNCERTAINTY

It could be understood why some schools were offering parents more options in determining how their children should be educated. By the spring of 1932, the economy had weakened precipitously, a fact that was showing up in enrollment figures. Porter Sargent surveyed 250 leading day and boarding schools across the country, learning that there had been an 18 percent drop in attendance. Sargent explained, however, that given the state of the economy, 18 percent fewer private school students wasn't that bad. Industry in the United States (essentially the gross national product) was down 33 percent, suggesting that private schools were doing quite well, all things considered. New England and West Coast schools were least affected by the economic crisis, and boarding schools hurt less than day schools. Many private schools, just like public schools, had or were planning to cut teacher salaries (or teachers themselves) as budgets shrank.[11]

Wholly dependent on private sources of revenue rather than taxation, private schools were indeed feeling the pinch in the early 1930s. There were now several thousand private schools in the country, although Morton Snyder of Rye Country Day estimated that they served just 1–2 percent of the nation's children. Tuitions ranged from the hundreds of dollars well into the thousands (girls' boarding schools were typically the most expensive). It was initially those in finance who had transferred their kids to public schools but now, three years into the Depression, more professionals and business owners were doing the same as "a pall of uncertainty" hung over the scene. Admission offices were receiving considerable numbers of letters of cancellation whose quantity ran in inverse proportion to stock and commodity prices.[12]

Sargent had put the number of dropouts at 18 percent but in the summer of 1932, Snyder reported that many schools were at just 50 percent of their previous enrollment. A fair share of parents had made "tentative reservations," waiting until late September to commit to registering or not. (October 1 was often the deadline.) Just like weaker banks, weaker private schools were the first to go under. Now, some schools that had struggled through the last few years were suspending operations until further notice. To their credit, most private schools were doing whatever they could to keep as many of their employees employed, waiting for what all agreed was an inevitable recovery.[13]

Happily, school administrations did not have to spend too much time and effort chasing down delinquent parents. Credit was often extended, particularly to those parents who otherwise paid the tuition bills on time. ("With tactful insistence, the schools get their money," Snyder reported.) Endowments were proving to be the saving grace of many a school treasury; bond yields were down but still providing a source of operating revenue. Still, just staying in business was a daily concern, much like any other enterprise during the worst days of the Great Depression. Many businesses were lowering the prices of their products due to the shortage of cash, but most private schools were resisting lowering their tuition, thinking that would not be in the long-term interests of their "brand."[14]

Things became yet bleaker in 1933, however, effectively forcing some private schools to offer tuition discounts. A survey made that year by the Tome School showed that 40 percent of the nation's boarding schools were planning to reduce their rates for the 1933–1934 school year, although few of the top ones in the Northeast were going that route. The Tome School, based in Port Deposit, Maryland, adopted a sliding-scale plan, in which tuition was based on the size of enrollment. The more students, the lower the tuition, a sensible idea given that it didn't cost much more to teach and board, say, 200 pupils than 150. (The plan was modeled on the efficiencies to be gained from mass production, in which per unit costs went down with greater volume.) Tome trustees proposed that other private schools follow the same formula, believing that it was a good and fair one during the economic crisis.[15]

That plan differed greatly from Father Frederick Sill's "Kent School Plan." At the time, the Kent School in Connecticut, which was and is associated with the Episcopal Church, figured out what the average expense was per pupil and informed parents of that amount. Parents then paid tuition based on what their "conscience and income" prescribed, certainly an interesting way to go about it. Needless to say, more financially oriented private schools were not inclined to allow parents to pay what they wished. Household income had shrunk every year since 1929, pressuring schools to enroll as many qualified students as possible while keeping tuition at a level at which operating costs could be met.[16]

That was quite a challenge for most private schools given the continual drop in registrations, however. Joseph G. Branch, head of the National Association of Schools, issued a dire warning in March 1933; unless Federal aid was provided to them, he warned, most of the nation's fifteen thousand privately owned schools would be forced to close in the not distant future. (Quite a few small denominational colleges in the South and West had gone belly up or were forced to merge.) A half-million instructors were employed in these private schools, and it was the prospect of a "jobless army" joining the ranks of the unemployed that was so concerning. Branch was leading a campaign to lobby Congress for at least a loan, although history had shown the aversion of taxpayers seeing their money go to private interests.[17]

A year later, however, things appeared to be turning around in the nation's economy, with the much-anticipated recovery looming on the horizon. To show her support for private schools and their pupils, Eleanor Roosevelt, an outspoken voice on human rights and the wife of the president, appeared at the Spence School on Manhattan's Upper East Side to offer some advice to four hundred local girls. The girls, all seniors, came from Spence, Katherine Gibbs, Brearley, Calhoun, Chapin, Finch, Gardner, Horace Mann, Lenox, Nightingale-Bamford, St. Agatha, and Todhunter.[18]

True to form, given her own life's work, Mrs. Roosevelt told the girls, most from very privileged backgrounds, that they would find "the abundant life" only by doing things for other people. Roosevelt was aware that many of these girls would not have to earn their own living but urged them to "pay your own way" by serving society in some way. The wife of the president was also not above doing a little recruiting. "The government needs citizens with character to produce public servants with character," she told the audience, seemingly trading on her own experience. (After being privately tutored, Eleanor Roosevelt completed her education at a finishing school in England.)[19]

Teachers at private schools seemed to understand Mrs. Roosevelt's recipe for "the abundant life." Although some private schools were big money-makers, others were nonprofit or barely broke even, hardly in a position to make teachers rich. Still, at one school, teachers chipped into a scholarship fund for older children whose parents could no longer pay the full tuition, even though the teachers' salaries had been cut. The good news was that some teachers who had accepted pay cuts during the lean years to keep their jobs were being "refunded" by administrations that were now in the black.[20]

Good news also came with N.W. Ayer's annual study of private school enrollments. Commitments were up 57 percent for the 1935–1936 school year over the previous year, a sure sign that more families had discretionary funds and that the economic crisis was in the rear-view mirror. Thirty-seven percent of the 140 schools surveyed reported that they would be at full capacity, well over the previous year's 23 percent. Finally, 96 percent of the schools now had as many or more pupils as they had in 1934–1935, the turnaround almost complete.[21]

With most private schools having survived the hard times, journalism dedicated to the subject switched gears to helping parents choose the right one for their child. Parents Magazine took the lead in this regard, publishing a series of articles that presented the decision as a critical one. "A mistake in the choice of a school may mar the entire career of an otherwise promising individual," one article by a self-described "mother of four" warned, no doubt putting considerable pressure on already stressed-out readers.[22]

That anonymous writer in general recommended boarding school for boys, thinking that a few years away from home were "a splendid preparation for the wider freedoms of college life." A caveat was attached, however, as it was difficult for anyone to stand out at larger schools where there were many high achievers. If your child is not a brilliant student, great athlete, or natural leader, think twice about sending him to one of those A-list schools in the Northeast, as he very well might get lost in the sea of averageness. That is sadly what happened to one of her sons, as she recalled. "He craved the distinction of some unusual accomplishment," the mother wrote, and his inability to find one did him no favors in building his self-worth later in life. A smaller, less prestigious school would have been a better choice, a lesson for her readers.[23]

Parents Magazine also helped answer the more basic question of why parents should choose private school over public school. Again, a mother was asked to write such a piece in 1935, editors likely thinking there would be more credibility from parent to parent. After some friends suggested private school for the couple's two boys, the usual objections arose. Private schools produced spoon-fed snobs, she and her husband replied, and the local public school was just fine. Crowded classrooms, a rigid curriculum, and lack of attention from teachers made them rethink their decision for their younger, more introverted son, however, and off to private school he went. The couple was happily surprised by the experience. "There is a spirit of scholarly endeavor and achievement more in line with native ability," the anonymous mother wrote, finding little of the snobbishness they had feared.[24]

A year later, *Parents* again asked a mother to offer her thoughts on why parents should consider private school for their children. Like many others of middle incomes, Nina Warren Wilhelm and her husband believed that any money spent on education should be for college rather than secondary school. Good grades from a public high school would be sufficient for their two boys to get into college, they reasoned. The reality turned out to be much different. Little time was spent on preparing for college entrance exams at their local high school, they learned, partly because just 10 percent of the seniors went off to college. Concerned that their boys would flunk the test and have to spend a couple of years studying to retake it, the couple found the money to send their sons to prep school.[25]

A SERVICE TO BE RENDERED

Such personal stories accounted for the continuing rebound of private schools. In their annual survey, N.W. Ayer found that more than 80 percent of the schools reported increased enrollments for the 1936–1937 academic year versus the past year. Boarding schools, which had been hurt worst by the Depression because of their higher expense, both in tuition and living expenses, were gradually returning to their 1929 levels. Just 10 percent of them had been full in 1935–1936 but now 30 percent of them were, with a higher percentage anticipated for 1937–1938.[26]

Was all well in American private schools? Not according to Claude Fuess, headmaster of Phillips Academy in Andover. Sounding a lot like Eleanor Roosevelt, or perhaps even George Boyce, Fuess asserted that private schools like his were failing in their obligation to train students for public service. "Education should prepare boys to live and not to make a living," he stated in 1937, not proud of his own school's record in graduates going on to careers in government. The United States should be more like England in this regard, Fuess held, as Parliament was chock-filled with Eton graduates, and a startlingly high proportion of Cabinet Ministers had attended Harrow. Congress, on the other hand, was not packed with graduates of Andover, Exeter, or Lawrenceville, however, begging the question why this was so. (Henry L. Stimson, the former Secretary of State, and Thomas D. Thatcher, former Solicitor General, were rare exceptions; each had attended Andover.)[27]

Future careers in public service or otherwise, droves of American pupils were once again heading to the nation's private schools. With thousands to choose from, it was no easy task to choose which was the right one; dozens of catalogs might be scattered on the dining room table for months. (Dad or mom being an alumni could make the decision process easier.) A tour of schools made it clear that each one had a particular atmosphere or what today we might call a vibe. Schools could be formal or informal, scholarly or artsy, or luxurious or spartan; a parent or child often immediately sensed if a certain school should be put on the shortlist or if one should get back in the car as soon as possible.[28]

Most of the literature devoted to helping parents choose a private school was oriented toward boys. Boys were more likely to attend a prep school and there were many more for them, reflecting their greater chance of going on to college and pursuing a career. *Parents* did due diligence by equipping readers with daughters what to look for in a girls' boarding school. Just like boarding schools for boys, there was a wide variety in the late 1930s—big and small, country and city, progressive and traditional, college-focused or "finishing," and cheap and expensive. More so than boys, girls often wanted to attend schools where their friends went, putting that criterion at the top. Choosing a school based on the wealth or social standing of the pupils' parents was also not uncommon for girls, as some upper-middle-class mothers wanted their daughters to be among the upper crust. This could backfire, however, as A-list girls might want to have nothing to do with a B-lister.[29]

Finishing schools were in some ways a world unto their own. Finishing schools, which were sometimes referred to as "charm schools," were primarily designed to teach teenage girls of means social graces, primarily etiquette, as well as the rituals of the upper class. Many such schools were in the country in the late 1930s but only a dozen or so concentrated in Connecticut, Maryland, and Virginia were considered truly fashionable and exclusive. Finishing schools often had large endowments and were unapologetically more business ventures intended to help girls enter society than agents of scholarship.[30]

Because they targeted the super-wealthy, finishing schools had been least affected by the Depression. A palpable sense of Britishness pervaded American finishing schools, one reason why the horsey set was so attractive to them. A school was likely to have dozens of horses of its own, but girls were known to bring their own. (Fox hunts could also be part of the curricula.) About a quarter of finishing school graduates went on to college, however, evidence that the students didn't spend all their time as equestriennes or learning where the butter knife should go in a place setting.[31]

Writing for *Forum and Century* in 1938, Marian Castle did not hold back her distaste for finishing schools. Americans usually disregarded the peculiar habits of the very wealthy as they rarely intersected with the lives of the "lower" classes, but Castle felt that finishing schools and what they represented had no place in contemporary society. "They are Victorian survivals of the smuggest sort," she wrote, "preparing girls for a world that has ceased to exist." One might think that such out-of-date institutions would have died out, but they were flourishing as some of the richest and most powerful people in the nation sent their daughters to get "finished." Castle held that because they ignored the many social, economic, and political problems of the day, finishing schools were not just anachronistic but "dangerous" and "a potential menace."[32]

A few months later, Sven Nilson responded to Castle's claims that graduates of finishing schools were not adequately prepared for modern life (or even marriage). Courses in current events, economics, and government could be found at some finishing schools, he pointed out in the same publication, and "domestic science" was part of the curriculum at many of them as well. While conceding that it was unlikely that graduates of finishing schools would go on to become leaders, the truth was that precious few of those attending the most academically rigorous private or public schools would ultimately change the world in a significant way. And was learning a foreign language or gaining fluency in art history really inferior to studying organic chemistry? Nilson wondered. "No education can be an education for life unless it takes into consideration the life the individual may reasonably expect to live when he or she graduates," he posited, a reasonable argument.[33]

The one thing that certainly could not be found in a finishing school was boys. (They might be invited to afternoon tea at more progressive ones.) There were of course plenty of coed private schools, which were a popular choice for girls who liked to have boys as friends or for "shy girls" whose mothers wanted them to meet boys. (Future husband hunting also no doubt played a role in girls going to a coed school, as the median age of a first marriage for a female in the late 1930s was twenty-one.) And while teachers at an all-girls school were usually just women, coeducational schools had both men and women as faculty, something that was considered important by parents thinking it was better to have a gender mix in instruction.[34]

For both girls and boys, choosing a school was more often than not a process of elimination. The distance between home and school reduced the pool considerably, particularly given the fact that commercial air travel was not yet common. Then there was the cost, as tuition could still be in the hundreds or the thousands. Once those two basic criteria were met, there was the much tougher part—comparing curricula and extracurricular activities. After that came evaluating the intangible but crucial variable of atmosphere. With all those factors in play, it can be seen how the process could be a daunting and emotional one. Parents and the child could disagree on which school was the winner, with many a tear shed attempting to reach a consensus.[35]

Naturally, each school made its best case regarding why it was extraordinary in some way. Indeed, while administrators of private schools were educators, they seem to have picked up a lot of marketing lingo along the way. Terms like "pioneer," "trailblazer," and even "heaven" might very well be found in a private school catalog, with some admission office copywriters not above taking a swipe at the "czarist regimental regime" of public schools. Mary Elizabeth O'Conner, however, was not impressed. "How glib! How convincing! How smug! And what an advertisement!" she observed in the *Journal of Education* in 1937, questioning the self-acknowledged, much-promoted superiority of private schools. O'Conner understood, however, how many parents and the American public at large were persuaded by such puffery, thinking that hearing was believing.[36]

Private schools' criticism of public schools may have just been part of their sales pitch, but O'Conner took it seriously. The vast majority of students went to public schools, after all, making them an essential and valuable part of American life. Public schools weren't very good at promoting themselves, however, putting them at a sort of competitive disadvantage. Still, misrepresenting public schools as being a kind of totalitarian state in private school propaganda was doing damage to the nation's overall educational system, she believed.[37]

THE HAUNTING SWEETNESS

There were signs, however, that private and public schools were becoming more partners rather than rivals. Since the Civil War, providing public funds to private schools was generally considered off-limits as governmental policy, something that contributed to the divide between the two basic paths of education. Recently, however, federal aid to students in private and parochial schools had been provided through the Federal Emergency Relief Administration and the National Youth Administration, each a New Deal agency. While that was a new development that broke with policy over the past three-quarters of a century, religious schools in the Colonial and early national periods could and did receive public aid, making it a return of sorts to the original conception of how education should be funded.[38]

Floyd W. Allport, a well-known professor of psychology at Syracuse University (and brother of fellow psychologist Gordon Allport), had an especially keen read on the respective roles of public and private schools in America. Allport had great respect for the nation's public school system, thinking its success spoke for itself. Still, there was a solid place for private schools, he believed. "Because the modern world is so complex, and since children differ so widely in character and needs," Allport wrote in 1938, "there is a service to be rendered by different kinds of institutions." Over time, he explained, the responsibility for the development of a child shifted from family and home to outside experts who specialized in different dimensions of life. Health, recreation, and religion had all been compartmentalized, making it entirely consistent that a scientific approach to education exemplified by public schools had also evolved.[39]

While not in itself a bad thing, Allport continued, this division of a child's life into components inherently ignored the viewing of a boy or girl as a whole human being. "This is the point at which a private school can render an important service," he wrote, believing that such a school could "supply the homelike values and opportunities in a way that a public school is not equipped to do." At boarding schools, in other words, students formed an "educational family," with teachers acting as surrogate parents. "His fellow students are not merely inhabitants of the same classroom, but comrades in play, in household duties, at meals, and in religious activities," Allport concluded, making them siblings by proxy.[40]

Parents may have not thought about it as deeply as the renowned psychologist, but they were avidly enrolling in private schools. Seventy-one percent of private schools anticipated full enrollments for the 1938–1939 academic year, a few percentages higher than the previous year. Girls' preparatory schools enjoyed the greatest increase, with 78 percent of them expecting to be at maximum capacity (a 10 percent jump). The Depression was over, very good news for the American private school.[41]

The financial windfall that private schools were experiencing at the close of the 1930s might have had something to do with the NEA's opposition to their receiving federal aid. Private schools had received some such assistance through the Works Project Administration, but the times had changed considerably over the past five years. Willard E. Givens, the NEA Executive Secretary, made his organization's position clear in 1939. "From the beginning, the National Education Association had advocated Federal aid for public schools and for public schools only," he stated, against states using such money for private schools. A bill had been raised in the House to permit states to allocate federal funds for textbooks and some other expenses, but Givens planned to lobby against it.[42]

The Southern Baptist Convention also opposed the bill, fully aware that Roman Catholic schools represented the largest share of religious private schools.[43] Such opposition could be understood given the separation of private and public schools since the Civil War. The division between the two paths of education reflected that between church and state (sometimes quite literally), in which sectarian interests were purposely kept apart from the nonsectarian to preserve democracy and decentralize power. Additionally, taxpayer money going to an exclusive cause just wasn't a very American idea, especially when that cause appeared to have plenty of financial resources on their own.

The NEA and Baptists were going against the grain of the times, however. In 1939, there were 3,256,415 students enrolled in 2,843 privately

supported schools in the country, according to data collected by the
National Bureau of Private Schools. The number of private school students
had grown by a quarter-million in the past year alone, and some 450,000
were expected to graduate in the spring. Americans were more attracted
than ever to private schools, and those schools were becoming an ever-
bigger piece of the nation's educational pie.[44] Shouldn't private schools
receive support just like public schools given that they each helped train
the next generation of adults in their own way?

Regardless of how they were funded entirely privately, the value of
private schools could not be overestimated by some parents, although the
reasons for that varied greatly. That the British elite sent their kids away to
their version of boarding schools at an early age was for the more status-
oriented enough reason to do the same, perceiving that as the preeminent
model of Western education. A fair share of parents who were confident
that their child would be college-bound were troubled by the likelihood
that 90 percent of the students in their local public school did not have such
plans; they looked to private schools as setting higher standards of academic
performance. For others, it was more simply the knowledge that their child
would be in bed by 10 p.m. rather than getting into some kind of trouble,
as most boarding schools had strict curfews.[45]

Getting teenagers out of the house and away from rowdier friends played
a role in choosing boarding school. "When adolescence dawns accompanied
by its vagaries, its irritations, its frequent rebellion against discipline and its
definite challenge to change from a child dependent on parents into a self-
reliant person," wrote Mary Thurman Martin, "many fathers and mothers
decide that going away to school is the experience best calculated to meet
the needs of this age." Thus begins the search for a school, initially often
by having heard about a certain one or by knowing that a cousin or friend
of a friend had gone to a supposedly good one. School tours would, on the
surface, seem to provide all the answers one needed to know about each
place, with stops along the way including the dining rooms, study hall, a
classroom or two (empty), the library, the gym, sports fields and courts, and
dorms (also empty, the students being in class).[46]

But again, the physical surroundings were not enough to convey the
more important information. Were the students happy? Was the classroom
experience stimulating? The opportunity to meet with current students
or teachers was usually not offered, ignoring the fact that education was
not a solitary affair but had much to do with relationships. Some parents
were known to bring along a long list of criteria, with each criterion rated
on a scale of one to ten. The winner would be the school that received the

highest number of points. But even such a thorough, quantifiable system couldn't capture whether or not a child would find any particular school a good place to spend a few years.[47]

Most passionate about private schools, however, were probably those who had attended one themselves. Decades may have gone by, but the emotions attached to one's dear old alma mater had only intensified. Powerful memories had been forged during their formative youth, and many recalled the years spent at boarding school as the happiest of their life. "When I close my eyes, I can see the gates, rearing their mellow dignity and beauty under great trees," glowed Millicent Taylor in remembering her time at school. Sights, sounds, and smells could be forever etched in one's mind, a sensory blend that would never be erased. It may have been corny, but for Taylor and many others, years spent at the contained universe of a school away from home were treasured. "The haunting sweetness of dream days spent during one's teens at boarding school remains a special and precious thing," she mused, as profound an endorsement as one could imagine.[48] The lives of those attending boarding and day schools at the close of the 1930s were about to be interrupted, however, as another world war altered the course of history.

③

THE 1940s: A WORLD IN ITSELF

"In the midst of American free education, private schools flourish and serve."

—Eugene Randolph Smith, 1940

In 1949, a new novel titled *Lucifer with a Book* appeared in bookstores. The novel by John Horne Burns was set in The Academy, a fictitious private school that borrowed freely from the actual ones whose stature had grown considerably in recent years. Classrooms, the chapel, faculty meetings, athletic fields, social events, and dormitory life served as backdrops for the story that took place over one academic year.[1]

All quite fitting, but Burns, who was intimately familiar with private school culture, turned his story into an over-the-top satire of the iconic, often beloved American institution. (He grew up in Andover, taught at the Loomis School in Windsor, Connecticut, and graduated from heavily prep-school-populated Harvard.) There was the benefactor whose millions endowed the school, the autocratic headmaster, the judicious teachers, the bullies, the smart Jewish boy (president of the student council), and the single African American (who is expelled for a minor offense). Repressed sexuality sweeps through the narrative (Burns was gay), which presents The Academy as a hotbed of materialism and false Puritanism. The book was mercilessly attacked by critics, no doubt in part because many of the

reviewers had attended or taught in such a school and didn't like the institution so ridiculed.[2]

Thankfully, although The Academy was said to be based on Loomis,
much of the melodramatic and salacious goings on in the novel were the
product of the author's imagination. The real-life American private school
reached new heights in the 1940s, a function of increasingly resource-
strained public school systems. World War II naturally served as a major
disruption to private schools, as a good number of teachers and staff joined
the effort. Like public schools, private schools were assigned the mission to
help win the war, elevating the importance of community service. During
and immediately after World War II, however, the role of private schools
within a democracy was scrutinized by critics thinking the institutions were
too much worlds unto themselves.

A CONFUSED WORLD

The beginning of a new decade was naturally an opportune time to reflect
on the state of the American private school. There were about thirty million
pupils in the nation's educational system in 1940, with roughly 3 percent
of that number enrolled in independent schools of some kind. Private
schools had evolved considerably from their earlier days when they were
usually run by an individual, family, or partnership as a business venture.
Now, it was more likely that the schools were incorporated and operated
as nonprofits, and there was much more adherence to state laws regarding
education. Boards of trustees were typically composed of local citizens of
good standing, easing concerns that the schools existing outside of political control could be agents of subversiveness. Although not taxed, being
nonprofits, private schools saved states money by taking students out of the
public school system, a fact that headmasters readily pointed out to critics
claiming that such institutions had no place in a democracy.[3]

The core reason for being for private schools, however, remained essentially the same. Private schools could approach education in their own
particular way, an attractive thing for parents wanting their children to be
immersed in a certain religion, language, or culture. Boarding schools, for
those who could afford it or receive a relatively rare scholarship, served an
important role for families which for some reason could not easily accommodate children living at home. As well, the greater financial resources of
private schools encouraged more personal instruction than typically possible in public schools because of the latter's larger grades and classes. (The

average class size at private schools was ten to fifteen pupils, while forty to fifty students could be found in a large public school classroom.) Finally, faculty at private schools were said to be more scholarly and professional than those of public schools; the former's service orientation allowed a closer association between teachers and pupils.[4]

If all that wasn't enough, there were the bigger and better physical settings of private schools to consider. Often spread out on large grounds in bucolic surroundings, private schools could convey a sense of freedom not found in overcrowded, institutional public schools. Facilities tended to offer newer, more complete equipment, something likely made possible by a millionaire writing a very large check to show his or her appreciation to the school. With less red tape and designed to serve the special needs of a child, private schools were nothing less than a godsend to more fortunate Americans.[5] The ability for private school teachers to choose their own textbooks and other materials and employ their own form of pedagogy was yet another advantage and, if one thought about it, a more democratic approach to instruction than one dictated by state-controlled boards of education.[6]

Alongside those legitimate reasons to consider sending one's child to a private school was the desire among some of the more supercilious to separate the boy or girl from what William Oliver Stevens called "the vulgar herd." For that segment, it was the thought of their loved one wearing an Eton-style tie along with striped trousers that represented the most appealing aspect of an exclusive school. (Such a uniform, sometimes completed by a top hat, could be found in England but not likely in the United States.) The wish to purposely distance oneself from the hoi polloi did no favors to private schools, Stevens believed, as it violated the belief that we were a genuinely democratic, classless society. (The fact that the American private school actually predated the nation's public schools was not considered or conveniently forgotten by critics of the former.)[7]

Happily, private schools were starting to shed their image as a kind of country club for children. In the 1920s and 1930s, boarding schools especially had often been selected by parents for their comfortable dormitories, wide range of sports offerings, and the contacts their children would likely make. The quality of landscaping or the number of tennis courts could have been deemed higher priorities than teacher ability. That had begun to change by 1940, however, as it became clear that the United States was an actor on a global stage in which education played a major role. "Attention has turned from the structure of the buildings to the use that is being made of them," Edward Cooke Willcox noted in *Parents*, with classrooms being "called upon to produce a generation capable of facing the tremendous problems which are now presented to a confused world."[8]

With the stakes raised in education, comparisons between private and public schools intensified. The mixing of children by gender, household wealth, and generations as Americans (and sometimes race and ethnicity) was commonly and understandably seen as a strong plus of public schools, as it reinforced the powerful ideas of community and a sense of place. The principal downside was that standards of instruction in public schools could be set not for the median but, in reality, the lowest common denominator to maximize graduation rates. Worse, perhaps, was that a fair number of students wished to be anywhere else than a classroom and longed to be liberated when they turned a certain age (often sixteen).[9] From this perspective, were public schools more "democratic" than private schools, and, if so, was that necessarily a good thing?

The simple fact that private schools were allowed to exist in the United States could be taken as a demonstration of democracy. The same could not be said to be true in totalitarian countries in which the state held power over education and pretty much everything else. That was a point made by James McConaughy in a February 1941 talk made to the Association of Private School Teachers of New York and Vicinity. McConaughy, president of Wesleyan University (and former Lieutenant Governor of Connecticut), warned his audience that, regardless of whether Hitler was defeated in Europe, the United States government could assume control over all education in this country within the next decade. That was the direction that education had taken in the twentieth century as states became increasingly involved in the workings of their public schools, making it reasonable to think that eliminating private schools was next on the agenda.[10]

Two months after McConaughy made his rather gloomy prediction, Reverend Samuel Wilson, president of Loyola University, echoed the prospect of private schools effectively coming under governmental control in the not-distant future. For Wilson, it would come much sooner, a result of the United States entering the European war, which appeared imminent. Massive defense expenditures would encourage the federal government to look for new sources of revenue, he explained, with the coffers of private schools ripe for picking. If taxed at both the state and federal levels, it would be difficult for smaller private schools to offer their current services, forcing them to close or possibly merge. Already viewed with some suspicion, private schools were vulnerable to attack, and another world war served as an ideal justification to take them over or put many of them out of business through Draconian financial measures.[11]

The run-up to the war also presented an opportunity for private schools, however. Contributing to the accelerating war effort was a means for private schools to both defend themselves and demonstrate they were as American as any other kind of institution. In June 1941, for example, students from Brearley, Chapin, Spence, Horace Mann, and Finch enlisted in a campaign to raise money for recreational facilities for soldiers and sailors. The effort was led by the women's division of the United Service Organizations (USO) for National Defense, with students from Sarah Lawrence and Hunter Colleges and members from Manhattan's Junior League also taking part.[12]

A few months later, students from several private schools in and around New York again showed their support for the Allied forces. The students contributed art they had created to the British War Relief Society; the 154 watercolors and drawings were exhibited at the American British Art Center and then sold for $5 apiece. Eight pictures were donated by Tina and Betsy Jolas, twelve- and fifteen-year-old sisters who attended the Lycee Francais, a French school in Manhattan.[13]

Things would get far more serious in just a few weeks. The attack on Pearl Harbor and the entry of the United States into the war changed the lives of all Americans, including those of schoolchildren, both private and public. Two days after Pearl Harbor, New York City held its first air raid drill, with one million students sent home or led into safe spots. There had been no warning of the drill, and, with no real emergency, the kids were happy to have early dismissal. Oddly, however, private schools were not invited to take part in the drill or even notified that one had taken place. Parents, hearing about the alarm over the radio or from the police, called the schools or rushed to them to fetch their children. Administrators were equally confused, wondering why they had been ignored by the city and its Board of Education. It would have been disastrous had it been a real air raid, and administrators urged officials to include them in future alarms.[14]

THESE TROUBLESOME TIMES

While the war altered the trajectory of everyday life in the country, the show, as it is said, must go on. Children still needed to go to school, making the selection of one as important as ever. "Even in these troublesome times, when all the talk is about the production of armament and the fighting of battles, some of us must think as calmly as we can about the education of our youth," noted Rudolph D. Lindquist in June 1942. Lindquist was the headmaster of the Cranbrook School in Bloomfield Hills, Michigan, a prestigious boarding school that remains so today. Current conditions in both home and community could make "growing up a serious problem," Lindquist suggested, particularly given the disruption that the war had caused. A "24-hour-a-day-school" like his could be the solution to the problem, as boarding schools offered "a stabilizing routine" for teenagers who could benefit from more structure in their lives.[15]

Lindquist made a solid case that conformity and authority were good things when relocated outside family life, a view that boarding school administrators often proposed to parents experiencing trouble with their adolescents. The headmaster was also prepared to respond to concerns that private schools like his were "undemocratic." Public schools were hardly egalitarian, he argued, as the quality of education ranged dramatically between poor communities and wealthy ones. In some areas of the country, just $50 was spent each school year on each pupil while in others it was $200 to $300. (His school spent $500, a figure that Lindquist was sure to point out.) Private schools were more democratic than public ones in this sense, as the former took the great variability in social class and regionality out of the equation.[16]

An interesting thesis, no doubt, and one that was likely used by administrators of many private schools. Sensibly, private schools tended to be concentrated in areas of the country where more people and more money could be found. Greater Boston could be said to have been the capital of private schools in the United States, but Manhattan, because of its density and wealth, was a strong contender in the 1940s. That borough of New York City was home to the oldest existing private secondary school in the country: the Collegiate School had been founded in 1638 by the Collegiate Dutch Reformed Church. Other extant private schools on the island that were founded centuries ago were the Trinity School (1709), Columbia Grammar School (1764), and Friends Seminary (1786).[17]

Alongside those traditional schools in Manhattan were a handful of progressive ones—that is, those that emphasized learning by doing or employed experimental pedagogical techniques. These included the Little Red School House (originally started by the city's Board of Education but later spun off as independent), the Lincoln School of Teachers College, the Ethical Culture School, the Dalton Schools, the City and Country School, and the Walden School. There were the girls' finishing schools, of course, and what might be said to be their male equivalents: the Allen-Stevenson School, Buckley, St. Barnard's, and a few others. There were no less than four French schools, where American children had the chance to associate with a bona fide young French countess or duke. Choir boys, meanwhile, might be found at the Cathedral School (run by the Cathedral of St. John the Divine), the Grace Church School, and the St. Thomas Church Choir School.[18]

With the war in full swing in 1943, educators across the nation took the time and effort to offer advice on how curricula could be adjusted during the emergency. Many private schools had deemphasized the liberal arts to make room for war-related subjects like aeronautics, meteorology, map reading and interpretation, and radio communications. There was a decided shift in mathematics and science classes to potential military applications, and knowledge of foreign languages took on greater importance. Some schools were enabling students to complete secondary school in three years rather than four to allow them to graduate before military service.[19]

Schools owning plenty of land were in the fortuitous position of expanding course offerings in agriculture, animal husbandry, and dairy farming. In the summer, students could be found working on farms to help grow much-needed food during the war years. The industrial arts too gained favor in private schools, with students possessing some mechanical ability instructed to make something useful on a lathe or woodworking machine. This was also excellent training for a job in industry should the boy want to go that route, just as the agricultural courses laid a good foundation for farming.[20]

While such changes in curricula made sense at the time, the bigger issue was the very survival of private schools. A myriad of challenges had arisen due to the war, including higher costs, high labor turnover, and food and other rationing. In addition to these operating issues, students, particularly older boys nearing graduation, were on edge, not knowing what their future held. The double whammy of a decrease in alumni gifting and lower return on invested endowments was having an appreciable effect on schools' bottom lines. Rising taxes and a leveling of household income were also wreaking havoc with the financial statements of private schools in the early 1940s. As well, Americans were necessarily focusing on essentials during the war, and there was no doubt that private schools were considered a luxury item.[21]

Private schools responded to this latest threat in different ways. Many were putting their students to work, something that would have previously been deemed anathema. But with a labor shortage, such a move made sense and was further justified by the notion that some scrubbing or other job was a good reality check for the more privileged. Other schools had, for the time being, adopted a tuition system based on ability to pay, opening the door to students whose parents normally could not afford the median $1,500 annual tuition. Asking the federal or state government for financial assistance was out of the question, as that was a long shot even in peacetime. To attract more students of means, some boarding schools were pitching themselves as excellent opportunities to get used to being away from home, living and working with a large group of people, and gaining some discipline before entering military service.[22]

If looking at the glass half-full rather than half-empty, boarding schools were in a very strong position. Home life had been seriously interrupted, with fathers serving in the armed forces or having taken a lucrative job on the homefront, and mothers working in a war plant or volunteering in some way. Older siblings may have enlisted or been drafted, further disrupting family life. Public schools, meanwhile, were seriously short-staffed, further straining their limited resources. Boarding schools, while experiencing major challenges of their own, existed in a kind of a bubble, making them appear as a haven for the duration of the war. "Proverbially a world in itself and busy with its own activities, a boarding school is inevitably less close to the war than is the average community," observed Laurence G. Leavitt and Dorothy H. Leavitt in *Parents* in 1943.[23]

While boarding schools appeared to have some valid selling points during the war, private schools overall had taken quite a beating. Porter Sargent certainly believed so, stating as much in the latest edition of his iconic *Handbook of Private Schools*. In the twenty-seventh (!) edition of the book, Sargent claimed that academic requirements had been lowered dramatically and faculties were thin at best, not surprising news. Many schools had closed as the government leased or purchased them for training recruits, housing personnel, or rest and recuperation for returning veterans. Sargent found the thought of blueblood students waiting on tables, making beds, and cleaning rooms rather horrifying, although boys at Kent and some other elite schools had always done such chores. St. Mark's and Hotchkiss were loaning out some students to nearby farms; this too was not in the spirit of the prep school.[24]

EVERY WALK OF LIFE

Even if they did have to occasionally use a scrubbing brush or a pitchfork, boarding school students enrolled in significant numbers for the 1943–1944 academic year. N.W. Ayer's survey revealed that while there had been a big drop at colleges, preparatory schools for boys, girls, or both were thriving, likely for the reasons experts had pointed out. Sixty-two percent of the nation's private schools were at 90 percent or greater capacity, a very respectable figure. Interestingly, it was the more expensive schools that were doing best, a reflection of the economic war boom. Military schools were of course overflowing, so much so that some were buying or renting nearby houses to use as dorms for boys.[25]

Many cadets would after graduation go to officer training school and become commissioned officers. Graduates of nonmilitary private schools were likely to become officers if they joined the armed forces, however. According to a survey of twenty-eight thousand alumni of forty independent schools serving in the military, 67 percent were commissioned officers, a startlingly high figure. One could interpret the figure in any number of ways, including that such graduates were prone to being high achievers. One could also conclude that those with an impressive academic record, money in the bank, and connections in high places were more likely to accept the rank of captain or major than be an enlisted soldier.[26]

Either way, that two-thirds of the alumni of private schools who were serving in the armed forces were commissioned officers could be taken as an affirmation of the value of independent education. Paradoxically, the prospering of private schools during the war was occurring alongside a distinct movement toward centralization of government. One theory to explain this was that there was a growing recognition that all children, even "average" ones, were individuals, some of them inclined to benefit from a private school education. From this perspective, the right to choose which school one's child should attend was entirely democratic, as it was in the best interests of the boy or girl and, in a grand sense, society.[27]

In May 1944, *Fortune* magazine published a study of independent schools that received much attention. From a purely statistical standpoint, independent schools for boys were the proverbial drop in the bucket. Just twenty thousand of the 3.5 million secondary school students in the United States attended a private school that was nonmilitary and non-Catholic. While small in number (about half of 1 percent), *Fortune* pointed out, the students' families skewed heavily toward high income, elevating the significance and influence of private schools. Eighty-six percent of the graduates of the one hundred or so institutions included in the study had gone on to college before the war, a very high percentage. (Twenty percent was the national average in public schools.) Most of those graduates went to Ivy League or other prestigious colleges (Harvard, Yale, William, and Dartmouth accounted for a full half), more evidence that the private school was a launchpad for the elite.[28]

The *Fortune* article and the media coverage it received no doubt made more parents consider the advantages of sending their child to private and specifically boarding school. (Many of those Ivy Leaguers had attended one of the latter.) Could taking a child out of the home be harmful? Would the child lose his or her love for me? Was a boarding school worth the money? These were questions that parents asked themselves when trying to make a decision. Psychologists made the case that adolescents need opportunities for self-expression that are more likely to be found outside the comforts of home and family. Modern life, especially in cities, no longer offered the chance for building self-discipline and "character," sociologists added, more reason to start packing Jack's or Jill's bag.[29]

Such traits had been emphasized by private schools during the war due to necessity, but it appeared that they would extend into the postwar years. Discipline and cooperation in the classroom, sports, and work programs were being stressed in the final months of the war, laying the groundwork for students to ultimately assume positions of leadership. Caring for the grounds and all the other jobs students had been assigned (some were shoveling snow off railroad tracks) would pay off dividends in peacetime, authorities believed. Such work programs would continue after the war, a 1945 survey by the Secondary Education Board revealed, as they demonstrated that private schools were indeed democratic.[30]

Another way for private schools to showcase their democracy was for more of their graduates to pursue careers in government. Claude Fuess, still headmaster of Phillips Academy in Andover, revived that theme in 1946, seeing too many of his alumni and those of other top schools enter the private sector for the financial rewards and prestige it offered. The war was over, but it was an anxious time, a good reason why the government needed the kind of leaders that private schools produced. Duty and responsibility were at the heart of the private school experience, Fuess argued, making it natural for them to choose careers in public service.[31]

Another theme of the past—governmental aid to private schools—surfaced soon after the war. In 1947, Senator Robert A. Taft (R-OH) proposed passage of a federal aid bill to raise school standards in thirty-three of the country's states. The Cold War had begun, putting a spotlight on the nation's educational system, whose quality of instruction ranged widely by region. Like previous such proposals, however, the bill ran into opposition, as the use of federal money for private schools was objectional to many groups (including, again, the Freemasons). It was hard to argue against equal opportunities for all American children, but making private schools a stronger competitor to public schools was a bad idea, the opposition argued. Others suggested that the decision on how to use the funds be left to the states.[32]

Supporters of the Taft bill countered that leveling the field of public education was certainly a worthy goal but quite an ambitious one that would require much more than some federal aid. The truth was that in many communities across the country, the local public schools weren't close to providing what some parents were seeking for their children's education. School "fit," direction in course of study, a broad, nonrigid curriculum, a faculty interested in the development of the "whole" child, and counseling services were just some of the criteria that private schools were simply far superior in providing. Given that private schools offered members of the community a valuable educational alternative, shouldn't those institutions also benefit from federal aid if it was made available?[33]

Either way, less-than-rich parents had to figure out a way to pay tuition for the school that was better suited for the child assuming they had not received a full scholarship. Most private schools at the time billed parents in two big chunks, one in the fall and one in spring. Dividing a year's tuition into halves led to sticker shock for many, creating a new business opportunity for finance companies. Several companies were offering the service, with two of the more popular being the Tuition Plan and the Baltimore Plan. Annual tuition was divided monthly rather than halves, much more in line with how earners got paid. About 3 percent was added by the finance companies, but the charge was considered well worth it by parents not sure they could come up with a small fortune every six months. Some families were actually choosing less costly schools because of how tuition was billed; the monthly plan made it possible to go with their top pick.[34]

The top pick may very well have been Phillips Academy at Andover. As America's oldest and arguably most prestigious private school, Andover held a special place in the nation's educational landscape. (It remains among the top-ranked schools in the country.) For a rare feature article for a particular school, Henry F. Pringle and Katherine Pringle visited Andover in 1947, reporting their findings in the *Saturday Evening Post*. "The boys of the academy look very much alike," was their first observation, not just in their clothing but in physical appearance. The same prep look could be found in other well-known Eastern private schools like St. Mark's, St. Paul's, Lawrenceville, and Hill, suggesting they were indeed a breed apart from their public-school kin.[35]

For those not acquainted with boarding schools, especially one as rarified as Andover, the article in one of the most popular magazines of the day offered a host of interesting insights. The school was hardly a year-long summer camp, for one thing, with academics emphasized. (One-third of the students flunked out.) While there were some blue bloods, most of the students were from upper-middle-class families in which the father was a businessman. Yale, Harvard, and Princeton were graduates' top choices for college (in that order), although the class of 1946 went on to thirty-four different institutions. Drinking was not permitted but smoking was for juniors and seniors. There was a strong code of discipline, yet dinner rolls were known to become airborne during meals, with staff generally tolerant of such teenage boy behavior to let off steam.[36]

Andover and its sibling located just a few miles north, Phillips Exeter, were said to be different from other private schools by their reported commitment to preserving democracy in education. "No boy who is interested should let financial need deter him from applying" for admission, stated Andover's prospectus, a progressive idea that addressed the widespread criticism directed at "elitist" private schools. Andover defined itself as "an independent and non-denominational school whose students come from every walk of life," countering the impression that it catered exclusively to the wealthy. Almost one-fifth of the school's 750 students received some financial aid, a significant percentage at the time.[37]

From today's perspective, however, Andover (and virtually all other private schools in the country) were nowhere close to being diverse and inclusive. While nondenominational, Andover remained overwhelmingly Protestant; just ninety-six Catholics and fifty-four Jews were included in the student body.[38] No mention at all was made of race in the article and no people of color could be found in the photos that accompanied it, making it clear that preserving democracy in education had its limits in the late 1940s.

A NEW SPIRIT

Despite its noble effort to diversify its student body in terms of family wealth, Andover was a world apart from the nation's urban public schools. More teachers, equipment, and everything else that went into running a school came with more money, a basic economic fact that left a great divide in resources between public and private schools. In New York City in 1947, the Public Education Association (PEA) had had enough of the sorry condition of the city's public schools and decided to go on the offensive. Simply put, more money from New York State needed to flow to the city's schools to pay for the teachers, nurses, classrooms, textbooks, library books, and supplies to support a very large population. The PEA launched an aggressive media campaign to make its point and pressure state legislators to take action.[39]

Many parents who sent their children to private schools fully endorsed the PEA campaign. These folks wished they could send their kids to the city's public schools but, after looking at the one they were zoned for, decided that a private school was the only real option despite the high cost. (Some public schools had no playground, a dealbreaker by itself.) Bennet Cerf, the writer and publisher, was one such parent who reluctantly chose private school for his child. Cerf, along with other notables including Elmer Rice and Richard Rodgers, had happily graduated from Public School No. 10. "No parent in his right mind who can afford a private school for his child today would enter him in any but a few of the existing public schools in New York City," Cerf wrote in the *Saturday Review of Literature*. Parents were also moving out to the city's suburbs to take advantage of their better public schools, the beginnings of what would become a mass migration in the 1950s and 1960s.[40]

While it was the most populace city in the country, New York hardly had a monopoly on less than adequate public schools. (There were some in Queens and the Bronx which were quite good.) The baby boom was well underway by 1948, further straining public school systems across the nation and making more parents consider private institutions. Buoyed by the growth of private schools during and after World War II, the National Council of Independent Schools was becoming a force to be reckoned with in educational circles. The organization had been founded in 1943 (with W.L.W. Field of Milton Academy serving as chairman) and had made considerable progress in its five years of existence. About two hundred private schools had joined up along with six hundred others which shared membership through various societies or associations.[41]

While competitors in a sense, private schools understood there was power to be gained by banding together. Private schools remained under attack by more conservative forces who continued to hold that such institutions were by their very nature nondemocratic. In addition to lobbying for private schools, the National Council of Independent Schools was devoting considerable effort to improving relationships with public schools, a smart move to more firmly locate the former under the big umbrella of American education. (Many private schools were rebranding themselves as "independent schools" to deemphasize their exclusivity.) The organization also acted as a clearing house for all kinds of information relating to independent schools, including management, finances, fundraising, legal matters, and curricula development.[42]

Private schools were taking steps to change their lingering image as ivory towers for the cultural elite. "Life in a private school can be very precious but most of us in charge wish to swing our gates wide open to community needs, for we want our schools to become more democratic," wrote Crosby Hodgman, the headmaster of Beaver Country Day, in 1948. Philips Andover Academy's Adult Education Program was the best known of such gate swinging; residents living within twenty miles of the school could attend adult education classes for just a couple of dollars. A good number of schools allowed all children to use their playgrounds when there wasn't a public one nearby, and others opened up their gyms, hockey rinks, or swimming pools to public school students. Lectures too could be "come one, come all." (Helen Keller had recently spoken at Beaver Country Day.) "When the school is shared with others," Hodgman added, "the students learn a kind of generosity which is needed in the world today."[43]

Historically separated from their respective communities (hence the expression "town and gown"), private schools were attempting to find common ground with locals. "A new spirit of public and community service has lately characterized the independent school," Dorothy Greener observed in the *Christian Science Monitor*. Avon Old Farms, a private school for boys in Connecticut, for example, had been loaned to the army during the war as a rehabilitation center for blinded veterans. A few years later, it was hosting local clubs and community organizations on its beautiful grounds and holding charitable dances in its large hall. The Loomis School was doing much the same, opening its doors to the Daughters of the American Revolution, League of Women Voters, and local historical society. Choate and Hotchkiss, also in Connecticut, were lending their facilities to their neighbors.[44]

Private schools may have been better neighbors than in the past, but that didn't mean they deserved to receive federal aid. That remained the view of some education officials as the bill proposing that all schools be eligible for funds smoldered in Congress. Willard Givens of the NEA had ratcheted up his opposition, claiming in 1949 that it would be unconstitutional for nontax-supported schools to collect federal money. (Such money was actually already being used in seventeen states for helping pay for transporting children to sectarian schools—bus service, basically—but the Congressional bill would make it possible to use the funds in many other ways.) Givens stated that the Constitution was being violated in all those states, despite the decision by the New Jersey Supreme Court that the aid could be used for transportation. Edgar Fuller, executive secretary of the National Council of Chief State School Officers, was another vocal opponent, even if the money directly benefited the students rather than the schools themselves.[45]

The issue of federal money aside, the American private school had had a very good run through the turbulent decade of the 1940s. Public schools

had become synonymous with mass education, in which output was prioritized over thinking. Rather than relying on a pedagogical approach based
on the memorizing of facts, private schools were said by their supporters
as ideally equipped to draw out the natural talents and abilities of students.
With smaller classes and significantly greater resources, private schools
were well suited to deliver individualized instruction, something that was
considered much needed to safely navigate the country through the dangerous postwar era.[46] A new set of challenges was in store for the American
private school, however, one that no one could predict.

4

THE 1950s: A SERVANT OF PUBLIC RESPONSIBILITY

"The private school is a servant of public responsibility administered by private funds."

—Allan V. Heeley, 1951

In 1959, two Chicago-area parents were asked why they had decided to send their respective children to private schools rather than the free, quite good public schools. "We had a terrible time getting our oldest into Mount Holyoke, my own college," explained a mother, saying that "Jane hadn't been impelled to do all she was capable of doing" in public school. "Now we are sending our younger child to a preparatory school that accepts only those intending to go on to college," the woman continued, noting that the school "surely does put on the pressure and, for the first time, Sally's really working."[1]

The second parent, a father, had a similar story. "I always thought I'd send my kids to public high school," he told a reporter, the reason for that being that "I wanted to be democratic, you know, as we all do." Why was the man now, as he put it, "straining the family budget to pay tuition to a private school"? "I want my boys to have to work hard at the old subjects, math, English, science," he said, adding that the school had "teachers who are able to get the most from their pupils and classes small enough for individual attention."[2]

Such stories sounded not unlike the "marketingese" that could often be found in the promotional catalogs of private schools. The stock of private schools rose through the 1950s, with independents commonly seen as "naturally superior" due to their not being subject to the resource constraints of public schools. Enrollments ballooned as more parents found the money to give their kids what was believed to be a better education. Still, private schools were not immune to the political winds that blew across America this decade, and it was becoming increasingly difficult for administrators to ignore the issue of race.

A THING OF SPECIAL WORTH

Things got off to a rocky start for private schools at mid-century. By a vote of sixteen to nine in March 1950, the House Labor Committee said no to federal money going to private (and thus parochial) schools, even though the aid would have been limited to bus service. The proposal for such had been made by one Representative John F. Kennedy (D-MA), who wanted the funds to be part of the $300 million bill that had been approved by the Senate but was deadlocked in the House. "So far as I am concerned, I won't vote for the bill," JFK told reporters after the vote; his Catholicism no doubt played a role in the denial of bus service for nonpublic schoolchildren.[3]

There was more than anti-Catholicism at work in the House vote. The Cold War had intensified, fueling more suspicion toward any activity or institution that could be considered "un-American." Private schools had long been viewed by some as nondemocratic entities because of their exclusivity, putting them in the bull's-eye of more conservative politicians. Only publicly funded, *free* schools thus should receive aid, these elected officials argued, although such schools were not really "free," as many homeowners grumbled when paying their property taxes.[4]

Advocates of private schools vigorously defended their right to decide where their children should get educated. "Wasn't freedom of choice the very essence of Americanism?" they asked, adding the fact that independent schools saved taxpayer money by drawing students out of the public school system. Also entirely American was the accepted practice for wealthier consumers to spend their money on products and services that cost more because they were seen as superior in some way. Private schools were viewed by some parents as education of a higher quality, and they were willing to pay for the additional expense out of their own pockets. Turning the tables, it was not capitalists but Communists who felt it was wrong to enjoy nonessentials, making private schools wholly consistent with our economic system. Finally, all taxpayers contributed to public schools, so it could not be said that supporters of private schools were disregarding their civic duty in any way.[5]

Such economic logic did little to persuade the anti-private school contingent that the institutions fostered divisions in social class—this too labeled an un-American act. "There is an impression that boarding schools and country day schools are gilded hothouses in which the progeny of brokers and bank presidents are tenderly nurtured in an atmosphere of genteel exclusion until they are old enough to own their own steam yachts and polo ponies," the novelist John P. Marquand Jr. observed in 1950. Private school educators insisted that the formula of better teachers and smaller classes added up to more individualized and thus superior instruction, but it appeared impossible to counter the belief that the institutions were primarily designed to keep the nation's upper crust at the top of the ladder.[6]

Trying to set the record straight was Allan V. Heeley, headmaster of the Lawrenceville School in New Jersey. The title of Heeley's 1951 book, *Why the Private School?*, acknowledged the wildly different views that Americans had toward the institution. Given Heeley's position and the fact that the book had been sponsored by the Tuition Plan (one of the major pay-as-you-go financing companies), the work was not surprisingly a solid endorsement of private schools. As his definition of the American private school suggested, Heeley viewed the institution as filling a vital role in what was undeniably a complicated and diverse educational system. The headmaster of one of the most prestigious independents unapologetically stated that private schools offered education for the superior student, making them a valuable alternative to the overburdened public school system.[7]

For Heeley, the admission standards alone made it clear that private schools were about scholarship rather than elitism. Leaders would naturally come forth from private schools, but this was not their primary purpose, as some believed. As well, after the war there had been a trend in public education towards practical courses such as "Creative Living" and "Life Adjustment," making private schools' emphasis on the classics more necessary. Immunity from what had to be taught and how was another strong plus for private schools, especially given the current intolerance for thought or action that strayed from the conventional. Last, Heeley claimed that boarding schools like his were more democratic than many public schools in that the students of the former subscribed to a common culture. "The regime provides no opportunities for ostentation by the well-to-do," he made clear in the book.[8]

Heeley's strongest argument for private schools rested on the fact that people weren't equal intellectually (or really any other way). Because of that, it was the responsibility of the nation's system of education to shape students' minds on an individual basis. "It is the task of democratic education to discover each person's ability and to nourish and cultivate it as a thing of special worth," he wrote, with private schools better equipped to achieve such a thing. "The proper education of the superior individual imposes special conditions," Heeley added, believing that the absence of public support and political control of private schools encouraged those conditions to exist.[9]

The most powerful case for private schools in America was, however, evidenced by their demand. There were plenty to choose from in the early fifties, with more guidebooks being published to help parents choose which one was right for their child. There were national, regional, and local such books available in most parts of the country, the definitive one still being the late Porter Sargent's *Private Schools* (the man had handed off the job to his son). Another one was James E. Bunting's *Private Independent Schools*, which went into more detail (curriculum, daily schedule, and a photo of the main building) for each school than provided in Sargent's book.[10]

Bunting's book also provided some good data. There were about seven hundred private schools in the country, with enrollments ranging anywhere between 20 to 750 students. Total enrollment was roughly one hundred thousand, with day school tuition averaging $500 and boarding school $1,400. More scholarships were being offered than before the war; fifteen thousand to twenty thousand students were estimated to be receiving some level of financial assistance. More than half of the schools were in the Northeast (36 percent in the Mid-Atlantic and 21 percent in New England), with 18 percent in the North Central, 16 percent in the South and Southwest, and 9 percent in the West.[11]

Interestingly, the National Council of Independent Schools, the leading advocate for private schools, conceded that the industry, if one could call it that, had some major problems. "The sporadic growth of fly-by-night institutions without standards of any kind confronts independent schools with the same problems which medical schools met and solved in the early 1900s," a spokesperson for the organization stated in a 1951 issue of *School and Society*. As well, claims that the institutions were "gilded hothouses" had some basis in truth. "The independent school, like the public high schools in prosperous suburbs, sometimes deals with students whose chief spiritual staff is a silver spoon and whose main intellectual reliance is a successful ancestor," the article continued, one challenge being to "find a means of imparting to all . . . graduates a lasting motivation."[12]

James B. Conant, president of Harvard University and probably the leading authority on American education at mid-century, was certainly no fan of private schools. He held that the exclusive nature of independent secondary schools contributed to community divisiveness, saying so much to the American Association of School Administrators at its 1952 conference in Boston. Hearing about Conant's comments to that group, the National Catholic Education Association was quick to respond. "Private schools do not undermine the unity of American society," the organization declared in a statement, adding that "the goal of successful living together in the United States is harmony—not uniformity."[13]

WE DON'T GIVE A DAMN

With the Red Scare of the Cold War in full bloom in the early 1950s, however, concerns that private schools were not espousing democracy as much as they should were running rampant. "McCarthyism" was sweeping through American life including education, its goal to root out communism and Communists wherever they might exist. The House Un-American Activities Committee (HUAC) and its supporters were investigating possible subversion within the nation's secondary schools, both public and private. Not surprisingly, the subject was top of mind at the 1953 meeting of the Secondary Education Board, where some 1,400 teachers from 250 institutions had gathered. The consensus among the private school faculty was to not bow to pressure to suppress either subject matter or teaching methods in the wake of the current House and Senate investigations.[14]

Some of these administrators and teachers were not afraid to make known their thoughts on the matter, even if there had been interest in what was going on in their schools or classrooms. Russell B. Fairgrieve, headmaster of the Southern Arizona School for Boys in Tucson, explained that he had not withdrawn any textbooks from his school despite urging by "patriotic organizations." Clemewell Lay, co-headmistress of the Emma Willard School in Troy, New York, also stood firm. "We have our convictions on what ought to be taught and we follow them," she said, feeling that "students should know all forms of government and what's going on in all other countries."[15]

For Perry Smith, headmaster of North Shore Country Day in Winnetka, Illinois, the investigation of his school by the *Chicago Tribune* and

American Legion in 1950 had backfired. Accusations of un-American pedagogy had been made but served to strengthen the bond among students,
faculty, and trustees. "We know now that we can meet an attack and survive
it," he explained. David Lanier, director of admissions at St. Mark's School
in Southborough, Massachusetts, put it more directly. "We don't give a
damn," he declared, even admitting that students in one class had been
assigned to read the Communist Manifesto (but didn't like it).[16]

The US Supreme Court's 1954 *Brown v. Board of Education* decision
declaring that state-sanctioned segregation of public schools was a violation
of the Fourteenth Amendment and was thus unconstitutional would have
an even more profound impact on private schools than fears they were hot-
beds of communism. Well before the decision officials in Southern states
pondered what possible steps to take should segregated public schools be
banned. No less than seventeen states practiced segregation in education,
so it was unlikely that there would be a single course of action. Many states
were discussing ending free public education altogether, something that
obviously would have major implications for private schools. The governors
of both Georgia and South Carolina declared that should the Supreme
Court disallow state-sanctioned segregation of public schools, they would
abolish public schools and lease them to private operators for $1 a year,
permitting them to still keep white and Black students apart.[17]

It might have been worthwhile for the governors of Southern states
considering such absurd legal machinations to pay a visit to Elisabeth Irwin
High School, a coeducational private school in Greenwich Village where
a student's race was inconsequential. Elisabeth Irwin was sometimes
described as the most public private school in New York City as its two
hundred students were highly ethnically and racially diverse. Ninety percent of its graduates went on to college, an extremely high rate even among
traditional private schools. The school was essentially an extension of the
Little Red School House private elementary school which had been spun
off from the city's Board of Education in 1932.[18]

Since they were up north anyway, the governors could also have benefited from a tour of the Stockbridge School in Interlaken, Massachusetts.
The headmaster of the school, Hans Maeder, had a remarkably progressive
view of human relationships and passed it on to teachers and students. "We
are trying to instill in our youngsters a sense of equality among people,"
he explained in 1954, distinguishing between equality and tolerance. (The
former suggested there was "comparable value" while the latter implied
condescension toward an "inferior" group.) Along with embracing the

concept of equality, respecting individuals' right to be different ran through the school's curriculum and culture, with "difference" including skin color, language, religion, and all other markers of personal identity.[19]

Regrettably, such a lesson was not often taught below the Mason-Dixon line in the 1950s. Following the *Brown v. Board of Education* ruling, some southern states (notably Georgia, South Carolina, and Mississippi) continued to announce that they would get rid of public school to maintain segregation in education. Was this legally possible? Robert Kramer, a Duke University law professor, said that if such an attempt was made, it was likely the federal government would step in to dash the plan. The "Private School Plan," as it had become to be called, was on shaky legal ground, Kramer believed, as state money would still be used by the now "private" schools.[20]

More to the point, perhaps, the Private School Plan was going against the grain of the times on a national basis. Just like many white parents, a good number of African American parents were discouraged by what Gerald Fraser of the *New York Amsterdam News* called "the overstuffed and understaffed classrooms" of public schools, especially in big cities. A private (often parochial) education for their child was the obvious answer. "They are taking advantage of their higher incomes and private school scholarships which are handed out liberally to Negro students in attempts to make the schools more democratic," Fraser noted.[21]

Not all private schools were receptive to opening their doors to African American students in the mid-fifties, however, even if their parents could pay the full tuition. M. D. Cartwright, a columnist for that same newspaper, published the contents of a letter that a friend had forwarded to her which made that sentiment quite clear. A friend of Cartwright's wanted to send her daughter, Mary Elizabeth, to "one of the ivy-league, swank boarding schools," and the friend asked Cartwright, who held a doctorate, to write a recommendation for the child. Cartwright was happy to oblige, and her friend applied for admission to a "swank" boarding school for girls.[22]

Cartwright's friend soon received a letter from the headmistress of the school that explained why Mary Elizabeth was being denied admission. The headmistress made it known that her school had "no quota or restrictions on children of either different backgrounds or different races," but she worried that Mary Elizabeth wouldn't be happy there. While Mary Elizabeth sounded like "a wonderful girl indeed," the headmistress wrote, she was concerned that Mary Elizabeth "would find herself, at times, both alone and lonely." The girls at the schools were not often kind, the headmistress explained, and picking on one or two students was not unusual.

"Mary Elizabeth looks like such a sweet child that I personally would hesitate to place her in this situation," the headmistress added in rejecting the application.[23]

M. D. Cartwright had some definite thoughts on the matter which she presented in her column. "She thinks she is being honest, even when she places the responsibility for hate based on race on her little charges," Cartwright wrote, believing that the headmistress was disingenuous in framing the rejection as being in the best interests of Mary Elizabeth (who happened to be class president). Cartwright knew several African American students who were attending predominantly white private schools, with none of them finding themselves "alone and lonely." Beyond that, Mary Elizabeth was hardly the sensitive girl portrayed by the headmistress and, having attended a Northern public school, was entirely comfortable being around white students, kind or otherwise.[24]

THE PRIME SOCIAL DUTY FACING THE COUNTRY TODAY

Despite the array of social, economic, and political issues swirling around them, private schools were more than weathering the storm. Since 1920, enrollments had steadily increased save for the dip during the Great Depression, with one source claiming that 12 percent of America's youth attended an independent school in 1955. Enrollments for both private and public schools had of course soared in the postwar years as the baby boom filled and then overflowed classrooms. Over the past seven years, public school enrollment rose from twenty-four million to almost thirty-one million, while that of private schools went from 3.1 million to 4.3 million. Parochial schools were doing particularly well, something attributed to Catholic parents wanting their children to get the same kind of faith-based education that they had received.[25]

With the increased popularity of private schools had come, inevitably, specialization. While private schools were often chosen by parents for their ability to help a child get into a top college (the "prep" in preparatory), more attention was being paid to the strengths of particular schools. A school may be selected based on its form of spirituality, sports facilities, concentration on the arts, or implementation of an innovative curriculum. Somewhat like public schools, private schools had shifted more toward practicality and preparation not just for college but life.[26]

While the numbers were fuzzy, as there were many ways to define private schools (another source claimed there were about three thousand independents, with just 2 percent of the school-age population as students), there was no doubt that such institutions had become a bigger and more important part of American life. Fred M. Hechinger made the interesting case that there had been three major and overlapping developments in education throughout the nation's history. One was the creation of the public school system ("the bedrock of an open society," according to Hechinger), and another was the formation of the parochial and other sectarian schools. The third was the presence of independent schools, whose purpose was to offer educational freedom to those not finding it in either of the other two options.[27]

Of course, much has changed in independent schools in two centuries, particularly in the last few decades. Porters, waiters, and maids had once been staples of higher-end boarding schools, but that kind of service was no more. Scholarships were far more prevalent than they had once been, with some schools offering up to a third of the student body at least some financial assistance. Admission had been virtually guaranteed to a child from a family of wealth, but that practice too had gone away. Some fathers still "pre-enrolled" their sons at birth to the school they had attended, but even that didn't guarantee admission when the boy came of age. In short, private schools had been heavily democratized, a fact largely lost on critics who complained that the institutions were, more than anything else, "nondemocratic."[28]

In a sense, Hechinger continued, the shedding of the social exclusiveness that had been very much a part of the appeal of private schools had brought them closer to their original identity and intent. Academic rigor had been the focus of both the Collegiate School and the Roxbury Latin School in Boston at their respective founding in the seventeenth century, while public service had been at the core of the first boarding schools in the eighteenth century (the latter a response to the philosophy espoused by Benjamin Franklin).[29]

The claim that private schools' independence allowed for more experimentation in methods of teaching and learning was true, but in fact, most institutions stuck to the same subjects found in public education. Still, some progressiveness could be found, mostly by offering students the freedom to choose activities or courses outside traditional pedagogy. At the Putney School in Vermont, for example, students might be found doing some farm work in the morning and writing poetry in the afternoon, while getting good grades at Choate allowed a pupil to take applied classes in things like aeronautics, radio, or navigation. Time was simply more elastic at boarding schools, allowing opportunities unlikely to be found at most public schools.[30]

All these benefits may or may not have explained why enrollments at private, nonsectarian schools in the South and border states were booming for the 1956–1957 academic year. With a few notable exceptions, school administrators denied that desegregation was a major factor, claiming the usual reasons—more children, dissatisfaction with public schools, and a good economy—for the bumper crop. The Hockaday School in Dallas admitted desegregation played a role in its gaining one or two new students, as did the Allen Academy in Bryan, Texas. It was more likely for race-sensitive parents to move to the whiter suburbs than switch their child from public school to private school. Expectations had been for many new private schools to be formed for white parents not wanting their children to be exposed to African American students, but this had so far not been the case. One such school in Beckley, West Virginia, had opened but had already gone out of business.[31]

Desegregation had also yet to change much in Northern private schools. That did not appear to be the case judging by a letter hundreds of alumni of Groton received in February 1957, however. The letter read:

> As desegregation is clearly the prime social duty facing the country today, Groton wishes to do all a school can towards complete eradication of the evil of segregation. . . . In consistence with the Christian doctrine and the teachings of the Bible . . . , Groton announces its irrevocable intention to increase the number of Negroes from a few students to not less than one quarter and not more than one third of its total enrollment.[32]

Groton was in the upper echelon of private schools (FDR and the current governor of New York, Averell Harriman, were a couple of its notable graduates), making such a bold decision something that many other independents were likely to follow. "Groton pledges, if necessary, the full use of its entire endowment funds toward scholarships for this purpose," the letter continued, a remarkable thing indeed.[33]

Not surprisingly, phone calls and telegrams from the alumni poured into the Massachusetts school, most of them, no doubt, expressing concern about the trustees' decision. The shocking letter was, however, a hoax. Groton was "open to all qualified candidates regardless of race, religion, or creed," a spokesperson for the school stated, but had no plans to dramatically alter the racial composition of its student body. There were currently three students of color at the school, with little reason that would change much in the foreseeable future.[34]

If used the way the letter writer proposed, Groton's endowment funds were hefty enough to offer many such scholarships. Most private schools had no endowment whatsoever, however, relying primarily (85 percent, according to one source) on tuition to keep the places running. Some teachers were jumping ship, finding better-paying opportunities in public education or private industry. Many parents of children attending private schools had financial struggles of their own, not at all the wealthy swells of the past. Average tuition was now about $2,000, and then there were all the extras like sports jackets and train fare. "The most worrisome parental question is 'Can we afford it?'" Terry Ferrer, education editor of *Newsweek*, noted in 1957, that rising inflation made it more difficult to answer "yes."[35]

Alongside the challenge of keeping faculty members, administrators of private schools had to consider how desegregation could affect their institutions. Groton's claim about ignoring race in admissions was questionable at best based on the numbers, and there was no question that many if not most private schools practiced discrimination in terms of both race and religion. While private schools fell outside the legal parameters of the Supreme Court's federal decision, they did often receive tax and other benefits from their home state. These could be in jeopardy should state legislatures decide to apply the same policies that were required in their public school system.[36]

Seeing how the issue was being handled by private colleges and universities gave a clue to where things may be headed for private K–12s. A quota system was frequently in use in higher education, with limited admission assigned to specific minority groups. The Eisenhower administration had recently appointed a Civil Rights Commission to investigate how that system operated, however, making it uncertain whether it would be around for the long term. In his new book *Racial Discrimination and Private Education*, Arthur S. Miller outlined many of the issues in play, particularly the degree to which the Fourteenth Amendment applied. "No State shall make or enforce any law which shall abridge the privileges or immunities of citizens of the United States . . . nor deny to any person within its jurisdiction the equal protection of the laws," the amendment stated, language that could indeed reshape the contours of private schools.[37]

A NEW AND ACUTE NEED

By the 1958–1959 academic year, some private schools were showing signs of proactively admitting more students of color in the wake of *Brown v. Board of Education* and possibly further federal legislation regarding segregation. The integration of public schools appeared to be now having a trickle-down effect throughout the private school universe, in other words, even in some areas that bordered the South. After Horace Mann, a public elementary school in Washington, DC (which Vice President Nixon's two daughters had attended) integrated per the Supreme Court ruling, for example, Sidwell Friends stepped up its efforts to admit more African American students. (Nixon's daughters were sent to that prestigious private school after graduating from Horace Mann.)[38]

Brown v. Board of Education also served as a bellwether of the direction education was taking in the United States. By overriding states' control vis-à-vis segregation, there was every reason to believe that the federal government would make further inroads into the management of public schools. If the past was prologue, more "mass education" would likely drive more parents to choose private schools for their children if they could afford to do so. "Bona-fide private schools, financed by private funds and operated in privately owned buildings, are today a major success in American education," David Lawrence proclaimed in 1958, seeing further gains to be made by independents in the years ahead.[39]

As expected, the Private School Plan—Southern states' ploy to get around federally mandated desegregation—was foiled by the US Supreme Court. It was Arkansas that was attempting to put the plan involving the leasing of public schools to private operators in place, something that the Court termed an "evasive scheme." (Virginia was going the same route.) Soon after that, the Circuit Court of Appeals stopped the Little Rock School Board from shifting public schools into a private corporation, keeping the Arkansas city's four high schools closed. (Nine schools had closed in Virginia.) "The segregationists are being stymied at every turn," the *Pittsburgh Courier* made note.[40]

There was, however, one more option for the segregationists—private schools of their own design. Within a few weeks, about 125 Little Rock high school students had reportedly applied to a new private school in Conway to be run by Conway Baptist College. Conway was thirty-two miles from Little Rock, however, making even the principal of the new school unsure how many students would show up to formally register. Faculty members from the college would also teach the high school students, the principal announced, this too not a strong incentive for the displaced students to appear in Conway.[41] If those downsides weren't enough, any new school would not be accredited, putting seniors planning to go to college at a distinct disadvantage. In Virginia, some white students were attending classes in clubs, churches, basement "rumpus rooms," and, in one case, a restaurant—places of learning that were unlikely to impress an admissions officer.[42]

Needless to say, none of these surrogate "schools" appeared in a new guide to private schools in the United States. Clarence E. Lovejoy's *Lovejoy's Prep School Guide* was the latest publication to help parents navigate their way through the increasingly complex world of independents. The guide included descriptions for more than 1,800 schools, whose annual tuition ranged from $0 to $7,000. (All of the most expensive were for "emotionally upset or otherwise handicapped children.") Denominational schools were included, something not typical in previous guides, with listings for Roman Catholic schools, Jewish yeshivas, and Mormon seminaries. New York State led the way with 253 institutions, with a surprise runner-up—California, with 120. Pennsylvania (116), Illinois (114), Massachusetts (106), New Jersey (76), and Connecticut (71) were next.[43]

Lovejoy's introduction to his guide was at least as interesting as the listings. There was "a new and acute need" for private schools in the suburbs, he wrote, a function of the population shift taking place across the country. City folks were flocking to suburban areas in droves in the late 1950s, many of them to escape what they viewed as urban decline. Current residents of those areas were not pleased to see new bond issues proposed for the building of new schools or the expansion of older ones that were needed to handle thousands of new students. Because it meant higher property taxes, these issues were often voted down, creating a need for additional private schools for the new residents.[44]

Whether suburban, urban, or rural, private schools were achieving record attendance. Enrollments for 1958–1959 were up 4 percent over the previous academic year, according to Ayer's annual survey, with most filled.[45] The majority of schools had also increased their tuition, making balance sheets look very good.[46] As well, fundraising efforts were proving to be more successful, adding yet more money to school bank accounts. Not surprisingly, much of the financial windfall was going toward the first order of business—raising teacher salaries and improving their benefits. Still, operating expenses were continuing to rise and there was growing pressure to offer more scholarships, making it seem like there would never be enough money for administrators of private schools to not worry about their budgets.[47]

The strides made in fundraising served as especially good news given the rather lackluster record that private schools had with regard to philanthropy. Top schools might receive big checks from alumni to add to their already fat endowments but that was more the exception than the rule. Average private schools were not often chosen by donors, and many parents had enough trouble coming up with the tuition and expenses, much less a significant gift. Private schools considered themselves to be a "blind spot" in the universe of philanthropy, understandably thinking they were being ignored by wealthy individuals looking for ways to give away some of their money to a good cause. Recently, however, corporations and foundations were coming to the rescue by giving schools generous grants, funds that were very welcome by administrators.[48]

While keeping faculty was the first priority, additional revenues were also being spent to keep buildings standing up. New schools in the suburbs had no such problem, but many older ones in the city were showing clear signs of their age. Built in the first decades of the twentieth century for small student bodies, urban private schools were a half-century later not only figuratively but literally bursting at the seams. Space was at a premium as enrollments doubled or tripled, and facilities originally designed for students while Teddy Roosevelt or William Taft was president were now woefully adequate. Gymnasiums in particular were small and in poor condition, especially when compared with the beautiful new ones found in suburban independents.[49]

As the disconnect between academic excellence and shoddy surroundings became too great to overlook, building campaigns became a common pursuit among private schools in larger cities. With land purchased courtesy of munificent benefactors, the ground was broken and architects were hired to construct new structures in modern design, often creating a collegiate-like campus. The result was more classrooms, modern labs, bigger libraries, an auditorium, a suitable gym, and covered play spaces, although public parks would still have to be used for swimming and sports that required extensive running.[50]

Despite new buildings and greater financial stability, however, it wasn't clear sailing for private schools. The term "reform" had entered the vocabulary of American education, much in part due to a book that was published in 1955: Rudolf Flesch's *Why Johnny Can't Read—And What You Can Do about It*. The book was a scathing indictment of America's educational system, particularly the way that reading was taught. *Why Johnny Can't Read*, which would remain on the bestseller list for thirty-seven weeks, put a major scare into the general public through its argument that we were losing the Cold War by raising a largely illiterate generation.[51]

Flesch claimed to have come up with the idea for the book after offering some "remedial reading" tutoring to a friend's twelve-year-old son. The boy was not "slow," Flesch determined, but rather was receiving the typical shoddy education in an ordinary American school. After investigating how reading was taught in a public school system, he wrote up his findings, setting off a bombshell in the world of education.[52] Improving the reading skills of "academically untalented" students became a priority within education, a response to *Why Johnny Can't Read* and a reaction to the "intelligence race" embedded in Cold War tensions.

Public schools were of course the focus of proposed educational reforms, but private schools recognized that it was in their own best interests to raise their standards in reading and elsewhere. With enrollments growing and forecast to spiral sharply upward as baby boomers reached high school age, independents bore a heavy responsibility in the nation's educational system. As well, colleges were becoming more particular in their admission standards, with no guarantee that students were accepted just because they had attended a good private school. Like public schools, independents were exploring different approaches in curriculum and other facets of the academic experience to address what was perceived by many as a "crisis" in American education.[53] Such efforts were well worth the investment as the American private school entered the turbulent 1960s.

THE 1960s: ISLANDS OF INTEGRITY

"It is our business to establish and maintain with determination islands of integrity."

—Esther Osgood, 1960

In March 1960, some 2,500 teachers and administrators from 550 private schools across the country gathered in New York City for the 34th Annual Conference of the Independent Schools Education Board. The focus of that year's meeting was morality and spirituality—characteristics that the educators felt were mightily lacking in the students who came out of their institutions. "The world today needs a hardy new generation, alert and well-informed, and fired by high ideals and a dauntless moral courage," stated Esther Osgood, executive secretary of the organization. While the graduates of American private schools were pleasant and well-educated, they were at the same time "spineless young people who love security, avoid trouble if they can, and have no strong belief in anything," Osgood told the group.[1]

Harsh words, perhaps, but sentiment that was frequently ascribed to the nation's youth through the postwar years. The Cold War was still decidedly chilly, with international politics and world events heavily informing educators' views regarding the responsibilities of the younger generation. Private school administrators felt that it was incumbent for their institutions to use their privileged position to, as Osgood expressed it, "educate hearts and souls as well as intellects."[2] No one could predict the course that the 1960s would take, of course, but such a goal would be realized in a way that Osgood and her colleagues could never imagine.

WE COULDN'T CARE LESS

Educational reform was still very much a priority as the decade began, although there was no consensus on how it should be achieved and by whom. The historical divide between public and private schools had by no means gone away, with the current "crisis" sometimes serving to further separate the two camps. At a 1960 meeting of the NEA, for example, Edgar Morphet, a professor of education at Cal Berkeley, fired a salvo at private schools, labeling some of their supporters as "dishonest or subversive." Such supporters were trying to undermine the nation's public school system to attract students (and tuition dollars), he claimed. Morphet had heard public schools called "godless institutions" by private school promoters, an unfair and untrue label, and it was no secret that the latter often suggested that the former had low educational standards. One ad run by a private school had, according to Morphet, asserted that the main aim of public schools was to teach students how to use a telephone and get along well with others, something obviously untrue.[3]

Many parents did believe that private schools had higher educational standards, however, and were choosing them on this basis for their children. Ayer's survey for the 1960–1961 academic year revealed that 93 percent of private schools in the country were full, with many of the registrations having been completed before the summer. As well, 41 percent of the schools had higher enrollments than the previous year, another sign that independents were in strong demand. About 30 percent of the schools had expanded in some way, a means of accommodating additional students.[4]

Enrollment in California's private schools had since the end of World War II increased 144 percent, far more than public schools despite the sharp rise in population. Noticing the trend, the *Los Angeles Times* sent a reporter out into the field to investigate the story, with Mary Lou Loper coming back with a five-part series that editors put on page one.[5] Even if private schools were for some parents a means to express their social and economic status and for others a dumping ground for their "problem children," they still had a place in American society, Loper concluded. "If one aspect of the American Way of Life is based on the premise that every child should be guaranteed a tuition-free public education of the highest quality," she wrote, "then freedom of choice is equally important."[6]

The popularity of private schools hardly meant that many Americans believed that they should receive federal aid. Henry Cabot Lodge Jr. certainly did, saying as much on national television in October 1960. No line should be drawn "between private and public school boys," the former United States representative to the United States stated on the CBS show *Face the Nation*, with the caveat that federal funds should be used only for the construction of new schools. Lodge's view on the issue was considered important, as he was the running mate for Vice President Richard Nixon, who was campaigning for the 1960 presidential election on the Republican ticket.[7]

A few weeks later, the Democratic candidate, John F. Kennedy, narrowly won the election, putting more emphasis on his position on the issue. Since his early political days in the House of Representatives, the first Roman Catholic president had vigorously supported aid for private and parochial schools. Congress had recently not passed a bill for federal loans to non-public schools, and Catholics remained opposed to any bill for aid in which private and parochial schools were excluded. Long-term, low-interest loans to private institutions would be Constitutional, argued Catholic leaders, who were lobbying to get that provision in the latest Congressional bill. (JFK, who had proposed that bill as a US Senator, held the loans were not Constitutional.) Regardless, by running their more than twelve thousand schools, Catholics saved the American taxpayers almost $3 billion annually, they pointed out, a more than fair exchange for the loans if legally allowed.[8]

The decision on the matter lay in the hands of the US Supreme Court, with Americans strongly divided on the issue. Some notable African Americans, such as the Reverend Dr. Gardner Taylor, a Brooklyn-based Baptist minister (and only Black member of New York City's Board of Education), were clearly against federal aid for private schools. Public schools were "the true child of civil government in desperate need of funds and facilities," he stated in 1961, not wanting to see any potential aid diverted to privately funded independents. The vast majority of African American children attended public schools, of course, leading Taylor to believe that "any division of public funds for private education would disproportionately affect these young people." Taylor also feared that Southern segregationists running their own private schools would be in a stronger position to try to have *Brown v. Board of Education* overturned if they received federal funds.[9]

Others feared that private schools receiving federal aid would lead to greater de facto segregation in large cities like New York. Some envisioned a public school system comprised of African American, Puerto Rican, and low-income Jewish families alongside a private school network consisting of middle- and upper-class whites. Recent data showed that there already was a sharp division in school choice according to race and ethnicity, leading to the theory that additional financial support for private schools from the government would draw even more whites to them.[10] Jewish groups, meanwhile, blanketly opposed federal aid to private schools, wanting to keep sharp lines between church and state.[11]

Meanwhile, as the Supreme Court weighed its decision, the baby boom continued to churn out more school-age children. About 4.5 million elementary and nine hundred thousand high school students were enrolled in Catholic schools for the 1961–1962 academic year, much higher numbers than the roughly eight hundred thousand and three hundred thousand who were respectively enrolled in private schools. There were seven times and ten times as many public school students, respectively, in a massive wave that was showing signs of overwhelming the system. More happily, integration was still rolling out state by state and school district by school district, with no major incidents. "We couldn't care less," said one Little Rock student, who was white.[12]

In a climate of what was sometimes referred to as "mass education," one could see how parents viewed private school as a means of helping get their children into top colleges. That view, however, was becoming an increasingly dated one, as admission directors of upper-tier colleges assigned less weight to the high school from which a senior graduated. The "Seven Sisters" (or "Heavenly Seven") had long been considered the woman's equivalent of the Ivy League, for example, but the actual figures were surprising. The composition of the freshman class at Mount Holyoke was 72 percent public/28 percent private, and those of Barnard were not much different (69 percent/31 percent). That there were so many more graduates of public schools than of private schools certainly had something to do with the heavily skewed ratio. These percentages might have been reversed a few decades back, illustrating the more level playing field between public and private schools in the 1960s, at least in terms of college admissions.[13]

The irony was that it was more difficult than ever for a child to get into a good private school. "Twenty-five years ago, all that was necessary to get a teen-age boy or girl into a private day or boarding school was the requisite cash and a fairly decent academic record," noted James V. Moffatt, director of admissions at The Hill School in Pottstown, Pennsylvania, in *Parents* in 1961, not a particularly high bar to clear. Now, however, there were often aptitude tests, competitive entrance exams, interviews, input from teachers, and alumni considerations at many private schools to screen candidates. Just one of three applicants was admitted to good private schools and one of six to excellent schools, tough odds to beat unless one was an academic star.[14] At least one advisory firm, the Independent School Admissions Advisory Center in Wallingford, Connecticut, was helping parents and students get into the private school of their choice, an industry that would balloon in the decades ahead.[15]

Seeing graduates of public schools take spots at elite colleges and universities that had once been reserved primarily for private school grads, administrators of independents realized they had better bolster their curricula. The principal aim of preparatory schools was to prepare students for college, after all, making that the focus of new programs such as advanced courses (the precursor to today's Advanced Placement, or AP classes) and accelerated courses (in which more material was taught at a faster rate). Enriching extracurricular activities was another way that private schools were trying to distinguish themselves from public schools (and justify their expense). Colleges were so far responding favorably to such programs, boding well for students who had signed up for them in hopes it would impress admission officers.[16]

Even if they no longer gave seniors the inside track to admission to an Ivy League or Seven Sisters college, boarding schools remained a much sought-after form of education among a certain set. American boarding schools traded heavily on their older British counterparts but differed in important ways, the first being their greater popularity across the pond; about 2 percent of children in the United States attended independent boarding schools while 7 percent of English children attended either Public Schools or Preparatory Schools. Public Schools were (confusingly to us) private, and accepted students aged thirteen-plus, while Preparatory Schools catered to students aged eight to fourteen. (The latter was preparation for the former.) There were very few American boarding schools for children under age thirteen (eighth grade, typically), making the concept of sending a wee one away for months at a time a distasteful one here.[17]

THE CONDITION OF PRIVILEGE

The growing popularity of private schools in the United States, whether boarding, day, Catholic, or parochial, was leading admission officers to rely more heavily on standardized tests. Such tests were seen as a means to evaluate candidates on an objective basis, as the validity of all the other criteria could vary widely. More than twenty-three thousand students registered for admission tests during the 1962–1963 school year as part of their application to a private school for the following year. Courses to prepare students for the Secondary School Admission Test (SSAT) created by the Princeton-based Educational Testing Service were being offered, with parents advised by test administrators that being alumni of a certain school no longer guaranteed admission for their children. Getting into a top private school had become nearly as difficult as being admitted to a top college, something no one could have predicted a generation earlier.[18]

The greater competition for admission to private schools went beyond a spike in applications. The integration of public schools was making administrators of private schools take a hard look at the racial composition of the student bodies. As independents, they were under no legal obligation to integrate but it was becoming increasingly difficult to defend race-related admission standards. Encouraging more African American students to apply and, if warranted, offering more scholarships was the most direct route to parallel the integration of public schools.

Addressing the overt racial imbalance could take many forms, however. The Dalton School in Manhattan, for example, was taking proactive steps to diversify by partnering with a nursery school in a new middle-income housing co-op in East Harlem which had been predominantly rented by African Americans. Dalton was "conscious of its condition of privilege," said Jack E. Kittell, the headmaster of the highly exclusive private school, framing the program as part of its continuing effort to be of service to the community.[19]

A look at the racial profile of private schools in Washington, DC, offered valuable perspective on the situation in the early sixties. The city was considered a good litmus test of private school integration because of its poor public schools, segregated housing, and, of course, it being the nation's capital. Eight of the nine major private schools in the area enrolled at least one African American during the 1962–1963 academic year.[20] The specific breakdown on the number of African Americans with the entire student body was:

Beauvior School: eight to ten of 240;
Georgetown Day School: sixty of 240;
Hawthorne School: ten of 132;
The Landon School: one of 500;
National Cathedral School: fourteen of 450;
The Potomac School: none of 500;
St. Albans: ten of 400;
Sandy Springs Friends School: six or seven of 111;
Sidwell Friends School: seven of 1000.[21]

While the percentage of students of color was certainly low from today's perspective, it was significantly higher than what it had been a decade earlier. Private school administrators recognized that offering more scholarships was key to attracting academically qualified African American students, putting more pressure on fundraising efforts. (Entrance exams were colorblind.) Finding scholarship money wasn't always easy, however. Running a medium-sized school was said to cost thousands of dollars each day when taking into account salaries, books, materials, and equipment, with tuition as the primary source of revenue.[22]

That was typically not enough, however; financial support from alumni and patrons was often needed to simply keep the schools running. A windfall was obviously very welcome, as administrators of Mercersburg Academy in Pennsylvania could attest after receiving a million-dollar-plus gift from a particularly grateful (and rich) alumnus. Choate, The Hill, Haverford, and Lawrenceville had also recently been beneficiaries of million-dollar checks, with that kind of money usually used to construct new buildings to expand enrollment.[23]

Enrollments were indeed expanding, as were the number of private schools themselves. Between 1953 and 1963, the number of independents had risen from fourteen thousand to seventeen thousand, according to Federal Welfare Department data, with about 6.9 million or 14.3 percent of the total school-age population. (The number included parochial schools.) Not only was the high birth rate over these years contributing to more private schools and students but so were "juvenile delinquency" and racial conflict, some experts were saying. (White parents were said to be sensitive to both those issues.) Benefiting most perhaps from this growth were boarding school teachers; salaries for them had risen by about 50 percent between 1958 and 1963, a result of the strong demand for junior high–level teachers in public schools due to the baby boom.[24]

Private schools' "ace-in-the-hole" when it came to attracting more students was to flaunt its various kinds of freedoms which stood in stark contrast to the limitations placed on public schools. According to an advisory trustee of the Polytechnic School in Pasadena, California, there were four such freedoms: the freedom to select students; the freedom to match the size of the student body to the size and abilities of the faculty; the greater freedom to choose teachers without having to adhere to (often irrelevant) state requirements; and the freedom to innovate and experiment in curriculum, pedagogy, and student-teacher relationships.[25]

To that last point, private schools were typically better equipped to offer unique learning opportunities for both enrollees and non-enrollees.

During the summer of 1965, for example, the Hotchkiss School in Lakeville, Connecticut, was hosting who the *New York Amsterdam News* termed "100 Negro, Puerto Rican, Chinese and some not-so-rich white boys." The "Greater Opportunity Program," as it was called, was an eight-week, experimental session that came about after the school's headmaster, A. William Olsen Jr., was asked by an alumnus when and how private schools would address the civil rights movement. (The Civil Rights Act of 1964 had been passed in July of that year, and the Selma to Montgomery March had been held in March 1965.)[26]

Out of that good question sprang the seeds for the "Greater Opportunity Program." Olsen chose The Rev. David P. Kern of the Bronx as field director of the program, who consulted with Kenneth Clark of the psychology department at City College of New York, the city's Deputy School Superintendent, and then school principals to help choose the students. Interviews with the students, most of them African American, came next, as it were they who it was believed would benefit from such a program which combined academics with outdoor recreational activities.[27]

A summer in the country was certainly nice for city kids, but the larger goal of the "Greater Opportunity Program" was to nurture their love of learning and encourage a willingness to take on academic challenges. Private schools were equipped to offer these qualities, which transcended race or economic background. African American parents were attracted to private schools for the same reasons as white parents—a more robust education, smaller classes, and greater individualized attention—than could often be found in the local public school. The National Negro Student Fund, a private nonprofit founded in 1964 that provided scholarships and other financial aid for bright African American students, was of considerable help in this regard. More independents were signing up for candidates who would be sponsored by the fund, although the process was a gradual one. The Ford Foundation chipped in $50,000 to the fund in 1965, another sign that it was gaining traction.[28]

Despite all the changes they had gone through over the decades, private schools had retained their identity as proponents of formal yet bespoke education. Choices in subjects to learn, methods of instruction, and even teachers were often offered to students, an obviously appealing proposition. Students were allowed to progress at their own pace and were encouraged to ask for help when needed. Freely expressing one's creativity was welcomed in art classes, especially in the free-wheelin' mid-sixties.[29]

Alongside these perks was a dedicated commitment to college placement for students nearing graduation. Guidance counselors at large public high schools were typically overwhelmed, while private school staff were known for taking the time and effort to write more personalized recommendation letters. Some parents on school tours were not shy about asking "What colleges do your graduates get into?"—a question that would be welcomed by some admission officers and deemed inappropriate by others. Whether or not that question was answered, parents may or may not have been pleased to learn that private school seniors now had just a slightly better chance of being admitted to a good college than a graduating public school student, all other things being equal.[30]

THE OLD SCHOOL TIES

With increasing pressure being put on private schools to effectively integrate in the mid-1960s, however, that chance was greater for qualified African Americans. In Washington, DC, the numbers had improved considerably since the count done during the 1962–1963 school year; more than 1,100 African American students were enrolled in the city's private schools in the 1966–1967 academic year. The number at Hawthorne had jumped from ten to fifty, and the number at the National Cathedral School had climbed from fourteen to twenty-two.[31]

The sharp increase was not just due to the ripple effect of desegregation. Many African American parents, just like white ones, were simply dissatisfied with the learning experience their children were getting (or not getting) in Washington public schools. (Even public school teachers had become inclined to send their children to private schools.) "The schools have deteriorated so badly that regardless of their race, people who can afford the cost are taking their kids out of public school," observed John A. Sessions, a member of that city's Board of Education. Many white parents were moving to the suburbs to take advantage of their better public schools but, because of suburban housing discrimination (and outright redlining), African Americans were more likely to choose the city's private schools (most of them Roman Catholic and parochial) as an alternative to public schools.[32]

For some students, the transition from public school to private school could be a challenging one. The Wadleigh Intermediate School 88 in Harlem was taking on that challenge by grooming a couple of dozen eighth graders for the shift via a class called "Preparing for Prep School." Admittance to the class was highly selective; students had to have a minimum IQ of 125, be two or more years ahead in math and reading, and maintain at least an 85 average in their major subjects. The junior high school was located in an impoverished area where the drop-out rate was more than 50 percent, "broken" homes were common, and drugs were frequently bought, sold, and taken, further distinguishing the students from other kids in the neighborhood.[33] There was, oddly, no public high school in central Harlem, although a new independent, Harlem Preparatory School, was opened in 1967.

The class at Wadleigh Intermediate had proved successful over its three years of existence; thirty-one students had so far gone on to prep schools on full scholarships. "Preparing for Prep School" was part of the Independent Schools Talent Search Program (ISTSP), which matched economically disadvantaged students with scholarship-granting private schools. Dartmouth and Mount Holyoke Colleges supported the program by inviting the selected students to take a summer course in what might be called Prep School 101.[34]

That course was no doubt useful for Wadleigh graduates now at the Westover School in Middlebury, Connecticut, a particularly posh institution for girls that bore no resemblance to Harlem. Other students were attending the Hun School in Princeton; the Oakwood School in Poughkeepsie, New York; Lawrenceville in New Jersey; the Northfield School in Massachusetts; Deerfield Academy in Massachusetts; the Wyanflete School in Portland, Maine; and the Dalton, Walden, and Birch Wathen Schools (all in Manhattan).[35]

The issue of race was initially a factor in the Wadleighites' experience when they landed at prep schools but more often than not eventually became less relevant. "For the majority of girls at my school, I am the first Negro that they have had any real everyday social contact with," said one student now taking classes with two hundred others from different backgrounds. (Many assumed that anyone from Harlem was by definition a "hoodlum.") "At first they didn't know how to react and suddenly it dawned on them that I was just like anyone else and that's the way they treat me—just like anyone else," she added. Rather than racial difference, it was getting comfortable with prep culture—its competition, fast pace, and day-to-day routine—that presented the greater challenge for the Wadleigh graduates.[36]

More African American students were ready to take on that challenge in the late 1960s. Fortunately, racial barriers had fallen significantly at even the elite private schools, with many of them actively seeking a multiracial student body. Ninety percent of 740 institutions claimed to have "open-door" policies with regard to race, a survey by the National Association of

Independent Schools found, with two-thirds of those 740 schools having at least one African American enrolled. In all, there were 3,720 Black students in the 462 private schools that had African American enrollment, which represented 3.2 percent of the student population.[37]

More of both Black and white students were applying to private schools as the turmoil of the late 1960s infiltrated an already troubled public school system. Getting accepted to a private school had become more difficult for some time now, but things went to an entirely new level in New York City in the fall of 1968. Public school teachers had gone on strike in September, affecting more than a million students. Although the city-wide strike lasted just thirty-six days, the event had become the last straw for parents unsatisfied with the public school education their children were receiving. A virtual flood of applications poured into the offices of the city's independents, more than at any other time in the schools' often long histories. Applications to Riverdale Country Day for Boys in the Bronx were 75 percent greater than any previous year, with far fewer open slots than could be accommodated despite the hefty $3,000 tuition. Some parents were telling Russell Ames, admissions officer at the school, that they were willing to "go into hock" if their child was accepted.[38]

The unprecedented application season called for unprecedented measures. Some schools were holding group interview sessions because there simply weren't enough hours in the day to hold individual ones. The Collegiate School (where eight-year-old John F. Kennedy Jr. was currently a student) had received requests from 1,847 potential applicants when it shut down its admission process, as there were only seventy-five to eighty openings. Private schools as far away as Boston were trying to scoop up applicants who had been turned away by New York City schools, assuming of course the families were willing to relocate.[39]

Even with the strike, there would likely not have been nearly as many applicants had the image of private schools not changed so much since the end of World War II. "United States private schools which confine their enrollments to children of the privileged few are fast becoming passe," noted Carolyn F. Ruffin in the *Christian Science Monitor* in 1969. Others agreed with Ruffin's assessment. "The days of the old school ties are gone," said Edward Yeomans, a consultant for the Boston-based National Association of Independent Schools. Not just active recruitment of minorities and awarding of scholarship money had metaphorically and often literally retired that iconic article of clothing that identified students with a certain school (or year or house). Private schools were exhibiting greater community involvement and cooperating more with their public school counterparts and, in the process, shedding some of their exclusivity and, to some, snobbishness.[40]

That kind of model had been set by two independents in particular: the Ethical Culture schools in New York City and the Society of Friends schools in Baltimore, Washington, Philadelphia, and Boston. (The latter, with its Quaker orientation, stressed the responsibility of individuals within a community.) The University School in Shaker Heights, Ohio, had moved in that direction by inviting inner-city students and teachers to its campus for tours and lectures and by sending some fifty of its own students to Cleveland public schools as tutors. Students from Shady Hill School in Cambridge, Massachusetts, were venturing into less lovely areas of Boston on clean-up missions and also tutoring inner-city kids on Saturday mornings.[41]

SEPARATE AND INFERIOR

Moving in the opposite direction were the 150 or so private schools in the South that were open only to white students. Spread out among eleven states, such schools had proliferated since the passage of the 1964 Civil Rights Act that prohibited discrimination based on race, religion, gender, or national origin. Schools that didn't receive federal funds or were concerned that they would lose nonprofit status were not subject to Title VI of the Act, however, allowing segregation to continue in private schools. Enrollment in such schools increased tenfold over the past five years, according to the Southern Regional Council. It was unclear how many students were enrolled in the schools, with that organization's monthly publication, *South Today*, claiming three hundred thousand. Most of the funding for the schools, which were nonaccredited and widely considered "substandard," was coming from the segregationist organization White Citizens Council.[42]

Segregationists certainly weren't happy with the October 1969 US Supreme Court decision that public schools had to desegregate "immediately" rather than "with all deliberate speed," as the previous ruling stated. The test case was in Mississippi, making many residents of that state (including the governor, the state attorney general, and the state superintendent of education) think that significant numbers of whites would withdraw from public schools in areas with large Black populations and enroll in the forty or so private, nonsectarian ones (most affiliated with the White Citizens Council). "What you're going to have here in the delta is all-black public schools, with all the white people either going to private schools or leaving the county," said one official, thinking "it's gonna be a problem."[43]

Although segregated schools advertised "quality education" (a reference to concerns among white parents that the arrival of African American students would lower standards), the truth was much different due to a lack of money. Tuition ran around just $300, and the members of the White Citizens Council were more racist than rich. Marvell Academy in Mississippi, for example, was operating in two cheaply constructed houses, quite typical of the sort. Faculty, if one could call it that, consisted of retired or uncertified teachers, and labs, libraries, and gyms were usually nowhere to be found. Southern legislatures had attempted to get state tuition grants to fund the segregationist schools but, as predicted, that plan had been foiled by federal courts. The Southern Regional Council concluded that such schools offered a form of education that was, ironically, not "separate but equal" but "separate and inferior."[44]

Regardless of their quality, whites-only schools in the South were "cropping up like weeds across the region," wrote Leon W. Lindsay of the *Christian Science Monitor*. No one could say for sure whether the schools would be a long-term, possibly permanent feature of "Dixie's" educational landscape or if their students would be back in public schools in a year. Not all of them were as bad as the Marvell Academy. The Walton Academy in Good Hope, Georgia, for example, appeared entirely respectable save for its racist ideology. Its headmaster had taken early retirement from the Atlanta public school system with twenty-eight years of experience and had every intention of making the institution accredited. Not only that, but the Academy was located in an actual school that had been vacated because of desegregation and consolidation. Faculty was state-certified, and money from tuition and fundraising seemed to be sufficient to run the place.[45]

Interestingly, Walton Academy and other seemingly legitimate schools cut from the same cloth maintained that race was not a factor considered for admission. Many claimed that they would admit a "qualified Negro applicant," although none had been accepted. (One African American had filled out an application at Walton Academy but never formally submitted it.) It was estimated there were one hundred segregated schools in Georgia alone, with about forty thousand students. Bible reading, strict regulations regarding clothing and hair (it was the late sixties, after all), and a palpable strain of patriotism were common features of the schools.[46]

Interestingly, segregationists in Georgia had an alternative to private school. By paying tuition to a public school in a neighboring county, white parents could have their children attend one in which there were fewer or no African American students. That's what some parents in heavily Black-populated Taliaferro County were doing to pursue "quality education," showing the extent to which segregationists would go to avoid what their governor had called "a social experiment."[47]

Southern segregationists' concern that integration would lower educational standards might have benefited from the knowledge that some African American students at private schools were hardly flunking out. "From the beginning, the (African American) kids that were admitted here were very good," observed a student at St. Albans in Washington, DC, in 1969, "they got A's, went on to Harvard and graduated Phi Beta Kappa." Far more was expected of African American students than white ones at that school and likely at other independents, in fact, with exceptional ability in either academics or athletics the key to being accepted. A similar sentiment was expressed at St. Albans's sister school for girls, National Cathedral. "If you're black, you have to be ten times better than everybody else," noted a student there, "you can't pretend you're just like all the others." Like Jackie Robinson in baseball, the first African American students accepted at National Cathedral were chosen for their superior ability, knowing that their performance would be more critically scrutinized.[48]

Much had seemingly changed in both private school culture and race relations over just the last couple of years. The Summer of Love had come and gone, with the events of 1968 ushering in a harder-edged climate on and off campuses. Elements of the Black Pride and Black Power movements had seeped into the social landscape of private schools; some African Americans were wearing "Afro" hairstyles and attempting to form Black student unions. African American students at private schools reported being caught between two worlds, one defined by their Black identity and the other by their being part of a white-dominated, privileged institution. Some felt they had a responsibility to join the fight for equal rights in their own way, particularly if they had come from the "ghetto." "I'm showing them that there are other Negroes than those that riot," said another St. Albans student, confident that he could compete with anyone when going out into the real world.[49]

Some lower-income parents of private school students were receiving state-funded grants to help pay tuition and other expenses. More states were providing some form of aid to independents, whether they were secular, Catholic, or parochial. Although the US Supreme Court was still deliberating the issue on a federal level, more than a third of the fifty states had directed millions of dollars of taxpayers' money toward tuition assistance, textbooks, transportation, and teacher salaries (as long as the subjects taught were not religious). In some states, laws had been passed to make this aid legal although in other states no such legislation had yet to be passed. Court challenges were common in cases where laws had been passed to allow the practice (sometimes called "parochaid"), brought on by those opposed to public money being awarded to private, often sectarian institutions.[50]

Most in need of aid were the nation's Catholic and parochial schools. While elite private schools were charging high tuition and turning away qualified applicants, religious ones were in dire financial straits. Things were so bad in Arizona that a committee of Roman Catholics recommended that all parochial schools in the state be phased out over the next five to ten years because they didn't have enough money to pay teachers and staff. Things weren't much better in New York State where there were no less than 1,400 Roman Catholic schools serving some seven hundred thousand students. Tuition was doubling at Catholic high schools in Brooklyn and Queens for the 1969–1970 academic year (but still a bargain at $600).[51]

The journey of private schools through the stormy 1960s fittingly ended with what was perhaps the most controversial proposal to date relating to the field. Rather than eliminate private schools, as many had over the decades put forward on the basis of their being "nondemocratic," one public figure in Connecticut made the case that it was public schools that should go away. Al Cashman, a teacher in Lyme who was seeking a Republican Congressional seat in the state, campaigned that government-subsidized private schools replace public schools as a means to end what he called "mediocrity in education."[52]

While the idea of shutting down free public education was no doubt anathema to many voters, there was some logic to Cashman's proposal. It was private colleges and universities that offered the best education at that level, he argued. So, he asked, why not apply the same model to elementary and secondary schools? Going further, Cashman pointed out that these same colleges and universities received federal aid, making it reasonable that K–12 schools be funded by the government. From there, Cashman's plan got a bit wacky (local groups of parents would form schools, he envisioned), but simply raising the possibility of such a thing indicated both the dissatisfaction with public schools and the value of private schools.[53] Things would get even wilder for private schools in the next decade as America experienced a collective identity crisis.

6

THE 1970s: THE REAL WORLD

"By definition, education involves change."

—Bartley B. Nourse of the Holderness School, 1979

Rumors had been going around in Connecticut in 1970 about a new private school bordering Hedgehog Mountain in West Simsbury. One story was that the school, called Westledge, had brilliant students who were doing advanced work. Another was that the place wasn't really a school at all and that the kids were allowed to simply run wild in the woods all day.[1]

Journalist Karen Branan decided to investigate and, after receiving an invitation to visit, entered one of the nine buildings spread out on 340 acres of woodland. There she found students sprawled out on the carpeted floor while a teacher offered the program choices for the afternoon: classes in French, physics, and social studies; creative workshops; woodland clearing; team sports; or independent study. The students were remarkably multicultural, with race, religion, nationality, or economic background not considered in the admission process. Rather, the only requirement to be accepted to Westledge was possession of what one teacher called "that certain spark"—that is, a special talent of some kind. Each student had a unique course of study, and no letter grades were given at the school.[2]

While hardly typical, Westledge pointed toward the direction prep schools would take in the 1970s. Formal preparation for college remained a goal, but training for what one educator called the "real world" was taking precedence. A deep recession and a society in major flux were the primary catalysts for this transformation, with legal decisions also playing a significant role in turning the American private school into a much different kind of institution by the end of the decade.

BOARDING-SCHOOL BLUES

Private schools unquestionably had a great run since the end of World War II but, as they say, nothing lasts forever. For the 1970–1971 academic year, most of the premier East Coast boarding schools including Williston, Tilton, and Pomfret still had openings in September, an unusual thing. Applications were down even at elite schools such as Phillips Exeter, Emma Willard, the Masters School, and Ethel Walker, making admission officers select students who would not have been accepted in previous years.[3]

What had happened? By 1970, the forces of the counterculture had caught up with boarding schools, making them be seen as pillars of the establishment (which they of course were). Some were beginning to shed their more anachronistic ways, but there was no getting around their image as autocratic institutions demanding conformity and adherence to strict rules. "Today's youth is not accepting the kind of authority that the school represents," noted David Pynchon, headmaster of Deerfield Academy, with the sexual revolution also playing a part in the rejection of single-gender schools. Administrators were recognizing the problem and taking steps to keep the applications coming in. Rosemary Hall, a girls' boarding school, had decided to relocate to Wallingford, Connecticut, which just happened to be home to all-boys Choate.[4] (The schools would eventually merge.)

Other factors were in play for what *Time* called the "boarding-school blues." The postwar economic engine had lost considerable steam, with rising inflation and a nervous stock market adding to a bleak financial climate. Tuitions had continued to climb, making it not easy for many parents to find a spare $3,600 or so every year. (Rosemary Hall was charging $4,500.) Besides the high cost, suburban public high schools were proving to be tough competition for independents in terms of academics. Top colleges were no longer favoring private schools in admissions to any significant degree, making more upper-middle-class parents wonder why they should invest in such an expensive education. Also, teenagers had more say in which school they wanted to attend and were reluctant to give up their current friends and the comforts of home for a strange academy somewhere in the country, no matter how prestigious it was said to be.[5]

Boarding schools were also suffering the blues due to changing perceptions regarding race, ethnicity, religion, and gender. More liberal parents had always been turned off by the exclusive nature of private schools but now, with both multicultural and feminist movements further heating up, institutions run by and catering to wealthy white Protestant males were, in the parlance of the times, major "turn-offs." At the same time, conservative parents were not happy to see the schools gradually accept more students of color and dubious economic backgrounds, particularly if a chunk of the former's tuition dollars were going toward scholarships for minorities.[6]

As more suburban teenagers opted for local junior high and high schools rather than boarding schools, more younger children were pouring into public elementary schools. The decline and closing of thousands of parochial schools across the country was having a direct effect on K–6 enrollment, with public school districts having to add classrooms and teachers to support the influx. This cost money, of course, making the budget-conscious Nixon administration take notice.[7]

Nixon himself commented on the situation as part of a March 1970 message to Congress on educational reform, in the process providing a solid endorsement of private schools (while consciously avoiding the word "private"):

> The non-public elementary and secondary schools in the United States have long been an integral part of the nation's educational establishment—supplementing in an important way, the main task of our public school system. The non-public schools provide a diversity which our educational system would otherwise lack. They also give a spur of competition to the public schools—through which educational innovations come, both systems benefit, and progress results.[8]

Everything that the president said was true, but the more important point was that private schools collectively saved American taxpayers billions of dollars a year by taking millions of students out of the tuition-free public school system. The number of students enrolled in private elementary schools was declining, however, partly due to the financial woes of parochial schools and partly due to more parents choosing nonreligious education for their children. Catholic schools accounted for 3.9 million or 93 percent of the 4.2 million students enrolled in private elementary schools, an astounding figure. Most high school students in private schools were in Catholic-affiliated institutions, but this number too was falling as the nation became more secular, cause for concern for the fiscally prudent administration.[9]

Spurred on by gradual desegregation, enrollments in Catholic or parochial and those in secular private schools were going in opposite directions. Between 1961 and 1971, enrollment in non-Catholic schools had doubled, increasing from 0.7 million to 1.4 million. Over this same period, enrollment in Catholic or parochial schools decreased from 5.3 million to 4.0 million, a function in large part of these institutions' financial troubles. By 1971, a quarter of all private school students were in secular academies, and the trend showed no signs of slowing down.[10]

While enrollment in Catholic private schools was falling fast, Christian independents were sprouting throughout the South directly due to the legal mandate of desegregation. In both the South and the North, urban white families concerned about the integration of public schools were relocating to the suburbs, particularly if the number of Black students rose above 50 percent. Establishing a private school was another option to avoid desegregation, however, and that's what thousands of parents in Southern and border states were doing in the early 1970s, abetted by organizations that supported the cause.[11] Between October 30, 1969, and September 30, 1970, sixty new "segregated academies" were incorporated in Georgia, a fair share of them in February 1970, which the Supreme Court had set as the deadline for full desegregation of public school systems.[12]

Many of these new private schools across the South had Christian names, suggesting that there was a link between fundamentalist faith and racist attitudes—an odd thing if true given the precepts of the religion. In Georgia alone, there was Augusta Christian, Bainbridge Christian, Berean Christian Schools, Colonial Hills Christian Schools, DeKalb Christian Academy, East Lake Christian Academy, Macon Christian Academy, and Rose City Christian Academy. Administrators of such schools insisted their students were enrolling not to maintain segregation but to be in a Christian atmosphere. Public schools were too secular, parents echoed, begging the question of why so many Southerners had come to that realization so suddenly.[13] In 1971, the United Klans of America announced it would open a private school in South Carolina. The organization which openly supported segregation in education (and everywhere else) had already been providing financial assistance to white-only academies in North Carolina, stated Grand Dragon J. Robert Jones in an interview on WBTV, a Charlotte television station.[14]

The Nixon administration had to date looked the other way when it came to segregated academies claiming tax-exempt status and deducting financial contributions. In 1970, however, Nixon disallowed such practices made by private schools that were racially discriminatory as it became clear that they were in contradiction to the intent of *Brown v. Board of Education*. Legal actions were being taken against the schools at the state level to stop the practice, and the NEA had come out in protest of it as well. Many were thus happy to see the president take action by effectively penalizing the racist institutions.[15]

THE CURRENT CRISIS

Nixon's support for private schools of all types, even if financially motivated, offered evidence that while they were privately managed, they served a public function. This was the principal argument made by those lobbying for state aid to private schools. In a 1972 essay for *Current History*, Otto F. Krauschaar elaborated on how private schools were in the public interest, something of which most citizens were unaware because they simply didn't know much about independent schools. In a 1969 Gallup survey, most respondents said they had little idea how independents were supported, how much it cost to attend, and what financial assistance might be available if they chose to apply. Still, the vast majority of those polled believed that parents (or children) should have the right to choose a school, a reflection of our pluralistic society.[16]

No one would agree with that sentiment more than Lester A. Waters Jr., a seventeen-year-old from West Philadelphia. Waters, who happened to be African American, had attended Overbrook High School but had switched from the public school to Miquon Upper School in Germantown. Waters considered his new school, which was private yet tuition-free, far superior to Overbrook, where teachers were known to insult and even hit students. Waters found the school's approach to teaching one of "brainwashing, molding, and propagandizing," making it not surprising that many of his friends had dropped out. At Miquon, "the students and teachers are on an equal level," he wrote for the *Philadelphia Tribune*, something that allowed each to learn from the other.[17]

Fortunately for students like Waters, there was no shortage of schools in the United States from which to choose, as Grace and Fred M. Hechinger noted. "One of the concrete benefits of selecting a private school is that it allows a choice of different educational philosophies and the parents' outlook," they wrote for *Harper's Bazaar* in 1972. That was particularly true in bigger cities. In New York, for example, traditionalists leaned toward Collegiate, progressives toward New Lincoln, and child-centered toward Summerhill and Montessori. While getting their children into such schools had been parents' focus for at least the past generation, however, now it was they who held more of the cards as the number of applicants fell. Parents were allowing contracts for reenrollment to slip past the deadline, waiting longer to decide whether to sign or not. Some private schools had taken out bank loans to meet payrolls while they waited for tuition checks to arrive (or not arrive) in the mail.[18]

Interestingly, what some were calling "the current crisis" in private schools was making them once again skew toward the rich. Needing students whose parents could pay full tuition, even in a recession, administrations were being a little more flexible about academic qualifications. A high proportion of children of the wealthy tended to destabilize schools by putting social status ahead of character, however, negatively impacting students of less means. Scholarships were down as well, this too reversing the impressive gains that independents had made over the past decade in terms of diversifying student bodies.[19]

With higher overhead and beds to fill, boarding schools in particular were cash crunched. Admission officers were sent across the country to recruit candidates, preferably those who lived in the biggest houses in the best neighborhoods in town. It was, admittedly, a hard sell, especially for teenagers taking in all the pleasures that were readily available in the early seventies. (I was sixteen in 1972 and can attest to most of them.) More schools were going coed, both to double the pool of candidates and satisfy students' wishes to be in the company of those of another gender.[20]

Even some of the top prep schools were deciding to partner in the recessionary early seventies. In 1972, Horace Mann and the Barnard School for Boys announced they would merge, something that made particular sense since they had adjoining campuses in the Riverdale section of the Bronx. Each school had raised tuition as enrollments fell, but lowering overhead by eliminating duplicate functions appeared to be the only way to avoid making severe cuts which would lower educational standards.[21]

Adding to the slew of problems for private schools was the devaluation of a liberal arts college education. Data from the 1970 Census revealed that there were twenty-five thousand different occupations in 441 groupings in the United States, making us a nation of specialists rather than generalists. A college degree once was a virtual guarantee of getting a good job but that was no more; there were now too many Americans with college degrees and

not enough jobs that required them.[22] If college preparation was the primary role of prep schools and a college degree was hardly worth the paper
it was printed on, what was the future of the American private school?

Until that question was answered, private schools, especially those in
Southern or border states, continued to struggle with the legal implications
of desegregation. In August 1973, a federal district court in Virginia ruled
that private schools could not practice racial discrimination—the first time
such a decision had been made. (Two sets of parents who had been denied
admission to two local schools had filed the suit, claiming it was based on
their race.) There was still no specific law addressing segregation in private
schools but the judge in the case cited the Federal Civil Rights Act of 1866
("all persons shall have the same right to make and enforce contracts as
is enjoyed by whites") in his ruling. (That act spun out of the Thirteenth
Amendment, which had abolished slavery.) There were major implications
to the decision, possibly affecting not just Southern private schools but
Northern ones as well if racial discrimination could be shown.[23]

Almost two years later, the issue remained unresolved, as the two schools
involved filed appeals. After another federal court affirmed the first court's
decision, the case went to the US Supreme Court, the key question being
whether a denial of rights had occurred. (The Justice Department had filed
a brief in support of the lower courts' rulings.) Again, the decision was
expected to be a landmark one, especially in the South where many whites-
only private schools had been founded as a response to court-ordered
desegregation of public schools (along with busing to force integration).[24]
Since 1970, the Internal Revenue Service had officially denied tax-exempt
status to segregated private schools but rarely enforced the policy despite
President Nixon's support for it.[25]

There were 3,500 such schools in Southern states in 1975, with a total
enrollment of roughly 750,000 students (10 percent of the region's white
school-age children). Another one of the "best" segregated academies was
Briarcrest Baptist High School in Memphis, which received accreditation
from the Southern Association of Colleges and Schools. All of Briarcrest's
1,432 students and 69 faculty and staff members were white, despite the
school's claim that they, much like Walton Academy, had open admissions.
No Blacks had applied, administrators explained, although they conceded
that it was desegregation that had led most of the parents to choose Briarcrest for their children. (Busing and sex education had been the last straws.)
Segregated schools in the South were not only dramatically reducing the
number of white students in public schools but tipping the balance heavily
toward African Americans, in the process hindering actual desegregation.[26]

While the Supreme Court considered the segregation issue, there were greater opportunities for African Americans to circumvent the various negatives of public schools and at the same time take advantage of the positives of independents. Most predominantly white private schools belonged to the A Better Chance (ABC) program which helped place economically disadvantaged students in such schools seeking greater diversity. Just a handful or so private schools had from their founding an "open admission" policy, the most notable one being Mount Hermon in East Northfield, Massachusetts. The boarding school had originally been for boys but in 1970 had merged with all-girls Northfield (both had been founded by Dwight Lyman Moody of Bible fame).[27]

By 1975, Mount Hermon had become one of the biggest prep schools in the country in both students (1,050) and campus size (4,400 acres). Just thirty-nine students were Black; however, the impetus for its president, Howard L. Jones, was to try to dramatically increase the percentage. (Jones had founded the ABC program.) With scholarship funds short due to the current financial plight of boarding schools, Jones had an interesting strategy to diversify the student body: find African American parents who could afford to pay the full $4,500 annual tuition and use some of that money to offer scholarships to less affluent Black students. A speculative plan, perhaps, but Jones was also keen on diversifying Mount Hermon's administration and faculty—something quite rare in the prep school universe.[28]

Boggs Academy, located in Keysville, Georgia, was the only accredited African American prep school in the country in the mid-1970s. Eighty-two percent of its students received some financial aid and 95 percent of graduates received college acceptances, each a high percentage by any measure. The occasional white student enrolled at Boggs, and the school had an exchange program with predominantly white preparatory schools to expose those of different races to each other.[29]

More Black and white students would soon sit next to each other in private school classrooms across the country. In 1976, the Supreme Court finally announced its decision that private schools did not have the right to deny applicants based on their race, rejecting the argument made by the two Virginia schools that they had certain constitutionally guaranteed principles. (Those were freedom of association, the right of privacy, and the right of parents to determine their children's education.) Racial discrimination had never been given constitutional protection, the highest court in the land noted, with the decisions made by the lower courts fully upheld. Private social organizations (such as country clubs) could restrict their membership based on race or other criteria, the court was careful to add, and private schools could still exclude applicants by gender or religion.[30]

THE STUFF OF FICTION

How much effect would the Supreme Court's decision have on the nation's twelve thousand or so private schools? Few private schools had an official policy of racial exclusion even if it was clear that African Americans were not welcome and would not be admitted. A few hundred schools in the South and border states did formally prohibit Blacks from enrolling at their institutions, and it was these "white academies" that were subject to the new ruling. Still, the decision "does not alter the panoply of economic and social reasons that produce all-white private schools even if those schools have no policy of racial exclusion," Thomas J. Flygare observed in *Phi Delta Kappan* in 1976, seeing no sudden flood of minority applicants to such schools. "A greater public awareness" that minority children could not be excluded from private schools because of their skin color was, however, a very good thing in itself, Flygare added.[31]

Just as the issue of segregation in private schools was resolved, at least from a legal sense, there seemed to be a sea change in their financial position. By the mid-seventies, the nation's economy was improving, good news to institutions that relied on a certain number of households having discretionary dollars to spend on nonpublic education. New England remained the nation's capital of independent schools, making it worthwhile to see how private schools were faring in that region of the country.

There was good news and bad news. Between 1960, more than fifteen New England independents had folded due to the inability to meet payrolls and other operating costs. More than twenty new ones had opened, however, as parents from across the country and abroad looked to the six-state area as the premier place for their children to receive an elite American education. Massachusetts remained number one in sheer numbers, with more than seventy-five boarding and day schools. There were now more independents in Connecticut than in California, even though the former had about one-seventh of the latter's population. One out of every four accredited high schools in New England was nonpublic, an amazing statistic.[32]

Prep schools that had been around since the eighteenth century had done what they had to in order to survive the major economic and social challenges of the early 1970s. St. Paul's School in Concord, New Hampshire, had an endowment of $40 million but had still decided to go coed in 1971 to fill open spots (and appease teenage boys). It and other schools, including Deerfield Academy, had also started to take in more foreign students whose wealthy parents could pay the full tuition.[33]

With admission to private schools more in demand at the nation's bicentennial than they had been in some years, parents were taking measures to improve the chances of their children being admitted to the school of their choice. Like now, competition was most fierce in New York City a half-century ago. Four-year-olds at nursery schools were taking the Educational Records Bureau (ERB) test, with a high score increasing the odds of a child getting into kindergarten at the city's most selective schools. An interview was the next hoop to jump through, a source of considerable worry among parents whose children were bright but not particularly loquacious or magnetic.[34]

In such a climate, both parents and educators were wondering about the repercussions of "failure" at such an early age. How would possible rejection affect the child? Was his or her academic career ruined before it had really begun? The ERB and testing in general was the source of much controversy as more schools, both private and public, used the scores to screen and sort students. Eighty private schools in New York (including Dalton, Brearley, Spence, and Buckley) and six hundred nationwide included the ERB in their admission process, although it should be said that parents were far more stressed about its taking than the children, who viewed it as a kind of game.[35]

Game or otherwise, admission officers relied on the results of the ERB in conjunction with an evaluation of the interview before inviting the child in question to take part in a playgroup to determine how she or he interacted with others. Only about one-third of applicants would make it through the admission process; boys-only Buckley, for example, accepted forty students from its pool of 125 applicants for the 1976–1977 academic year. Some private schools, notably Rudolph Steiner, which used the Waldorf approach to education, did not require the ERB, while others, including Dalton, used it but prioritized the interview and recommendations from nursery school-teachers when making their decision.[36]

Some of those four-year-olds lucky enough to get into a private kindergarten would over the years evolve into "preppies." The term was gaining currency in the late seventies as preparatory schools and the students who attended them became cultural archetypes, both positive and negative. "Prep school appeared to my romantic side and the stuff of fiction played in my head," recalled Hilary Cosell when she was told by her parents that she would be attending one to get a better education than that offered by her public school. (She was the daughter of famed sports broadcaster Howard Cosell.) What was that romanticized image created by the likes of movies with Hayley Mills and novels by J. D. Salinger? "Old-moneyed families, snub-nosed girls in spanking-clean uniforms," as Cosell described it in *Seventeen*, with "the preppies from the neighboring boy's school knowing the difference between a jib and a spinnaker sail."[37]

With that impression in mind, the fifteen-year-old Cosell herself became a preppie, arriving that fall at an ivy-covered Tudor mansion on the north shore of Long Island. With her gray skirt, gray blazer with the school crest on a breast pocket, and brown oxfords, she certainly looked the part. Internally, however, Cosell soon realized that she did not fit into prep school culture. As with many if not most boarding schools, there were not only a plethora of regulations but an honor system that required students to report classmates who violated a rule. Such students would end up in Saturday detention, leading Cosell to describe her school as a "maximum security prison." Daily chapel didn't sweeten the deal, and within a few months, she pleaded with her parents to be released from the institution.[38]

Thinking that the boarding school was an ideal feeder to Radcliffe or Vassar, Cosell's parents were surprised to learn that the education their daughter was getting was less challenging than the one she had received in her Westchester County public school and there were fewer electives. Not only that, Cosell found the students at her new school to be a homogenous, sheltered group, and she missed the diversity of her old classmates. There were thirty-plus students in each class in her public school, ensuring that there would be different types of people to learn from, even in upscale Westchester. After much fuss, Cosell finally got her way, and the following year she happily returned to public school. There was also a happy ending: upon graduation, Cosell was admitted to her first-choice college, Sarah Lawrence, a "progressive Radcliffe" of which even her parents approved.[39]

Now, having some time (thirteen years) to reflect on her experience, Cosell conceded that while she had made the right choice for herself, there was a mystique attached to private schools that she couldn't completely extinguish from her mind. "I never could quite escape the feeling that I'd been excluded somehow from a special club," considering its members "the chosen ones." Private school was just the beginning for this elite group, as from there they would go on to Ivy League colleges and become CEOs of major corporations. Such stereotypes and myths were firmly ingrained in Americans' consciousness, including her own, causing Cosell to investigate how much of them were true by looking at the data and interviewing an array of students, educators, and admissions officers.[40]

What did the journalist learn? First, as a whole, private school students circa 1977 were a different breed than those of decades past, not at all the children of the leisure class. More than half of the 280,000 independent school population came from families with annual household incomes less than $35,000, according to the National Association of Independent Schools, making them solidly middle class. One-third came from families with incomes of $25,000 or less, a far cry from yacht-owning plutocrats. The notion that contemporary preppies came from a long line of ancestors who had attended the same school for generations was also dispelled; 41 percent of new private school students were the first in their families to go to any independent much less the same one that dear old dad and grandad had attended.[41]

WHAT A DIFFERENCE

Much had apparently changed at prep schools since Cosell's unfortunate experience in 1964. There were rules, but the schools were no longer prison-like, with many ditching mandatory uniforms and daily chapel. There was a more relaxed atmosphere than in the past, and the curriculum too had become less rigid. Dalton had extended its progressive academic tradition, for example, and the Putney School was even more open-ended. For the more conservative, however, there were quite a few options, including the Cathedral School, St. Albans, and the all-girls Dana Hall, Emma Willard, and Westover School; and Groton Academy and the Holderness School remained boys only, at least for now.[42]

The ecology movement was in full bloom in the late seventies, and that became the focal point for Milton Academy in the Boston area. The 180-year-old institution wasn't known for being particularly progressive, but in 1978 it debuted a new building dedicated to alternative forms of agri-culture, aquaculture, land use, and energy-saving architecture. (The energy crisis had been just a few years back.) As interesting, students and teach-ers had constructed the building—a futuristic, solar-powered greenhouse. Organic vegetables were grown there and served in the school's cafeteria, but there was much more to the project. Milton Academy's greenhouse was "a socio-educational statement that updates a central purpose of American schools," as Bartley B. Nourse Jr. described it in *Phi Delta Kappan*, that purpose being to "prepare students for the real world."[43]

Milton's greenhouse symbolized the transformation being made by the American private school as the nation itself remade itself economically, socially, and politically. Preparation for the real world demanded a new and different set of skills, something more administrations were realizing as they charted the course of their institutions. While enrollments were up at private schools, fiscal restraint remained the order of the day, as the line between being in the black and the red was a thin one. Budgets were even tighter in public schools, with any programs considered unnecessary—music, art, physical education, notably—ripe to get cut by the state or district. A back-to-the-basics movement had taken hold in public education after student test scores revealed that the nation's schools were "failing," and dissatisfied taxpayers were increasingly voting down bond issues to raise budgets.[44]

In such a climate, it wasn't surprising that teachers in public schools wondered what life might be like in the world of independents. Teachers, especially those of "specialized" subjects, were getting axed left and right in many school districts across the country, making it understandable that conditions would appear to be better in a privately funded environment. Was the grass greener on the other side of the academic hill? More teachers were asking that question, especially those in California where Proposition 13 had dramatically reduced property taxes—the primary source of public school funding.[45]

James W. Peterson was one public school teacher who made the leap, telling his story in *Phi Delta Kappan*. Although based in California, Peterson's decision to move from public to private was made even before Prop. 13, when he saw untenured colleagues dismissed and classroom sizes balloon. Teachers were threatening to strike, all the more reason to jump ship if a good job opportunity arose. That it did, and soon Peterson was teaching at a private elementary school interested in expanding beyond its Montessori orientation. Familiar with both the public-school curriculum and the Rudolph Steiner approach, Peterson was quite a catch for the small private school with bigger plans.[46]

If there was a single takeaway from his experience, it was that while public schools approached education from a general, one-size-fits-all perspective, independents came at it through a particular philosophy. Whatever that philosophy happened to be, it was woven throughout the school's curriculum and practices, especially by teachers' pedagogy. Parents chose a school based on that philosophy, reinforcing it and making the school different from others. "What a difference this has made in my own teaching experience!" Peterson exclaimed, now seeing public education as a hodgepodge of teachers' varying approaches that lacked focus and continuity.[47]

Peterson went further in his praise for teaching in a private school. There was far more sharing of ideas among teachers, with staff meetings used to compare notes on subject appropriateness and other issues. Also, Peterson was allowed to teach what and how he wanted with little interference from administration. Most striking, perhaps, was the contentment level of students' parents. Unlike in public school, where parents could be upset by any number of things—homework, grades, or desired outcomes—the parents at his new school were remarkably satisfied and supportive, even those whose children were struggling. "These parents had paid their money and were getting what they paid for," Peterson concluded, sounding more like someone in the hospitality business or service sector than an educator.[48]

While Peterson's experience was a sanguine one, even he admitted that a certain amount of pressure came from the fact that parents were paying for their children's education. Parents were making a financial investment and were counting on a good return, a concept not found in public schools. The parents of public school students were delighted (and often surprised) by positive results, in other words, while those of private school students fully expected them. The key differentiating factor was, in a word, money, seemingly regardless of how much a parent happened to have.[49]

There were, of course, other significant differences between private and public schools. Independents had no obligation to use state-directed standardized tests; there were no Title I or special state programs; and there was no law dictating the length of class periods and recesses. Class sizes were smaller, of course, and private school teachers had much greater freedom to develop curricula and choose (or not use) textbooks. Staying "on schedule" was not a fixation, as in public schools, although that hardly meant that private schools approached education in a free-form, improvisational manner like a bebop musician. The curriculum at better private schools was highly structured and academically rigorous despite the lack of regulation, arguably their most compelling feature.[50]

It would be remiss to not point out one final distinguishing element of private schools—the ability to infuse education with a spiritual component. Recounting the life of Buddha or telling the Garden of Eden story in a classroom could be cause for a public school teacher's dismissal, a function of the wall built in the nation between church and state. Beyond its usefulness as a pedagogical tool, spiritual content added much to understanding the human experience, making its barring in public schools a glaring weakness to many educators. Until relatively recently, spiritual values had been very much part of the country's public education system, but the great sensitivity surrounding anything related to religion had changed that by the end of the seventies.[51] The 1970s had proved to be a decade of radical change for American private schools in many ways, but yet another major shift lay in store.

7

THE 1980s: A BENEFICIAL REVOLUTION

"Private schools have never been healthier or more vigorous than they are now."

—Denis P. Doyle, US Department of Education, 1981

"Though it has received comparatively little notice in the media," wrote M. Stanton Evans in *National Review* in May 1980, "a beneficial revolution is currently unfolding within the ranks of American education." What was that revolution? It was the "private school boom," Evans stated, citing statistics to back up his claim. Between 1965 and 1975, according to new Census figures, the number of students in nonparochial private schools in the United States had more than doubled, increasing from 615,548 to 1,443,000. No data was yet available but, with the economic rebound of the late seventies, it was likely that yet more students had entered nonsectarian private schools. Still, the demand had yet to be met; about three new independent schools were being founded every day in 1980, said Robert Baldwin of the Citizens for Educational Freedom. If the trend continued, there would be more private schools in the country than public ones by 1990, an astounding thought to consider.[1]

There was little doubt that the gains made by American private schools had come largely from parents' dissatisfaction with the nation's public school system. A host of problems, notably anemic academics, adverse student behaviors, and the erosion of traditional values, were driving more parents to choose a different kind of education for their children.[2] The 1980s would prove to be a historic decade for private schools, as economic, political, and social forces melded to create a perfect storm for independent education. A sea change was taking place in American society, and private schools were ideally positioned to take advantage of it.

AN IMPORTANT EXPANSION

Nowhere more than in New York City could that shift in cultural values be detected. For the 1980–1981 academic year, the city's 288 private schools looked to the past to chart their future. Firmer discipline, tighter dress codes, and a more traditional pedagogy were part of this reining in of school culture that administrators believed had become too loose in the wake of the counterculture. Being late to school or cutting classes would no longer be tolerated at most of the schools, as that was what students were likely pursuing during "free period" and "independent study." "We're definitely swinging back to a conservative time," said Emily Lewis of the Riverdale School, her institution like others planning to instill greater structure in the class day and emphasize basic skills over electives (like macrame) in the curriculum.[3]

Most parents approved of these changes, and in fact felt lucky that their child was enrolled in a private school. Getting into a top one was now more difficult than ever, even at the entry level, particularly in big cities. Only a third of applicants to kindergarten were accepted to their first-choice school in San Francisco, and Boston parents were applying to prestigious Commonwealth Day School more than a year ahead of the first day of kindergarten. "It's become a little more difficult to get into a private kindergarten than to enroll in college," noted Helen LaCroix, director of admission at the Francis W. Parker School in Chicago. Two-income families were driving the need for kindergartens and nursery schools, and the $2,000 to $4,000 tuition was not serving as a deterrent.[4]

Kindergarten to twelfth grade was a long way to go, but parents could foresee the intense competition for their children to get into top colleges in a dozen or so years. More immediate concerns were encroaching governmental interference with the public school system and the safety of students within it. Public schools still accounted for 89 percent of the nation's students, but the winds were clearly in favor of independents, at least among those who could afford the tuition or get financial aid.[5] More support for private schools came with the release of a new "Coleman Report." The original report that was published in 1966 concluded that desegregation could lift academic achievement of disadvantaged students. In his 1981 version, sociologist James Coleman reported that achievement levels of high schoolers in independents exceeded those of their public school peers.[6]

Coleman's latest findings that the learning experience in private schools was superior to that in public schools—a result of stricter discipline and higher academic standards—were not surprisingly controversial.[7] Still, the new report served as ammunition for supporters of private school tuition income tax credits, an issue that had been simmering for the past decade. The Reagan administration backed the idea, with US Secretary of Education Terrel H. Bell telling the Senate that the tax credits represented "an important expansion of educational opportunities for all Americans."[8]

Bell's comments reflected the now more inclusive nature of private schools. "The new image is much more sanguine and egalitarian," Donna Joy Newman of the *Chicago Tribune* proposed, adding that "middle-class and minority families who would have sent their children to public schools automatically are caught up in the age of consumerism." Parents were, in other words, approaching the marketplace of education from a more critical perspective, not willing to settle for an inferior product even if it was free. Beyond the academics, it was said that private schools were well-suited to build confidence and self-assurance, a skill set that parents wanted their children to have.[9]

With all factors seemingly working in favor of private schools in the early eighties, entrepreneurs found ways to get in on the action. "A growing band of ex-pedagogues, school admissions officers, psychologists and social workers who call themselves educational counselors," as *Time* described them, were serving as matchmakers between students and private schools. For a fee of anywhere from $250 to $600, the consultants found a school that was a good fit for a pupil, a welcome service given the large and complex maze of prep schools. More often than not, the student in question was having some kind of issue at his or her current school, making the consultant's job not an easy one given the demand for admittance.[10]

A coed institution was becoming a more popular choice among those shopping around for a private school. The coeducational movement could be said to have begun in 1970, when Phillips Exeter and Loomis Chaffee in Windsor, Connecticut, each decided to admit girls. Choate and Rosemary Hall joined forces the following year, and both Taft and St. Paul's went coed in 1971. Andover, St. Mark's, and St. George's in Middleton, Rhode Island, did the same the next year followed by St. Andrew's in Middletown,

Delaware, in 1973. Next came Hotchkiss and Middlesex in Concord, Massachusetts, in 1974 and Groton became coed with its 1975 merger with Emma Willard. Notable holdouts on the East Coast were Deerfield, Brooks School in North Andover, Massachusetts, Lawrenceville, and Hill.[11]

Private schools on the West Coast were following the pattern that had been set in the Northeast. The Midland School, Thatcher School, Flintridge Preparatory, Cate School, and Webb School, all in Southern California, went coeducational in the late seventies and early eighties, with everyone seemingly happy with the decision. Phillips Exeter, which had blazed the trail, was viewed as the model to follow by other private schools considering going coed. With its huge endowment, the school did not need the tuition dollars from increased enrollment that some others did at the time. Rather, "it is simply more natural for boys and girls to be educated together," as Andre Vernet, head of Exeter's committee, had expressed it. With little contact with those of a different gender, boys at the school acted as if they had never seen a girl during the annual "Dance Weekend" and when they got to college.[12]

John A. Bikales, a Boston-area high school student, offered an alternative perspective on the coed issue. While conceding that single-sex schools were "an endangered species," Bikales maintained that there was a certain value to them that shouldn't be overlooked. Speaking about all-boys schools, the presence of females can, for some males, "work an inhibiting influence on class participation and can add a social pressure which often works to the detriment of the educational purpose of the institution." The teen years were often insecure ones, he added, and being in the company of girls could for a segment of boys contribute to their lack of self-confidence.[13]

Many if not most single-sex institutions had gone coed due to financial pressures, but by the early 1980s, those were less of a factor in deciding to enroll girls (or boys) or merge with another school. While administrators now didn't avoid taking a look at their balance sheets, worried about possibly seeing minus signs, they did not have delusions of grandeur. Educators in independents viewed their schools as complementing, rather than competing with, public schools, offering parents an alternative for students with more individualized needs. Administrators typically wanted to keep their schools on the smaller size of the spectrum, knowing that specialization would suffer if they got too big.[14]

The statistics surrounding private school enrollments had always been inconsistent, with different assumptions and research methodologies leading to wildly different outcomes. Still, data from the National Opinion Research Center at the University of Chicago provided a few interesting insights about the state of private schools in the early eighties. First, while 10 percent of school-age children in the United States as a whole attended private schools, enrollments were highly regional. Seventeen percent of school-age children in Connecticut went to private schools—the highest percentage of any state—while just 1.5 percent in Wyoming did. Second, while enrollments at religious private schools had fallen precipitously, just 36.4 percent of all private schools had no religious affiliation in 1981. Finally, private schools remained overwhelmingly white despite significant gains made by minorities. Just 14 percent of students were non-white (6 percent Hispanic, 5 percent African American, and 3 percent "other"), putting diversity initiatives at the top of prep schools' agendas.[15]

HAVE YOU HEARD?

Data also showed that private schools were no longer just for wealthy families, with evidence suggesting that the student mix of prep schools had been reconstituted throughout the 1970s in terms of economic and social class. "The traditional elite constituency has changed decisively in the last decade to include more children of middle-class parents," noted Margot Slade in the *New York Times* in 1982. The reasons for choosing private school over public too had shifted. While private school had in years past been viewed as a means to demonstrate social prestige, carry on a family tradition, or gain entry to top colleges, it was the quality of education that now mattered most to parents.[16]

Income levels of households in which at least one child attended private school had indeed dropped. More families with annual incomes between $10,000 and $30,000 were now sending a child to a private school, and applications for financial aid had risen sharply. The divorce rate had climbed, and more women were having children on their own, resulting in a greater number of single parents who were keen on private school. As well, private schools tended to have longer school days and allow students to come in before classes and stay after, a big plus for working parents worried about adult supervision for their kids. Parents who had happily attended public schools were increasingly choosing independents for their children, not happy with the changes in the former that had occurred over the past generation.[17]

Two remarkable things about the "revolution" taking place in the sphere of private schools were that the number of school-age children in the United States was going down and the nation's economy was flat at best. A growing number of independents, knowing that some middle-class house-holds, even if they were two-income, couldn't afford to pay the tuition in a single year, were offering student loans at low interest rates, much like colleges were doing. Drawn to private schools' higher academic standards, as well as their smaller classes, greater specialization, and better teachers, more parents were willing to drive an hour or more from and to home, quite a sacrifice to make in the pursuit of a good education for their child.[18]

A 1983 survey by the National Association of Independent Schools con-firmed that it was private schools' higher academic standards that served as their primary draw. Eighty-one percent of the three thousand students surveyed said their academic skills had improved after their first year of private school, quite an endorsement. There were other interesting find-ings from the survey. Forty-five percent of the students reported that they had a say in where they went to school, the larger point being that parents still retained the majority vote. While more demanding academics was the main reason to opt for private school, other factors were the better chance of getting into a good college, greater independence, dissatisfaction with public school, a firmer sense of community, and, perhaps a bit oddly, an impressive campus.[19]

Within such a pro-private school climate, was it any surprise that a book with the title *The ABC's of Starting a Private School* was published? Although rather short at about a hundred pages, the book by Bonnie Schreiter was filled with useful information about the nuts and bolts of private schools, making it a great resource for readers who were thinking about founding their own. There were, after all, many things to consider, the first one being what purpose the school intended to serve. Bylaws, teacher contracts, health regulations, legal waivers, fundraising, and how to apply for tax-exempt status were just some of the other matters that went into organizing and operating a private school, a possibly lucrative business as the demand for them continued to grow.[20]

There was obviously a lot more to establishing a successful private school than just hanging out a shingle with a preppy-sounding name. The many parts of an academic machine had to run smoothly and work together as a single unit, with people of course the engine. An empathetic board of trust-ees, accessible administration, close (almost family-like) faculty, supportive parents, and appreciative alumnae were vital for any private school to carve out a niche in an increasingly crowded and competitive marketplace. Less red tape was one of the most distinguishing features of an independent, making flexibility an essential asset. (Paperwork alone was enough to drive public school teachers out of the occupation.)[21]

Starting a single private school was an ambitious exercise given all the moving parts but three leaders in business education in Chicago had much bigger plans. Richard Rosett of the University of Chicago and Dennis J. Keller and Ronald L. Taylor of the Keller Graduate School of Management were making plans in 1984 to roll out a national chain of independent elementary and secondary schools, approaching the concept like any other for-profit business. Their Education Corporation of America would offer consumers a better product than what the government was providing with public education, just as the private company Federal Express outperformed the US Post Office. The company would provide parents with "first-class, high-quality education at an affordable price," Rosett said, a selling proposition that he believed would be attractive to a large segment of consumers rather than those of upper incomes.[22]

The trio were in retrospect biting off a bit more than they could chew, but, against the backdrop of the "shop-til-you-drop" 1980s, it was hard to ignore the sense that private schools were becoming marketers selling a product or service to consumers. There had long been some element of that but by the mid-eighties, it was well on the way toward being if not already overt and unapologetic. The best boarding schools had no shortage of applicants (seven or eight times as many as openings), but many were seeking more minorities as they recognized their lack of diversity. At Boarding School Day in October 1984, held at the Buckley School in Manhattan, admission officers from dozens of New York City area schools welcomed parents and students from a variety of socioeconomic backgrounds. Attendees were, essentially, shopping around for a school, not unlike the process involved with buying a new car, weighing the pros and cons of each one presented.[23]

Some of the premier independents in the country, including Concord Academy, Phillips Exeter, and Phillips (Andover), showed up at Boarding School Day, which was sponsored by the Parents League of New York. Andover's minority enrollment had doubled in the past four years to 9 percent, but its administration wanted to raise it still further. Thirty-seven percent of Andover's students received some financial aid and 58 percent of the once all-boys school were now girls. Many of the conversations at Boarding School Day had to do with drugs, which had heavily infiltrated public schools and private day schools. (Some public high schools actually had drug-sniffing dogs searching for the stuff in lockers.) It was believed the problem was not as great in boarding schools as private day schools, part of why the number of applicants to the former had soared. Still, a handful of seniors at Choate Rosemary Hall had recently been expelled for using cocaine, an indication of how prevalent drug culture was among teenagers in the 1980s.[24]

Even if drugs had infiltrated campuses, interest in private schools continued to rise in the mid-eighties. Parents were now submitting as many as five or six applications rather than the two or three that had been the norm a decade earlier. With tests and interviews for each one, the process could be overwhelming, and it took months to hear back from admission offices with a letter of acceptance or, more likely based on the odds, rejection. Evaluating one's child in ways that a parent had never previously done could be an uncomfortable experience. Some parents of young children were having them take special tutorial programs that were said to raise scores on intelligence tests although school officials claimed they were generally useless. Coaching was discouraged, however, as it could give the school a false impression of a child's ability or maturity.[25]

Paradoxically, perhaps, the younger the child, the greater the stress associated with the admission process, especially in New York City, where the competition for private school admission to nursery, kindergarten, and first grade was most intense. It was not unusual for a certain type of parent to take a rejection personally, seeing their child's failure to be admitted to a top school as their own fault for not better preparing him or her for the competition. Rather than allow said child to have wasted his or her time on a playground, a father might ask, "Shouldn't I have insisted that the little one do brain-teasing puzzles?" A mother might respond, "Why did I not listen to Mozart when my baby's IQ was developing?" Another might think that she may have worn entirely the wrong kind of shoes to the interview.[26]

Manhattanites' anxiety reached a peak the second week of February when letters for the following academic year were sent. Those seven days could be apprehensive ones as normally rational adults exhibited rather bizarre behavior, such as peeking out of windows to see when the mail arrived. (A thin envelope was assumed to mean rejection, while a fat one suggested acceptance.) One mother labeled the seven days "Trauma Week," an indication of the stress parents felt. That level of angst may have been silly given that the applicants were tots, but some parents genuinely believed that rejection from the top dozen or so schools could derail their child from the fast track to an Ivy League college (and, by implication, success in life).[27]

The main topic at gatherings that week among that set—rapidly becoming known as "yuppies"—revolved around one particular question: "Have you heard?" For the other fifty-one weeks of the year, chatter among upper-middle-class Manhattanites most often centered on real estate, but for those seven days talk about prices per square foot was suspended. The long odds of getting into the cream of the crop—Trinity or Dalton—were a staple of the conversations. While long, the odds tended to be wildly exaggerated; one rumor was that Trinity had received two thousand applications for the 1985–1986 academic year when the actual number was three hundred. The "hot" school that year was the Town School on the Upper East Side (despite having been founded in 1913), making it not surprising that applications had tripled from the previous year.[28]

While competition was fierce for a limited number of spots, there was a certain comradery among parents going through the same painful experience. Empathetic looks were cast toward those who had received a letter with the message that their child "might do better elsewhere." Mothers were known to hide if the news was bad, however, too embarrassed to appear in public where one might run into friends asking the key question. Admission officers felt sorry for parents put in such an uncomfortable position, but such was life in the academic fast lane.[29]

MUFFIE OR MOPSY

It could be seen how given the trauma (or just drama) of the admission process, some Manhattan parents cut from a different cloth opted for a lower tier of private schools. (There were more than a hundred in the city.) Others were taking more extreme measures by choosing public school for their children upon learning how competitive it was at the uppermost level. Displays of wealth culture too could be a turnoff for those of average incomes. "When I saw parents hiring stretch limos to bring Muffie or Mopsy, I thought it was going too far," said one mother who dropped out of the race.[30]

Others decided on a different course for their child when seeing how few students of color there were at a school in which they had been interested. (Among the fifteen thousand students enrolled in Manhattan private schools, more than 80 percent were white, with that figure more than 90 percent in kindergarten and first grade.)[31] When questioned, "Do you have ethnic diversity?" one headmistress actually replied, "Yes, we have children from all the boroughs," nicely illustrating the point. Another administrator from the tony, WASPish Upper East Side considered diversity to consist of accepting students from the Upper West Side or Jewish children. Still, there were plenty of Gothamites eager, ready, and able to play the game, some of them beginning the process in the hospital shortly after giving birth.[32]

Much like real estate, K–12 education in New York City was a world unto itself, but a greater interest in private school was a national phenomenon. By the end of 1984—halfway through the decade—one out of every eight children in the United States attended a private school, quite a jump in just a few years. There were now some 5.7 million students in 27,700 private schools in the country, according to the Department of Education, with the number of Roman Catholic and parochial schools still shrinking. Private schools were roughly half the size of their public school counterparts in terms of student bodies, but the growing number of independents was more than making up for that.[33]

While the number of students in Catholic and parochial schools had fallen, those in Protestant evangelical schools were increasing. These schools were not the segregated academies of the South; rather, they were nonracist institutions that appealed to families seeking education with a moral and religious foundation. Enrollment doubled for such schools between 1978 and 1984, according to associations of Christian schools, reflecting the nation's embrace of more conservative values and ascent of the theological right. Enrollment in other religious schools, such as those with a Lutheran and Jewish orientation, had grown but not nearly as much as the evangelical ones.[34]

Asian Americans were also increasingly turning to private schools in the 1980s. A large number of Vietnamese, Korean, Chinese, Japanese, Thai, and Filipino families had recently emigrated to the United States, many of whom wanted the best education possible for their children. In New York, some parents were enrolling their kids in Prep for Prep, a program that helped place gifted minorities in private schools, with a program called A Better Chance taking a similar approach in Boston. (Private schools' rush to diversify in the late 1960s and early 1970s had in a sense backfired, as many minorities admitted had not been academically ready for the tougher work.) In Los Angeles, almost half of the student body of the Pilgrim School during the 1986–1987 academic year were Asian American, and the percentage was continuing to rise.[35]

Alongside private schools' gradual diversification, more schools dedicated to a particular minority group were opening across the country. "Minority families, like their white counterparts, have become increasingly dissatisfied with the public schools," noted Lindsey Gruson in the *New York Times*. (The dropout rate in many urban areas was 70 percent.) According to the Institute for Independent Education, there were 220 private schools for African American students, about sixty for Asian Americans, at least forty for Hispanics, and about a dozen for Native Americans in 1986. Most of the schools, which collectively served about forty-five thousand students, were in inner-city, low-income neighborhoods. The owners and operators of the schools were almost always themselves members of minority groups, as was the faculty.[36]

Until *Brown v. Board of Education*, African American private schools were a common feature on the nation's educational landscape. Desegregation of public schools had changed that, but now there was a revival in urban areas, and for the same reasons that all private schools were flourishing. In addition to taking refuge from the various problems of public schools, African American independents offered "an abundance of no-frills, task-oriented school spirit, smaller classes, and teachers who give them their personal attention," wrote Dr. Leonard Krivy in the *Philadelphia Tribune*. Materials and equipment were relatively scarce and there were typically no sports teams as there were in public schools, but that was viewed as a small price to pay for all the educational advantages.[37]

Competing to a greater extent with all-minority private schools, elite independents double-downed on diversity initiatives, and not for altruistic reasons. Administrators recognized that an education at an almost all-white institution was not good preparation for life after graduation. Parents were not getting their money's worth at such a school, it was agreed, a shortchanging on the return on investment they expected and deserved. Even in multicultural New York, a white child of means might have little interaction with African Americans and Hispanics, giving him or her a narrow understanding of American and global culture.[38]

To that point, the city's Independent Schools Admissions Association (whose advisory board included staff and parents from the Allen-Stevenson School, Bank Street, Brearley, Dalton, Day, Friends Seminary, Horace Mann, New Lincoln, Nightingale-Bamford, Saint David's, Spence, and West Side Montessori) was striving to recruit more Black and Hispanic children for kindergarten and first grade. Modest progress was considered to have been made to date, an understandable thing given all the variables in play.[39] Of the 870 member institutions in the National Association of Independent Schools, minorities accounted for 11 percent of all students, with Asian Americans surpassing African Americans for the first time in the 1987–1988 academic year.[40]

Private schools were diversifying in ways that had nothing to do with race or ethnicity. Rules regarding dress and personal appearance—a staple in most private schools—were becoming more of an issue for administrations as students sought ways to individualize themselves. Many American prep schools had long followed the tradition imported from British boarding schools that began in the mid-nineteenth century and was inspired by military uniforms. Boys at "public" schools wore uniforms (as the word implied) to encourage conformity, something Jonathan Gathorne-Hardy noted in his *The Old School Tie: The Phenomenon of the English Public School*. "A uniform does what is says—make one form," he wrote, making a pupil "easier to control and also stamping him with the image of the institution."[41]

It may have been 1980s America, but private school deans still preferred uniforms for their alleged ability to make students focus on academics rather than appearance and to set an aura of discipline. Uniforms often consisted of a gray or tartan skirt for girls with a white blouse and gray or khaki pants for boys. Students could typically choose polo shirts from a variety of colors, with sweaters and blazers consistent with the school's traditional colors. More formal schools required boys to wear rep ties. Shoes were brown or black, usually Oxfords, Topsiders, or penny loafers. Some schools carried crests on their jackets, often inscribed with a Latin motto, making them iconic signifiers of private school culture.[42]

There were signs, however, that dress codes were breaking down as students found ways to personalize their appearance. Some were not tucking in their shirttails, both to be more comfortable and to take a swipe at enforced properness. Jewelry was a gray area, with some schools allowing it and others not. Either way, students seemed to be wearing more of it as a means of separating themselves from the crowd. Hair too was generally undefined territory, although dyeing it in a primary color would frequently lead to a chat with the dean.[43]

GENTEEL POVERTY

Private school administrators had bigger fish to fry than some students striking a passing resemblance to Annie Lennox or David Bowie. A host of challenges confronted the nation's private schools near the end of the decade, many of them a function of their tremendous growth. There were now more than a dozen private school associations to which tens of thousands of independent institutions belonged, including the National Association of Independent Schools, the American Montessori Society, Christian Schools International, Friends Council of Education, National Catholic Educational Association, the Council of Independent Black Institutions, and the National Society for Hebrew Day Schools. A new book, *Private Schools of the United States*, offered information on fifteen thousand schools, a valuable resource for parents, students, and guidance counselors trying to decide which one was best for a particular child.[44] Amazingly, Porter Sargent's *The Handbook of Private Schools* was still being published as well (thirty-seven years after the man's death).[45]

Another new book was *Visible Now: Blacks in Private Schools*. The edited collection of essays offered interesting insights into the often highly charged relationship between African Americans and private schools, whether the institutions were primarily white or all-Black. The most compelling stories involved the friction that was known to develop when parents sought to make possible excellent educational opportunities for their children while at the same time imparting racial pride. Most African American enrollment in private schools remained in Catholic institutions, even though the majority of Black families belonged to other faiths. There was a long history of Catholic schools serving the needs of lower-income urban families, and this continued to form a key part of African American education.[46]

The fact that there were more independent schools and students was a good thing, but the growth had made it more difficult to attract and retain qualified teachers. Salaries were typically two-thirds to three-quarters of what public school teachers earned, a trade-off for what many private school teachers considered to be greater freedom and better working conditions. As in public schools, teachers in independents often moonlighted to make extra money and were open to a career change should a more lucrative opportunity come along. The teaching profession as a whole was at risk, experts believed, as living in "genteel poverty" had less appeal in the money-conscious late 1980s.[47]

The even larger issue private school administrators had to address was whether their offerings were worth the money. The two Coleman Reports had made it appear so, but much had changed in education since the publication of the second one in 1981. Private school students scored just slightly higher than public school students on two important achievement tests in 1986, a smaller margin than what had been expected by leading educators. Public school standards were believed to be improving under the mandate of educational reform, making administrators of independents wonder if they needed to strengthen their curricula to keep up.[48]

It may have been coincidental, but more stories about parents transferring their children from exclusive private schools to good public ones began to appear in the media. Given independents' relative lack of diversity, high cost, and no guarantee of offering a great education, it could be seen how public schools represented a better choice for some children. Private school students felt the need to compete with their classmates and excel in some way—academics, sports, or the arts—creating a level of pressure and stress not common in public school. Also, some parents felt more connected to their community with their kids in local public schools and liked the broader racial, ethnic, and economic mix typically found in them. To that point, there was a wider selection of friends from which to choose in public school, something kids were known to point out to parents who for other reasons were already thinking about not signing the private school reenrollment contract.[49]

In addition to achieving greater diversity, finding good teachers, and maintaining their academic superiority over public schools, many urban private schools had yet another challenge: fitting everything into a small space. Hallways may be doubling as libraries or computer rooms in some schools, with simply not enough room to squeeze in all the materials, equipment, and people. (It was not unusual for an urban private school to be housed in what had been a turn-of-the-century or older church, mansion, or brownstone.) With attendance at capacity, buildings were further strained, making the dream of a state-of-the-art science lab or full-court basketball court an elusive one. Annexing another building or moving to a new, larger one was easier said than done, and not just because of the expense. Neighbors in tony neighborhoods didn't want a big school on their block, envisioning hundreds of children getting in and out of buses every weekday on their now relatively peaceful street.[50]

Nightingale-Bamford on the Upper East Side of Manhattan was one such school experiencing growing pains in the late eighties. The exclusive school for girls had an expansion plan for its sixty-year-old building but it had stalled due to community opposition. Neighbors didn't like the idea of four more stories being put on top of the existing structure along with the construction of a new wing in an adjacent vacant lot. (Not only sunlight and air would be blocked, they argued, but the historical character of the street would be spoiled and the greenery damaged.) Property values would decline, the neighbors added, a common complaint when expansion plans for any school were announced. Not just city private schools were experiencing the problem but ones in older suburbs, with space at a premium due to residential and retail growth.[51]

Adding to the woes of private schools, even during what was unarguably a boom period, was a lessening of parental involvement in their student's education within certain circles. Such parents appeared to be busier in their own lives, whether professionally or personally, and were spending less time helping their children with homework, studying, and other school-related activities. Two-career couples had become the norm, particularly among parents who could afford tuition for private school, but there was a cost to greater household income. Educators were noticing that more students, most of them in preschool or elementary school, were lacking in basic skills and attributed the deficiency to a decrease in parental participation.[52]

How to address the issue? Educators were asking members of wealthier families' caretakers—nannies, au pairs, housekeepers, and tutors—to fill in for largely absentee parents by adding an educational role to their responsibilities. Surrogate parents found themselves meeting with teachers, going on field trips, and studying with children, sometimes even invited to classrooms to get a better sense of what was being taught and needed to be learned. While not ideal, it was a sensible adaptation to the realities of modern life, educators held, certainly better than having a generation of students with weak vocabulary or an inability to do simple arithmetic.[53]

Happily, however, not all parents were delegating the job. In some private schools, notably those with a religious orientation, parents were pleased to be involved in their children's academic life. A grassroots atmosphere pervaded such schools, with parents welcome to offer suggestions regarding curricula and programs. Admission committees sometimes included parents, as it was believed that the latter had a good sense of the kind of students who should be accepted. Some schools went so far as to see parents as the primary teachers of children, with faculty and administration there to provide support.[54] That level of cooperation was a rare thing in the universe of the American private school, however, something that would soon become apparent.

8

THE 1990s: REACHING
FOR THE RAINBOW

"You want students to celebrate their differences, but you want them to
feel a part of, and connected to, your school community."

—John Holden, head of St. Stephen's and St. Agnes School
(Arlington, Virginia), 1993

In January 1992, the administration at the Loomis Chaffee School was
faced with a tough decision: should the school distribute condoms to its
students? The independent boarding and day school in Windsor, Connecticut, for boys and girls in ninth to twelfth grades had a strict "no-sex" policy,
but a recent poll taken by the school newspaper, *The Log*, showed that 54
percent of the student body was sexually active. The AIDS epidemic was
sweeping the nation, making administrators consider handing out condoms
to students who requested them. The issue was "a health problem" rather
than one of birth control, staff members made clear, designating the infir-
mary as the site of condom distribution, should the school go ahead with
the plan.[1]

Needless to say, the original administrators of the Loomis Chaffee
School, which had been founded in 1914, did not have to face such difficult decisions. American private schools had evolved considerably over
the twentieth century, making them in some ways unrecognizable to those
who had trod the same paths a century or two centuries earlier. The biggest change involved the people who populated the campuses of private

schools, as the world of education and the nation as a whole addressed its institutional racism and other biases. More than anything else, diversity would come to define the narrative of private schools in the 1990s, adding an important chapter to its already extraordinary journey.

AN INDEPENDENT LOT

The twentieth century had indeed been a remarkable one for the American private school, but the final decade was starting as somewhat of a dud. Enrollments were slipping a bit from their 1980s high in many parts of the country, with a declining school-age population and weak economy the main causes. Having become used to continually rising demand, administrators were taken aback by the downturn, and ratcheted up their marketing campaigns. Letting real estate agents and relocation companies know that there were openings was part of the effort to increase enrollments, and schools were also asking alumni and parents to spread the word.[2]

Even in New York City, private schools were feeling the pinch. Teachers were being laid off, class sizes enlarged, programs cut, and more schools were merging. Tuitions were being raised, presumably under the assumption that there were a certain number of parents who would pay whatever it cost to keep their kids in private school. Those with middle incomes and without full scholarships were moving or considering moving to Long Island and Westchester for their good public schools as many had done in the past.[3]

The recession affected private schools in a variety of ways, none of them good. Corporate layoffs were having a trickle-down effect; it wasn't unusual for a handful of students at nearby schools to be affected. Vacations and home improvements were put on hold if it meant keeping a child in private school.[4] Families who had not previously asked for financial aid were now doing so, further straining school budgets, and more students were looking for part-time jobs as their allowances were reduced or eliminated. Some couples were refinancing their homes to raise the money, especially if they had two or three kids in private school, or borrowing it from their parents. Schools had become more understanding if a monthly payment was missed even though they needed the money to pay their own bills.[5]

Public schools were free, of course, and thus a more attractive option in a recession. Standardized testing had become the centerpiece of educational reform in the eighties, so it was not surprising that parents were interested in using a school's aggregate test score to help inform their decision between public and private. While states published scores for public schools, almost all private schools refused to release them, however, claiming that they didn't fully reflect their institution's overall educational experience and that results could be misleading. There were all sorts of variables to consider, but test scores were objective criteria that could at least narrow the field. "Our students outperform the national norm but here we treat the test as just another factor," said Margo Long of the Oakwood School in North Hollywood, California, a staple answer when parents asked to see scores to compare schools.[6]

Were private schools by default superior to public schools? It was a question that had been asked before but the harder economic times of the early 1990s were pushing it to the forefront of the national conversation regarding education. In New York City, fourth-grade students in private schools eked by those in public schools on proficiency standards on a challenging state test (55 percent to 52 percent), not reassuring news to strong advocates of independents. The city's more exclusive private schools had not participated in the test, however, reason to believe that the results were not a fair measurement.[7]

There was some evidence that private school students were better test takers than those in public schools. In Granby, Connecticut, a steady stream of public high school students had migrated to private schools located in other communities beginning in the late 1980s. SAT scores had dropped sharply in Granby over this same period, leading some to conclude that it was an example of "bright flight"—the loss of more academically equipped students to private schools. Public school officials were studying the data to try to account for the drop.[8]

Many private schools in other parts of the country, however, would have welcomed bright flight. The combination of the recession and dip in the high school age demographic was making private schools work that much harder to attract students. Independents had discovered marketing in the 1980s but now were stepping up efforts in that department via advertising, glitzy videos, more open houses, and alumni and parent networking events. Boarding schools were sending recruiters across the United States as well as to South America, Europe, and Asia, and reaping positive results in what had been largely untapped markets. Much of the messaging was geared toward letting candidates know that not just wealthy white children attended private schools, a perception that lingered despite the diversity initiatives of the last quarter-century.[9]

Many parents didn't require convincing to send their kids to a private school. Enrollments may have been down but concerns about overcrowding, drugs, gangs, and violence in public schools remained, making independents a very attractive alternative. "I have only one chance to give my kid an education," said one Texan mom after taking a full-time job to put her three kids in private school. Some parents were dipping into their children's college funds to pay the tuition for private school, thinking it was a better investment in terms of education. Average tuition was $6,400 in 1991, a significant amount given that 36 percent of the parents of private school students had an annual household income of less than $50,000.[10]

Some educators believed that money spent on private school could pay off bigger dividends than on an expensive college. Elementary and secondary school was where children "learn to study as well as increase their knowledge," stated Barbara Scott of the Kent School in Connecticut, thinking the priority should be to develop a good attitude and healthy work habits—things of which she felt private schools excelled.[11]

Public school supporters, meanwhile, felt equally committed to their form of education. Stronger community ties and greater cultural diversity were just a couple of plusses, they argued, with some students returning to public school after finding their independent school too monocultural and overly protective. One Cleveland Heights teen asserted that public schools "challenged students to be individual and gives you so much to become your own person," thinking the concerns about gangs and drugs were more rumor than fact. Another reported that public school helped him learn how to "deal with all kinds of people," and that there was too much handholding at private schools. "The kids have to be self-motivated and struggle with the human issues," said the latter's father, "but the outcome is a better and more responsible citizen."[12]

The very different opinions vis-à-vis the issue of public versus private schools were not surprising given the tremendous scope of education in general. Quality in both private and public schools varied wildly, for one thing, and the range of what both parents and students were seeking in an educational experience ran the gamut. Most of the focus was on academics, and deservedly so, but the truth was that parents often chose a certain school for a different reason—that is, religious orientation, educational philosophy, level of discipline, or attention to special needs. Within the private school universe alone, how could one objectively compare a traditional boarding prep school, an Afro-centric urban academy, and a suburban, predominantly white independent run for profit?[13]

For George E. Conway, headmaster of St. Anne's Belfield School in Charlottesville, Virginia, there were three factors that parents should look for when evaluating private schools. The first was effective leadership, particularly regarding the relationship between administration and teachers. Teachers were "an independent lot," Conway thought, especially better ones who had gone the private school route. Headmasters should be academically trained and have some teaching experience themselves to better understand the daily challenges that faculty face, he believed. Next for Conway was school size, which preferably should be small to allow for small class sizes. A couple dozen or more adolescents in a room did not make a good learning environment, and teachers were simply more effective when working on an individual basis with students. Finally, parental involvement was key for Conway, meaning the degree to which parents (not nannies) were invested (not financially) in the education of their children.[14]

A MESSY BUSINESS

Private school boosters had long spouted the benefits of their style of education but had little quantitative evidence to back up their claims. That changed with the publication of a study completed by the National Center for Education Statistics. Eighth graders in nonsectarian private schools were more than twice as likely as those in either public or parochial schools to study advanced math or algebra, foreign language, or laboratory science. They were also more likely to take part in fine and performing arts and play a sport. They watched much less television and did much more homework, making it not surprising that private school students entered college with SAT scores almost a hundred points higher than public and parochial schools.[15]

Welcome news, certainly, and a good defense against critics who labeled private schools as places that bore little resemblance to "the real world." Actually, some advocates of independent schools freely admitted that the institutions were not mini versions of the real world or even attempted to be. Rather, at their best, private schools were models of "an ideal world," an environment in which students could master the skills needed in a world that was often too real.[16]

Perhaps that noble idea was the basis for the Clintons to send their daughter Chelsea to private school. The news broke in January 1993, just a couple of weeks before the president and First Lady settled into the White House. The media made much of the couple's announcement, particularly because both Bill and Hillary Clinton had been big backers of public education. (Chelsea had attended public school in Little Rock.) That fall, Chelsea would be attending Sidwell Friends as an eighth grader, a school often described by journalists as "posh" (and charged a tuition of over $10,000). It was a "personal family decision," the White House explained, a line that other elected officials and school board members had used when they chose private school over public. Nixon's two daughters had attended Sidwell as did Teddy Roosevelt's son, making the Clintons' decision not too surprising.[17]

Still, the announcement fueled the fire surrounding private schools versus public schools and reinforced the image that the former were elitist institutions primarily tailored to the interests of privileged whites. While campaigning, Clinton had not only pledged to improve public education but had made a point that white students were the minority at the school that Chelsea attended. Decades had gone by, but there had been no resolution on whether income tax credits or vouchers should be provided by the government to help families pay for private school, turning the Clintons' personal decision into a political issue.[18] The last child to have lived in the White House, Amy Carter, had attended public school in Washington, drawing more criticism of the incoming president from his political foes.[19]

While it likely couldn't be said of Sidwell, there were many instances in which a private school had a larger percentage of minority students than the local public schools. (This was especially true for parochial or Catholic schools.) Nationally, minorities—African Americans, Hispanics, and Asian Americans—comprised 14 percent of all private school students in 1993, a significant increase from the 9 percent in 1982. (Four percent of teachers at independent schools were now minorities.) Additionally, there were independents where African Americans represented the majority of students, notably Piney Woods in Mississippi, the Harvard School in Chicago, Xavier Prep in New Orleans, and Girard College in Philadelphia (which was and remains, despite its name, a prep school).[20]

With more students of color came a change in how independents approached cultural diversity. While in the past, minorities were expected to assimilate into the white Protestant culture that pervaded most private schools, administrators now encouraged students of color to retain their cultural identity. This shift reflected the transformation of national identity from the "melting pot" to a multicultural one, in which ethnic, racial, and religious differences were celebrated rather than repressed. Private schools were "reaching for the rainbow," Stephen Buckley observed in the *Washington Post* in 1993, noting the reconfiguring of curricula, hiring of more minority faculty, creation of racially defined clubs, and diversification of boards of trustees.[21]

The trick was to accommodate multiculturalism within a particular school's community and traditions, some of which went back centuries. Courses in subjects such as Middle Eastern history and African American literature were being taught, and Black Student Unions were formed. There was concern among some parents and alumni that the school they knew and loved would become something much different as the diversity initiative swept through all aspects of the institution. Administrators were dependent on those constituencies for tuition and gifts, of course, making the issue a complicated one, especially given the fact that greater financial aid was typically part of initiatives. "This is a messy business," said Diana Beebe, head of all-girls Holton-Arms School in Washington, DC, "but you don't get anywhere without taking risks."[22]

With the recession of the early nineties over, however, administrators could spend more time on diversity initiatives and less on recruitment. A healthier economy wasn't the only thing boosting private school enrollments. Education reform had not lifted students' standardized test scores to any significant degree, and, in some states, they were dropping. Calls flooded into admissions offices in the spring of 1994 in Los Angeles after the most recent California Learning Assessment System test scores were released. Most of the area's students in grades four, eight, and ten were scoring below statewide standards in reading, writing, and mathematics, causing some parents to give up on public schools.[23]

Other parents were making appointments with admission offices for a completely different reason. Since the feminist movement of the 1970s, there had been claims that gender bias was embedded in public school education, primarily due to teachers prioritizing the academic success of boys over girls. These assertions had recently been renewed as research findings showed that public school teachers more often called on boys and often let them lead classroom discussions. In the wake of such studies, single-sex independents in certain parts of the country were experiencing a revival of sorts. In West Los Angeles, for example, all-girls schools such as Notre Dame Academy, Marlboro School for Girls, Marymount, and Immaculate Heart were seen as places where young women (as they were preferred to be called) could develop leadership skills, enjoy freedom of expression, and pursue excellence in all dimensions of academic life.[24]

Add in continuing safety concerns about public schools and a seemingly never-ending budget crunch, one can see how private schools were once again experiencing a rush of applications. No one could say with complete assurance that independents were superior to public schools because of all the variables involved, but some considered them to be an oasis in an arid educational climate. As in the 1980s, parents were seeking ways to give their kids an edge in more competitive markets, particularly if schools required the Independent School Entrance Examination (ISEE) (which now many secular secondary institutions did). Scores were crucial in the admission process and, given that a student could take it only once at that time, one-on-one tutoring was becoming more popular.[25]

Needless to say, the ISEE did not measure a student's character, ethics, or moral compass, something that was a growing concern to independent educators. Many private schools excelled in teaching young people academic skills but ignored the development of more humanistic traits that were central to individuals and society as a whole. Some prep schools did have in place a set of values that informed curricula, but anything to do with philosophy typically took a backseat to subjects that colleges liked to see on a student's transcript. Many students didn't know the meaning of words such as "integrity" or "virtue," this in itself a sign that a generation was being raised without much thought given to how to be a good global citizen. Parents were part of the problem, of course, as they too were likely more interested in their child getting into Harvard than him or her learning how to make the world a better place.[26]

A WORK IN PROGRESS

Private school administrators recognized that the best way to teach ethical and moral values to students was through action. Independents had long been accused of being "nondemocratic" institutions because of their exclusivity, and they were now embracing diversity in part to show that they had a moral compass of their own. Desegregation had served as the vehicle for public schools to become more diverse and, while it had taken a few extra decades, private schools were at the end of the twentieth century admitting significant numbers of students of color regardless of their families' financial status. In the process, the identity of independents was gradually changing from being bastions for economically privileged white Protestants to functioning as high-quality academic institutions that served Americans of all backgrounds.

The diversification of private schools served multiple purposes. "The current push is a result not only of what school directors call 'a moral imperative' but also of hard-nosed financial considerations," wrote Valerie Strauss in the *Washington Post* in 1995, noting that many African American families paid full tuition to DC-area independents. Achieving what some educators called an "equitable learning experience" for all students was not an easy thing, however, as genuine inclusivity was easier said than done. Again, changing the culture of a school that may have been founded before the Civil War took considerable effort involving both people and materials. Courses for staff and faculty on recognizing and addressing personal and institutional bias were sometimes part of the process.[27]

Diversity within private schools thus went well beyond admitting more minority students and hiring more minority teachers. Many independents celebrated Black History Month and Kwanzaa, and works by Toni Morrison and Alice Walker were just as likely to be on reading lists as those by F. Scott Fitzgerald and Ernest Hemingway. It varied by school, of course, but it was not unusual for about half of minority students to be African American and Hispanics and Asian Americans to comprise the other half. From a historical view, much progress had been made in terms of making independents more inclusive but "tensions and misunderstandings remain," noted Marilyn McCraven and Mary Maushard of the *Baltimore Sun*. Diversification at private schools in Baltimore was a "work in progress," they concluded after a thorough survey, a case of making two steps forward and then taking one step back.[28]

Private schools' reach for the rainbow often involved alliances with organizations that matched minority students with dozens of elementary and secondary independents in a particular area. Families were likely to hear of these partnerships simply by word of mouth, a fortuitous thing as a placement could lead to a life-altering experience. The process involved an application to an interview with the alliance followed by a tour of potential schools to find the right fit, as each institution had its own culture, philosophy, and approach. If accepted, families then filled out lengthy financial aid applications, as schools in the program admitted students without regard to their ability to pay the tuition. A summer boot camp to help prepare students for life in a private school was the final step; some of them were surprised to learn how much homework would be involved (and how much money the parents of some other students had in the bank).[29]

Not every applicant was selected, however, making some families take rather extraordinary measures if they felt that a private school was the better choice for their child. There were stories of grandparents using much of their Social Security money to pay for tuition and expenses, even if that meant occasionally eating at a community food bank. Others might forgo new clothes for as long as possible, not see the inside of a restaurant, or work multiple part-time jobs to come up with the necessary cash. Such stories, entirely true, provided hard evidence that independents were not just for rich folks, as some still believed they were. While it didn't mean going hungry, tuition for middle-class families was often a stretch; this also dispelled the myth that private schools were only for plutocrats.[30]

The sacrifices some would make to afford a private education for a child or grandchild were directly related to a lack of faith in public school. Even some staunch defenders of the nation's public schools were thinking an independent would be a better choice for young persons, if they were given the chance. Public education had been a marvelous thing from its beginnings in the late nineteenth century to the mid-1960s or so, many agreed but much had changed over the last few decades.[31]

John Rosemond, a psychologist and columnist for the *Hartford Courant*, was one such long supporter of public schools who appeared to be switching allegiances. To explain why, Rosemond listed a litany of "viruses" that had attacked the public school system: misguided tenure policies, top-heavy bureaucracy, school boards comprised of "wannabe politicians," an emphasis on social engineering and "self-esteem" versus academics, endless series of "reforms," and, last but not least, total failure in the arena of discipline. Private schools, on the other hand, typically did not give tenure, reinvested most of their money in education rather than administration, had volunteer boards, ignored "reform," focused on academics, and knew how to manage student behavior.[32]

Private schools were also by the mid-nineties inclined to require high schoolers to do some kind of community service as part of their increasing recognition that education went beyond academics. Collecting canned goods for local food banks was a common activity, particularly around Thanksgiving. Volunteering to serve meals in soup kitchens was another staple of students' community service, with graduation dependent on their completing a certain number of hours. Such service was not just about "giving back"; students were likely to learn much from the experience that could never be taught in a classroom. Visiting patients with Alzheimer's, building homes through Habitat for Humanity, and taking part in environmental cleanups served as other ways students were learning the values of citizenship.[33]

Boarding schools had been vigorous champions of community service for as long as anyone could remember, yet that didn't appear to be a major selling point for parents and students. Premier New England boarding schools such as Andover, Choate, Groton, and St. Paul's had lost nearly 10 percent of their enrollments over the past decade despite reeling in more international students. Northfield Mount Hermon and Kent were down as well, and a handful of boarding schools had closed. Meanwhile, the number of day schools (and students) had risen during this same period, a two-ships-passing-in-the-night within the sea of independent education.[34]

In a 1996 piece for the *American Scholar*, David V. Hicks parsed the reasons for what he called "the strange fate of the American boarding school." Boarding schools were hardly an oasis in education, a study by Louis M. Crosier had revealed; rather, the institutions were home to a host of "casualties of privilege" including drug use, bullying, eating disorders, and sexual activity. Then there was their cost, which was significantly more than day schools (double, in fact, on average). Finally, Ivy League colleges no longer looked to boarding schools as their main source of freshmen, making parents question their value relative to the required investment.[35]

As day schools continued to flourish, in part because parents could keep an eye on their kids, choosing the ideal one became seen as that much more important. For some time, tutors had been used to help students get into private school but now consultants were being hired to help parents select the independent that would represent the best match. The service cost hundreds and sometimes thousands of dollars, but that was considered small change given the long-term upsides of an individual being placed in the right school (and downsides of going to the wrong one). Consultants "packaged" their young clients in ways that made it appear to be a perfect match between child and school, even if the client happened to be applying to preschool or a private kindergarten. The perceived slide of public schools, rise in two-income households, and "echo boom" (children of baby boomers) were said to account for the burgeoning industry.[36]

IN THE SPOTLIGHT

One could take issue with any form of "packaging" of four-year-olds but still acknowledge the phenomenal ascent of the American private school. It hadn't been that long since private schools were "small, even suspect, players" on the nation's educational scene, as Peter W. Cookson Jr. expressed in the *Brookings Review*. Aligned with a certain class or religion, independents were indeed marginal institutions, particularly when compared to the country's massive public school system which promised equal opportunity and upward mobility for all, despite the glaring inequalities with regard to race and gender.[37]

Cookson argued that it was 1980 when "the tables turned," with public schools now the weak link in the chain. Private schools were now "in the spotlight," although there were many different kinds. (Researcher Don Erikson had identified no less than fifteen: nonsectarian, Roman Catholic, Lutheran, Jewish, Seventh Day Adventist, Episcopal, Greek Orthodox, Quaker, Mennonite, Calvinist, Evangelical, Assembly of God, special education, alternative, and military.) There were twenty-seven thousand elementary and secondary private schools with about six million students (12 percent of the nation's schoolchildren) in 1997. Most of the independents were concentrated on the East and West Coasts, with Connecticut still in the lead with 17 percent of the state's total number of students and Wyoming last with just 1.5 percent.[38]

For Cookson, the range of private schools was most striking at this point in their history. "It is a mosaic of institutions that vary by mission, size, and social exclusivity," he observed, although data showed that private school families were wealthier than average and that the overwhelming majority of students were white despite diversity initiatives. Private schools tended to be lumped together as offering a better educational experience than public schools but Cookson, who had visited dozens of them over the past twenty years, found some to be excellent, others mediocre, and still others terrible.[39]

Whatever their type or quality, private schools were experiencing high demand in the late nineties, so much so that a fair number of day schools were expanding or trying to figure out how to find more space. "People who would never have thought about sending their children to private school are now doing so," said Linda Kaiser of the Field School in Washington, DC, noting that the profile of parents filing applications had changed in the past decade. In the fortunate position of having to turn away applicants, administrators had to choose whether to maintain the current size of their school or grow, which usually meant having to acquire or lease out more real estate. More students in a bigger space (or different campuses) usually altered the atmosphere of a school, making the decision not an easy one.[40]

Given the number of new buildings—classrooms, libraries, gyms, and administrative offices—being constructed on and off existing private school campuses, expansion appeared to be the leading choice to accommodate more students. There was a certain competition among independents in any given market, making new building envy part of the decision to invest money to grow. The economy was strong, and the stock market was roaring, making it a good time to launch a major capital campaign.[41] New buildings also offered the opportunity to create technology centers or computer labs as it became increasingly clear that students would have to be digitally fluent in the twenty-first century.[42]

Another source of funding for capital projects, business operations, or tuition assistance was auctions. Private schools across the country were finding auctions to be both very popular and highly lucrative, as parents bid on donated products and services. You name it—trips, art, tickets to shows, dinner with a celebrity, or even a VIP parking space—might be auctioned off, with buyers and sellers coming away happy with the transaction. At some schools, auctions were being recognized as the biggest event of the year and an entertaining way to bring the community together.[43]

Meanwhile, as dollars rolled in, so did applications, many of the latter from high-achieving baby boomers who were passing on their competitive ethos to their children. Some parents were doubtful about their child with good but not great grades being accepted to a more prestigious school, given the long odds, and didn't quite know how to pay the steep tuition should they beat the odds. Such applicants may be put on a waiting list and, if eventually accepted, a frenzied period of coming up with thousands of dollars immediately began. (Annual tuition at more expensive schools cost more than a new car.) Parents were known to sell their house and move to a more modest one to quickly raise the cash, but it was considered worth the trade-off.[44]

Interestingly, experts such as Arthur Powell, author of *Lessons of Privilege: The American Prep School Tradition*, advised that it was not top students who benefited most from independent education but those who were in the middle of the pack. Public schools tended to focus on the two ends of the spectrum—that is, those who excelled and those who struggled, leaving those somewhere between without much attention. With smaller classes and more individualized instruction, however, private schools devoted as much of their resources to average learners as students who were on one or the other side of the curve.[45]

That was an appealing aspect of private schools to many parents, even if they had to answer questions like, "What animal or vegetable would your child like to be?" or "Which musical instrument does your child most resemble?" in interviews. Admission officers at independents had seemingly borrowed a page from Barbara Walters who in 1981 had asked Katharine Hepburn in an interview what kind of tree would she be. Such questions were designed to bring some creativity and fun into the admission process, but many parents fretted that they would respond with a "wrong" animal, vegetable, or musical instrument, thereby crushing their child's chances of getting into the school. "Admissions hell," as some referred to it, also might involve bribing children to incentivize them to sparkle in interviews, have them take IQ tests to supplement their package, or contact anyone and everyone who had some connection to a particular school. Every word of the essay typically required would be painstakingly scrutinized to present a child in the best light possible without being considered classic parental bragging.[46]

Private schools' use of but not obsession with standardized testing was yet another reason why some parents were going to extreme measures to receive a letter of acceptance. As a central part of educational reforms, "teaching to the test" had become the norm in public schools, a concern among many that this was not an ideal learning experience. Much was made of the results of such tests, with considerable pressure placed on schools, districts, states, and of course, students to do well on them. Independents placed significantly less emphasis on standardized tests, employing them more as guidelines than measurement tools, an attractive thing for those who viewed education in more holistic terms.[47]

The absence of other restrictions associated with public schools was pushing more parents to independents. Faith-based institutions were committed to developing not just children's minds but their souls as well, explaining why 85 percent of the nation's private schools were religiously affiliated. Even in nonreligious classes, teachers were free to discuss God and other subjects that could get a faculty member of a public school fired. Spirituality may have had little to do with academics, but religious schools won a disproportionate percentage of US Department of Education Blue Ribbon awards, a program that recognized exemplary student achievement.[48] While a particular faith-based school could be managed or even owned by a religious institution, it was likely that administrators emphasized humanistic and universal values as a reflection of their commitment to diversity and inclusion.[49]

Diversity initiatives continued through the late 1990s, yet enrollment figures for students of color had flattened out, with several reasons said to account for that. Some private school administrators simply didn't know how to recruit more minorities, and many families didn't know that such schools, often in suburban, mostly white communities, existed. Other parents who were aware of such schools and knew that administrators were seeking more students of color opted to keep their kids in public school out of concern they might be marginalized in predominantly white institutions. Outsourcing the recruitment process to professionals with expertise in the area often resulted in higher numbers.[50]

Even with those cited reasons, educators were somewhat puzzled and decidedly concerned by the leveling off of diversity in private schools. Aggressive recruiting efforts had been in place since the 1960s, many schools were flush with money, and the nonwhite population was continuing to expand, a seemingly perfect formula to attract more students of color. There was an even greater dearth of teachers and administrators of color, compounding the problem. In New York City, elite schools such as Fieldston, Brearley, Spence, and Friends Seminary had formed committees and task forces to examine attitudes about race, ethnicity, and class, yet they too had hit a wall. Minority students reported feeling uncomfortable on campuses, with too much attention paid to their race in both classroom settings and among friends.[51] A new century was about to begin, however, offering hope that American private schools would realize their full potential.

9

THE 2000s: THE GARDEN OF EDEN

"The blood is flowing on Park Avenue."

—Bill Dennett, a Westport, Connecticut-based private
school consultant, 2005

In April 2002, a truck from New York City arrived in Clay, West Virginia, carrying some very special cargo. Inside were hundreds of expensive gowns, shoes, gloves, jewelry, and other accessories, which were soon put on display in a "boutique" in the Clay County High School gym. The clothing had been donated by girls from the Hewitt School as what was dubbed "Operation Prom Dress." Such dresses cost hundreds of dollars, much more than what the average family in Clay County could afford to spend on an article of clothing that would likely be worn just once. (The annual tuition at Hewitt was about equal to the median annual household income of a resident of the Appalachian town.) A contingent from Hewitt arrived a week later via private jet to help out with the operation. "All of our students are young women of privilege," said Linda Gibbs, head of Hewitt, "which is why we believe strongly that those who have much have an obligation to give back."[1]

Operation Prom Dress rather glaringly showcased the elitist reputation of private schools while also demonstrating their commitment to community service. Not much had changed in that regard, as independent schools had long been seen as exclusive institutions that recognized they had an obligation to serve the public good. What was different about private schools compared with their past was that they had become a bigger piece of the nation's educational pie. In the 1999–2000 school year, there were 27,009 private schools in the United States, with 5.3 million students. The country had become much more secular over the years, but independents remained heavily denominational. Seventy-nine percent of all private schools had a religious affiliation, with 30 percent of them Roman Catholic or parochial. Still, about the same share of students were enrolled in private schools as in the past several decades: 10–11 percent.[2] The first decade of the twenty-first century would be a volatile time for the American private school, however, as it rode a wild economic roller coaster.

IT'S ALL ABOUT MONEY

The tone of the new decade could be said to have been set when it became apparent how many heads of private schools had decided to retire or look for different jobs. In New York City alone, the heads of Dalton, Riverdale, Spence, Brearley, Chapin, Calhoun, Lycee Francais, Manhattan Country, United Nations International, Horace Mann, Ethical Culture, Fieldston, Windward, and City and Country had over the last few years cleaned out their desks. Soon to go were the headmasters from Collegiate, Hewitt, Poly Prep, and Buckley. What accounted for the mass exodus? A loss of authority and demanding parents had something to do with it, but it was more the pressure to raise big money that had led to the departures. Board members were judging performance in financial terms and were prepared to ditch headmasters who didn't meet fundraising goals. "It's all about money, all day long," explained Sandra R. Bass, publisher of the newsletter *The Private School Insider*.[3]

Fortunately for those headmasters who wanted to keep their jobs, there was no shortage of parents willing to pay full tuition, assuming their children were granted admission. There was a bumper crop of applications to private schools in 2000 as the robust economy, propelled by the dot-com explosion, made money not an issue for many families. The high numbers of middle-school-aged children were also creating what some considered unprecedented demand for a slot at A-list schools. Even students with excellent grades and great test scores were being turned away because of low admission rates (27 percent at Hotchkiss, 31 percent at Choate, and 32 percent at Miss Porter's).[4]

Some parents, however, had to pay no tuition at all to Miss Porter's, and not because their children had been offered a scholarship. Miss Porter's, like most independents, waived tuition for students who had a parent who worked at the school, a huge perk for middle-class families. Students still had to meet admission standards, although Miss Porter's would pay half the tuition of another private school if the student didn't meet its qualifications. The benefit was equivalent to anywhere between 25 percent and 50 percent of a teacher's or staff member's salary, making it a compelling selling point in attracting good talent.[5]

Finding good talent was no easy task for private school administrators. Not only was there a national teacher shortage but independents paid less and provided fewer benefits than public schools, putting the former at a distinct disadvantage despite offering smaller classes and more autonomy. (Paradoxically, teacher turnover was higher in private schools, yet teachers were more satisfied with their working conditions.)[6] The opportunity to be innovative by tweaking the curriculum was wonderful but teachers had to pay their bills, making the decision a difficult one for those who had multiple offers.[7]

Private school administrators realized that they would have to bring their teacher salaries closer to what public schools were offering to stay competitive. If nothing else, there were now more students to teach. Incoming classes were larger and both retention rates—the number of returning students—and "yield"—the number of students accepted who choose to attend—were higher. Boarding schools, which had recently hit a rough patch, were now trending upward as parents' bank accounts swelled.[8]

There were other reasons why enrollments at private schools were at record levels. Even in districts in which public schools were considered outstanding, those who could afford it were opting for an independent simply because the latter was bound to be smaller. (It was not unusual for a public high school to have ten times the number of students than a private school.) There was thus a much better chance of making it onto a sports team at an independent, as there was a greater likelihood of getting called on in a classroom discussion. Some students loved being part of a big school while others felt more comfortable in a more intimate setting, and it was the latter for whom private schools were ideally suited.[9]

By the fall of 2001, however, the dot-com bubble had burst, deflating many parents' financial portfolios in the process. What might be a $20,000 annual tuition plus fees bill was one thing in a bullish economy but something quite different in a bearish one, making some rethink the commitment they had made to private school. For the super-rich, $80,000 spread out over four years was petty cash while for others it brought on sticker shock, a fact that presented major implications for admission officers. Financial aid requests would undoubtedly go up and alumni donations would likely go down, meaning the bottom line of independents would be impacted by the stock market tumble. Endowments too were not what they were just a year earlier, and this was an indication that revenue streams would be reduced, at least for the short term.[10]

While some parents balked at the cost, the advantages that private schools offered were sufficient justification to not change anything, if it was at all possible. They weren't called prep schools for nothing, after all; independents were designed from the ground up to help students prepare for college, the first step being acceptance to one's institution of choice. In that respect, the smaller size of private schools effectively stacked the deck for their students, as fewer numbers allowed greater participation in clubs and other after-school activities—something college admission officers liked to see on applications. Many independents also built in time during the school day for "free periods," allowing yet more opportunity to belong to (and often be president of) a club or other kind of group. Winning an award of some sort was also much more possible in a school of three hundred versus three thousand; this too was likely to impress highly selective colleges, particularly elite ones that offered early admission decisions.[11]

With all those advantages, it was not surprising that even in a down economy, the efforts to get into a selective private school were intense. Particularly in highly competitive markets like New York and Los Angeles, test preparation classes and consulting services to help students applying for middle school at an independent had become a tidy cottage industry. Although the business was unregulated, parents would happily pay whatever it cost to have their child do their best on the ISEE, SSAT, or High School Placement Test. That one happened to be a straight-A student, star athlete, or musical prodigy didn't seem to matter; if only insurance, prepping for the test was deemed worth the time and money, especially since it had become the norm in more affluent areas. Seventy-five percent of the applicants to the Brentwood School in Los Angeles were estimated to have taken prep courses, for example, with the owner of a firm offering such services there describing their appeal as "sort of like having a personal trainer."[12]

The nation's economy had further worsened after 9/11, but demand for private schools remained as great as ever. Parents were putting off the purchase of that new SUV they had wanted to instead invest the twenty grand in their child's education, as there would always be another car to buy. "The phones are still ringing, people are still sending me letters and knocking on our door to ask for a spot," said Steven J. Nelson, headmaster of the Calhoun School in Manhattan. (One hundred ninety applications had come in for the fifteen spots in the school's kindergarten.) In New York especially, parents were more concerned about security, that too making some see private schools not as a luxury but a necessity. "My child will be closely watched, and the teachers will know him better," explained one mother applying to Calhoun (and to eighteen other schools).[13] To that point, a 2004 study by the Heartland Institute found that the rate of violent crime against students was nearly twice as high in public schools than in private schools.[14]

While the doors of private school admission officers were being loudly knocked on, that didn't mean that there was no room for improvement. There were many schools that parents could choose from, and administrators wanted to attract the top students to maintain or enhance their reputation. Strong academics were expected, making a school's facilities and amenities a way to differentiate itself from the competition. Many schools were investing tens of millions of dollars on upgrades like fitness centers, ceramics rooms, cappuccino machines, and, in the case of Lexington Christian Academy in Massachusetts, an indoor climbing wall.[15]

MARCH MADNESS

Such things were certainly nice, and would no doubt encourage some parents to choose one private school over another, but there were bigger issues at stake. Independents were spending considerable energy trying to figure out how to make their institutions more attractive to African Americans, Latinos, and Asian Americans, something quite more challenging than installing a machine that made delicious coffee. Communicating the key benefits of private school—quality of education and tighter discipline—was recognized as the primary means of encouraging promising minority students to make the switch from public school.[16]

A new report issued by the US Department of Education showed the difference that private school education could make for many students. Students who attended private schools were twice as likely to get a college degree than students who attended public schools, according to data from "The Condition of Education 2002." Moreover, students who attended private schools and came from families of the lowest quartile of poverty in the nation were nearly four times more likely to get a higher education degree than comparable students who attended public schools, the report also showed. Private school students on average took more advanced courses before graduation than students at public schools did, one reason to explain the results.[17]

That was good news for advocates of private schools, of course, much better than the news that students in private schools were more likely to attend racially segregated classrooms than students in public schools. That was the finding from a new study by a group of researchers at the University of Arkansas, directly contradicting the findings from a 1998 study by Jay P. Greene, a senior fellow at the Manhattan Institute for Policy Research. The national average of minority students in classrooms was 37.4 percent, according to the Arkansas study, which considered classrooms with racial compositions within 10 percent of the national average to be integrated. The study revealed that 9.4 percent of private school students were in integrated classrooms, while 13.5 percent of public school students were.[18]

Those findings resonated with several recently published studies that showed that white students' choice between private and public schools was shaped by the racial composition of the local student population. In his study, Robert W. Fairlie explored whether Latinos were also enrolling in private schools to avoid being in classrooms where there was a majority of African American students. Fairlie's findings supported his thesis that there was such a thing as "Latino flight" from public schools into private schools, one that closely mirrored the decades-long "white flight" phenomenon.[19]

Private schools were now actively recruiting Latinos, with admission officers seeing them as the "new" underrepresented minority. As a result, many felt that both admission and acceptance of African American students at private schools were being overshadowed by the push for more Latinos. Also, more complaints about racial incidents were being reported by African American students, which some attributed to the post–9/11 discriminatory backlash that was focused on Arabs and Muslims but had a spillover effect on all people of color.[20]

Still, more working-class and middle-class African Americans were enrolling in private schools as part of what some called "Black flight." There were about two hundred thousand African Americans in Catholic schools in 2004, and another fifty-two thousand African American students enrolled in the nation's four hundred historically Black independent schools. The factors behind Black flight were the same as for whites and Latinos—the desire for a better and safer education than what public schools were providing, particularly in urban areas.[21]

The flight to private schools, whether by whites, Latinos, or African Americans, was coming at a cost, and quite a significant one. Tuitions were rising fast, especially in New York City, where demand remained strongest. In spring 2004, a number of the city's top schools including Horace Mann, Brearley, and Marymount announced their tuition schedules for the following academic year, with most of them hovering around $26,000. This was a 5–9 percent hike over the previous year and didn't include the $3,000 or so additional cost for transportation, books, and lunch. Parents were soon on the city's private school grape line, comparing contracts (bills) to see which school topped the list. (It was Trevor Day, Dalton, and Calhoun, in that order.) Horace Mann had made the controversial decision to standardize tuition across grade levels, meaning the cost of sending a kindergartener to the school was the same as sending a senior.[22]

Raising tuition was not the only means of increasing revenues, a goal shared by many private schools. Independents had for many years sold off land for an infusion of cash, especially in the hard economic times of the early 1930s and early 1970s. Now, however, some schools were finding more entrepreneurial ways to make bottom lines look better, something that board members and trustees were delighted by. Shattuck-St. Mary's in Faribault, Minnesota, rented out its wedding chapel and charged visitors to use its rope course, for example, while the Elmwood Franklin School in Buffalo, New York, had gone into the tutoring business. Georgetown Preparatory School in Washington, DC, was building upscale rental apartments on its campus, and in what was probably the oddest venture, the San Francisco School was partnering with a company called University Games to produce board games.[23]

Administrators defended such "extracurricular" activities by saying that additional funds were needed to pay for many things that parents now expected or desired in a private school. These included not only psychologists, diversity coordinators, and learning-disabilities specialists but also additional faculty who could teach college prep subjects like Chinese and advanced physics. Then there were the new field houses and science labs that seemingly every private school had on their wish lists, and the fact that many independents had had to raise the salaries of their current faculty or else lose them to public schools. The average endowment of a private school was just $7 million, not nearly enough to generate a revenue stream that could pay for all the facilities and amenities that were needed to stay competitive.[24]

The other factor in play was that in smaller markets, such as Buffalo, private schools were maxing out on the number of parents who could pay anywhere from $12,000 to $26,000 a year on tuition. One could imagine a scenario in which only children from wealthy families and those on scholarships made up student bodies, not unlike the mix that existed at private schools a half-century or full century ago. This would not be a good thing, all agreed, making the solution to keep tuition at a somewhat reasonable level so that middle-class families seeking alternative education could afford to pay it. That meant raising money from other sources, even one as farfetched as board games.[25]

Meanwhile, parents who could afford to pay full freight sent in their applications, hoping their children would beat the odds by receiving one of the thick acceptance letters. Some parents were known to take extreme (and ill-advised) measures to try to influence admissions officers, including tucking in a few hundred-dollar bills in applications and creating professional resumes for their elementary-age children.[26] Even younger siblings of current students were sometimes being rejected, as were "legacies"—children whose parents or grandparents had attended the same school. Admissions officers explained they prioritized the aptitude and personality of each child over family connections, not appeasing those who had assumed they were a shoo-in because Uncle Ned or Aunt Millie had gone there.[27]

In larger cities, where the competition for admissions remained especially fierce, the period in which letters were mailed had become known as "March Madness." (It overlapped with the National Collegiate Athletic Association [NCAA] basketball tournament.) Letters were typically sent out on the same date to try to minimize the panic that some experienced as they heard of acceptances and rejections from other parents. Some schools were closed for spring break while letters were being opened, although it wasn't clear whether that was intentional or not.[28]

It would be a difficult decision for many parents, but their children had a significantly better chance of getting accepted to an elite boarding school than a prestigious day school in larger cities. Boarding school enrollment was up just 2.7 percent over the past decade while it was 15 percent for day schools, making admission standards for the former more relaxed. The acceptance rate at Roxbury Latin in Boston was 13 percent in 2005, for example, while it was double that for selective boarding schools. (Second-tier boarding rates were 40–50 percent.) Many boarding schools also had day students, making the comparison one of apples to apples. The day school admission rate at Milton Academy was 16 percent while it was 42 percent for boarding, making it not surprising that there had been a surge in applications to the latter, no doubt many from students who had received rejection letters during March Madness.[29]

OPTING OUT

Despite the concern that private school tuition was now exceeding the limits of most middle-class families, particularly in smaller markets, the figures on contracts continued to rise. The costs of running a top-notch school were showing no signs of slowing, leaving administrators no choice but to charge more. In New York City, tuition and fees at pricier schools had surpassed $30,000, a number that even affluent families found rather alarming. This was the third consecutive year of marked increases, justified by higher overhead and bigger salaries to attract and retain qualified teachers. Enrollments had risen 12 percent over the past decade and were still trending upward, suggesting tuition would continue to balloon. It was believed that the No Child Left Behind Act of 2001, with its narrow approach and focus on standardized testing, was driving more parents to choose a different educational path for their children.[30]

Was there a limit to what private schools could charge and, if so, what was it? In the mid-1990s, it was said that there would be few takers for independent education if annual tuition surpassed $5,000. The same thing was said when it hit $10,000, $15,000, and $20,000, but now, after passing $25,000, it appeared there could be no magic number. The problem, however, was that many families that had paid full tuition and had given even more money in gifts were now applying for financial aid. The cost of a kindergartener attending an elite school in New York City was getting perilously close to the tuition at some of the nation's best universities (Stanford's was $33,000), something that just didn't seem right.[31]

Administrators explained that K–12 private schools like theirs had construction costs and had to keep up with ever-changing digital technology just like a university, but such information wasn't much help to parents wondering how they were going to come up with such a sizable chunk of cash every year. Parents who had more than one child were confronted with a real conundrum that demanded some creative thinking. Should we send one kid to private and one to public? Or perhaps we should send both to public for elementary and then both to private for middle and high? Or maybe both to private for elementary and then both to public for middle and high?[32] The possibilities were many, but it was sure to still cost an arm and a leg no matter which route was chosen.

The irony in such financial somersaults was that private school teachers were often less qualified, at least officially. "I have no formal education training, no teaching license, and no passing score on the Massachusetts Tests for Educator Licensure," wrote Alison Lobron, "and yet parents pay

more than $30,000 per student per year for me to teach their children."
It was true; Lobron taught English at Concord Academy yet had no official credentials of any kind. Yet, Lobron was considered qualified by her
administration simply because she was good at her job. Most of Lobron's
colleagues at Concord were in the same boat (she estimated that a quarter
of its faculty had some kind of state certification), and it was fair to assume
that that percentage was roughly the same for private schools across the
country.[33]

Parents likely weren't aware of which teachers were state-certified and
which were not, and perhaps didn't care much as long as their children
were doing well in school. They might have thought twice about paying
enormous sums of money to private schools had they learned of the results
of a new study released by the US Department of Education, however.
When certain scores on the National Assessment of Educational Progress
were adjusted for socioeconomic, race, and other characteristics, public
school students did just as well as or even better than private school students in some subjects. These findings mirrored those from a recent study
by two researchers at the University of Illinois at Urbana-Champaign,
although the methodology of both studies was questioned by researchers at
Harvard University.[34]

While researchers quibbled over sampling procedures and data analysis, reports that a public school education was just as good as that to be
had in an expensive independent appeared to affect parents' decision
regarding school choice. "Some parents are seeking an edge for the
kids—by moving them from private to public schools," observed Nancy
Keates in the *Wall Street Journal* in 2006 after talking to some who were
"opting out." Although it was tough to abandon a school that was nurturing and often set on beautiful grounds—one mother opting out called
her bucolic private school a "Garden of Eden"—parents were finding the
teachers at the local public schools to be excellent and that their children
were thriving in their new environment. The money being saved was
enormous, especially for parents who had more than one child in private
school.[35]

Keates found the shift to be taking place in all parts of the country,
although it was the best public schools in more affluent areas that were getting most of the transfers. Continually increasing tuition at private schools
was definitely a factor in the decision to opt-out; parents were seeing kids
in the neighborhood getting what appeared to be just as good an education
at the public school at no cost. Curricula were typically similar at private
and public, as were reading and math programs. A bonus was that district

public schools were often closer than the private school that a child had been attending, although some of the niceties of the latter—arts activities and extensive foreign language classes, say—were missed. Then there were the "values," which some administrators of independents emphasized upon seeing some of their students not reenroll.[36]

For many parents, the bigger issue was whether their children had a better chance of getting into a top college by graduating from a private school. There was no clear answer, but there was evidence that A-list colleges were admitting more public school students as part of their initiative to make their institutions more socially and economically diverse. Consultants advised that the heavy investment in private school was not money well spent unless the student finished in the top 10 percent of his or her class, as that is what got students accepted to the Ivy League and the like. Some middle-of-the-pack students felt that they would have a better chance at standing out in a public school than the independent at which they had been attending; this alone was a good reason to make the switch.[37]

In tonier neighborhoods, where sending one's children to an elite private school was the default position, the decision to go public was a countercultural one. A family in such an area could find itself as the only one on its street to have made that choice, making them appear to be rather odd ducks at block parties or other local gatherings. Such families may have made their decision not based on financial considerations but rather on moral ones, specifically that private schools were inherently exclusive. "No matter how progressive or egalitarian the private school, how much community service it promotes, or how large the scholarship fund, the fact is that some children are let in and others are not," stated a mom from Chevy Chase, Maryland, who had gone the unorthodox route. "Private schools also siphon off resources—financial, human and political—from the public schools, including those that need it most, to benefit an advantaged few," she argued.[38]

Private school administrators, however, were not at all unapologetic about the fact that their institutions offered an alternative form of education to parents who sought exclusivity and were willing to pay for it. A tour of some of the private schools in Los Angeles certainly made that clear; hundreds of millions of dollars were being spent on new construction as independents engaged in a "building race." Brentwood School was building a luxurious aquatics center, while the Windward School was putting up a new library with digital media studios and an indoor-outdoor reading area, complete with a fireplace. For writing annual checks of tens of thousands of dollars, parents not only wanted but expected the best in facilities and everything else that went into a twenty-first-century school. Technology was at the heart of the upgrades, as it had become clear that students' future careers would be grounded in the digital world.[39]

Tuitions couldn't pay for Olympic-sized swimming pools and a fleet of iMac computers, however, making the annual fund the primary means to raise millions in extra cash. "Appeal letters" were typically sent out in the fall, with language explaining that operating budgets paid for the essentials, but additional funds were needed to make the school the special place it was. Campaign goals could be anywhere from hundreds of thousands of dollars for smaller schools to millions for larger ones. On average, parents of current students kicked in 36 percent and alumni 20 percent of an annual campaign, with organizations, trustees, and others providing the remainder, according to the National Association of Independent Schools. Galas and auctions supplemented that pot of money, with the occasional "building fund" or "capital campaign" launched for a major project or expansion.[40]

DON'T GIVE

In 2008, one might have seen a few private school accountants dashing to the bank to deposit checks, lest they bounce like a rubber ball. The latest economic slump, triggered by the subprime mortgage crisis, was affecting private schools in some ways, none of them good. More parents were applying for financial aid and others decided to opt out completely, as even some assistance with tuition wouldn't be enough to pay the bills. Enrollments were dropping for the first time that many could remember, a situation compounded by a flat and, in some areas, declining birth rate. The "necessity" of a private school education was beginning to look more like a luxury, and one that was unaffordable.[41]

With many home foreclosures, higher unemployment rates, and increased cost of gas, it was indeed more difficult to justify the significant expense of private school. Enrollments that had been at—and sometimes exceeded—stated capacity were now lower, tightening independents' budgets and reversing their free-spending ways. Raising tuition was one option but that ran the risk of more parents dropping out; a common plan was to use the full tuition from parents who could afford it as financial aid for those who couldn't, an example of one hand feeding another.[42]

Adding to independents' financial woes was that much of endowment money was in the stock market, which had taken quite a tumble in the crisis. Special fundraising appeals were being made, but the portfolios of parents, alumni, and others had likely taken a similar hit. Administrators were counting on there being enough families for whom a recession was just a minor blip and a sufficient number of parents who would use their last penny to send their children to private school, if that's what it took.[43]

One family who had decided on private school for their children despite the economic meltdown was the Obamas. Just a week after Barack Obama was elected president in November 2008, he and his wife, Michelle, were shopping for a school in the Washington, DC, area for their two daughters. (Sasha was seven and Malia ten.) While campaigning, Obama had opposed tax-supported programs (vouchers) to families who wanted to send their children to private school but couldn't afford to do so, making the couple's decision, like that of previous presidents and First Ladies, a politically sensitive one. That Obama was African American added to the controversy, as there was a disproportionate percentage of Black students in less-than-adequate schools.[44]

Just a week later, the Obamas announced their decision, and it was not a surprise. Like the Roosevelts (Theodore's parents), Nixons, and Clintons, Barack and Michelle Obama chose Sidwell Friends after taking a look at a few other schools, including Georgetown Day and public school. Sidwell had considerable experience dealing with security and privacy for the power elite, however, making that a key factor in choosing the Quaker school. (Vice President Biden's grandchildren went there, as did Al Gore's son while Gore was vice president.) The two girls would be transferring to Sidwell from the University of Chicago Laboratory Schools, which was also private.[45]

The tuition for Sidwell was about $29,000 for each child, and that did not seem to present a problem for the Obamas, even in the down economy. (The presidential annual salary was $400,000.) Money seemed to be no object for parents and friends of private schools despite the moribund state of Wall Street. In November 2008, an auction for Trevor Day School yielded more than a cool half-million, just 15 percent below that raised the previous year, which had been a record for the school. Although it had a relatively small endowment, the school was in "sound shape financially," the head of Trevor Day told parents, with administrators from a host of the city's independents—Ethical Culture, Fieldston, Packer Collegiate, Calhoun, Trinity, Columbia Grammar and Preparatory, and St. Ann's—saying much the same.[46]

New York City was a universe unto itself, however, and thus not representative of the nation's private schools' financial health. Even in Los Angeles, where money often flowed freely, some schools were lowering their tuition to encourage parents to keep their kids enrolled. That was a rare thing for private schools, as it veered from the standard model of making slight increases each year to keep up with inflation and, if possible, offer more financial aid. These were unusual times, however, and without a decrease in tuition, there was the possibility of having a student body of just the rich and the poor. Keeping middle-class families at private schools was a primary goal of most administrators, and they were doing what they could to prevent a mass exodus.[47]

Smaller private schools were facing a major struggle just to survive in the economic crisis. Trinity Episcopal School in Galveston, Texas, was holding car washes and bake sales to raise money, and having staff members serve as substitute teachers as well to save precious dollars. Tuition there was just $5,000 to $8,000, leaving not much margin when parents lost their jobs and couldn't reenroll. Donations to such schools had also fallen, not surprisingly, as just paying tuition had become a stretch for many families. Families were taking several cost-cutting measures—camping instead of staying at a resort on vacation, swapping cars for one that got better gas mileage, and cutting one's grass instead of paying for a lawn service—to stay at the school.[48]

The Oakwood School in Los Angeles went quite beyond a car wash or bake sale to raise money during what some had begun to call the Great Recession. For its 2009 fundraising drive, the school was in the fortunate position of having Danny DeVito, Jason Alexander, Steve Carell, and other Hollywood notables take part in a short video humorously called "Don't Give" that ended up being posted on YouTube. "Don't give, unless you care about families who had a hard year and need some help with tuition," the stars told parents who had less of a hard year, the goal being to support financial aid and build the school's endowment. Other schools were asking donors to fund a scholarship for an individual student, an interesting approach that made giving more personal.[49]

That approach was consistent with what philanthropy professionals recommended to private school fundraisers. In *Philanthropy at Independent Schools*, a collection of essays, those who raised money for a living pointed out that 10 percent of potential donors contributed 85 percent of the funds brought in by private schools, meaning that development staffs should target those top prospects to literally get the biggest bang for the buck.[50] At many schools, the principal fundraiser was, well, the principal. In addition to running the academic side of what was in effect a business, heads of school had to be good schmoozers if they were to get large checks from the 10 percent. The best heads also knew something about construction, as much of the money raised often went to putting up new buildings or updating older ones. It was a hard job, explaining why salaries could be in the hundreds of thousands of dollars and why the turnover was so high.[51]

Heads of school might very well have weighed their career options when finding themselves in a much different economic environment than that of a couple of years earlier. Some donors had designated their money as "swing gifts" in capital campaigns launched during the good times, allowing them to make reductions should their pecuniary status change. A portion of them were doing just that, making administrators downsize their ambitious plans. In-progress projects such as artificial turf athletic fields (safer than grass), installation of SMART boards (retiring blackboards and chalk), gut renovations of auditoriums, replacing the wood floors of indoor basketball courts, and new study centers might have been delayed as available funds were redirected to financial aid.[52]

Also, a fair number of new construction projects were put on hold as helping families keep their children in school through tuition assistance took priority. Nationally, there had been just a slight decrease in enrollment at day schools while boarding schools, with their easier admission standards, were booming. More parents were requesting financial aid, however, as some of them had lost jobs as companies trimmed their budgets. Parents were also asking relatives for loans or dipping into their retirement savings, rather desperate measures that illustrated how important independent education was to them. Things would eventually stabilize, these parents believed, making efforts to avoid transferring a child to the local public school just a stopgap to get through the rough patch.[53] That belief would turn out to be untrue, however, as private schools entered what was perhaps the most contentious period of their long, mercurial history.

10

THE 2010s: AN EXISTENTIAL MOMENT

"Private schools find themselves now at an existential moment."

—Ginia Bellafante, *New York Times*, 2021

Had one been in Santa Monica, California, in the summer of 2016, one might have seen a group of a dozen or so children sitting on the grass in an office complex park in Santa Monica. Not unusual, of course, but these children, aged three and a half to five, were not playing. Rather, they were enrolled in KinderPrep, a weeklong "boot camp" intended to get them ready for the challenges of kindergarten. The program, offered by Academic Achievers, a private tutoring and admissions counseling company, costs $1,000, with some of the children enrolled for one-on-one sessions for $120 to $200 an hour. "When they get into kindergarten, there is no play," explained Elizabeth Fraley, the director of KinderPrep and other early education programs at Academic Achievers, adding that, "It's like first grade."[1]

One could take issue with anything that contributed to eliminating the play from kindergarten, but such has been the state of private schools over the past decade and change. The desire and pressure to get accepted to and eventually graduate from a prep school have intensified, a natural result of a more competitive academic climate. Top private schools appear to be resilient to ever-rising tuitions; among the more affluent, even $50,000 a year is seen as a good investment given the dividends an independent education can pay throughout one's life. Going to an A-list college remains seen as the launching pad for a successful career, driving the demand for prep school.

At the same time, however, private schools have never been so vilified as in recent years, with critics leveling a variety of charges against them. Independents are hardly the benevolent and noble institutions we like to think they are if even a fraction of the allegations made against them are true. The entire premise of private schools has been challenged in unprecedented ways, making us rethink the ethics involved in offering a limited number of children learning experiences that are unapologetically exclusive and wealth-dependent. In short, it's difficult to think of a dimension of American society that is more contradictory than the private school, revealing our sensitivity toward activities perceived as threats to our democracy.

PREP FACTORY

Naturally, prep school for kindergarten was viewed as not only preparing tots for the rigors of preschool but as something that would help in the admissions process. Getting accepted to an exclusive Los Angeles kindergarten was almost as difficult as gaining admission to one in New York City, making it understood why KinderPrep was considered a good investment by more affluent parents. (The admission process had become referred to as the "rug-rat race" in some circles.) It wasn't just about kindergarten, of course, as one level of education tended to lay the foundation for the next, and so on. Which kindergarten a child attended thus paved the way for elementary school, middle school, high school, and even college, or at least that was how it was perceived by many parents.[2]

The director of KinderPrep was not exaggerating too much in describing kindergarten as all work and no play. In more advanced kindergartens, at least, activities like building blocks were out, replaced by building math skills and reading comprehension (the nuts and bolts of Common Core, the multistate initiative designed to increase educational consistency on a national basis). Private elementary schools sought more mature children, encouraging the idea that it was never too early for a child to develop academically. Educators reminded parents that it was "just kindergarten," but it was easy to get caught up in the rug-rat race in certain parts of the country.[3]

Indeed, stories abounded about the steps parents in Los Angeles, New York, Chicago, San Francisco, and Atlanta would take to tip the scales of kindergarten admissions in their favor. There was the one about the "friend of a friend" who, right after giving birth, wrote a check for $50,000 to an especially selective school, and the one about the moneybags with a toddler or two who decided to fund the new building that a school just happened to need. Apocryphal, perhaps, but there was no doubt that more exclusive kindergartens closely scrutinized their applicant pool, sometimes quite literally. When shopping around Los Angeles for a kindergarten for her five-year-old twins, Christine Lennon was surprised to see her children in a school playground "with numbers pinned to their shirts like livestock at a state fair," as she wrote for *Town & Country*, the simulated playdate an exercise in social skills. It was rare to see rich people begging for something, as there was a price for almost everything, but that's what 1 percenters were doing when trying to get their kids admitted to one of the best schools in town.[4]

A few thousand miles east of Los Angeles, another set of parents were jockeying for spots in the choicest kindergartens in New York City. Acceptance and rejection letters were still typically mailed (email was gradually becoming the norm), but that didn't stop some parents from calling admissions officers by phone to get the good or bad news sooner. Moms and dads were lingering at preschool morning drop-offs to share their angst while waiting to learn whether their children were admitted to their schools of choice. Parents were also reporting updates on Urbanbaby.com and even posting their children's scores on the ERB test. Hundreds of applications were often received for perhaps a dozen open seats in kindergarten at a top school, making it understandable why the process was compared to a high school senior getting into Harvard or Yale. Indeed, acceptance rates at Harvard and Yale were currently running at 6.9 percent and 8.6 percent, respectively, similar odds for a four- or five-year-old trying to get into Friends Seminary, Poly Prep, or Mandell.[5]

In New York and elsewhere, parents frequently applied to both private schools and equally difficult-to-get-in public "gifted and talented" schools to hedge their bets. The former demanded a commitment and deposit months before admission decisions were made by the latter, however, meaning parents could be out thousands of dollars if their children were accepted by a gifted and talented school and they went that route. Some private schools required signed contracts for a full year of tuition with due dates shortly before admission announcements were made by public schools, meaning an important decision had to be made in a short amount of time, with tens of thousands of dollars at risk. The lottery system for the gifted and talented in New York City was compared to that of Powerball, but parents still applied, especially those whose children had scored highly on the ERB.[6]

Many families were no doubt happy to see that the ERB, a staple of the private school admission process, was losing some of its appeal. A high percentage of schools across the country required four- and five-year-olds to take the test as part of their applications, something that was said to put undue pressure on little ones (and cost more than $500). Extensive preparation for the ERB had made results almost meaningless, some admissions officers believed, with others saying that no test could accurately measure a child's intelligence. The ERB had entered the independent scene in the late 1960s, but much had changed in education over the past forty years, making it appear to be less of a reliable indicator of learning abilities.[7]

Ironically, one of the primary reasons to spend money on private school was to do well on another test—the SAT—that carried significant weight by colleges in their own admission process. According to the College Board's 2010 Group Profile Report, public school students had an average score of 1497 out of 2400 on the SAT, while the average score for students in independent schools was 1700, quite a spread. Some of the 200-point differential was attributed to self-selectivity (that better-educated students were more likely to go to private school in the first place), but it was believed that those same students worked harder as well (or at least spent more time preparing for the test).[8]

SAT tutors have been around for a couple of decades now as a supplement to the prep received during the school day. That was particularly true in New York City, where a related phenomenon was bubbling up: grade tutoring. In addition to high SAT scores, admissions people at top colleges liked to see As on students' transcripts, creating yet another business for expensive tutors. As end-of-year exams approached, students at Riverdale Country Day and other independents crammed with their tutors on specific subjects to avoid receiving dreaded Bs. Some parents were spending over six figures in a single year on SAT preparation (most often with Advantage Testing, considered the city's "prep factory"), subject prep with current and former private school teachers, and additional subject prep with consultants, all to get an edge in the intense college application competition.[9]

Parents of students at Riverdale Country also had to pay the school's tuition, of course, which seemed like a bargain compared to the tutoring bill despite breaking the $40,000 mark. That was a new record for New York City private schools and represented a 79 percent increase in just five years. Riverdale and other elite independents were not having trouble finding families more than happy to pay that amount of money each year but at that level, the makeup of the student population didn't reflect a cross-section of society. Tuition at Riverdale (and Trinity, Hewitt, and Ethical Culture

Fieldston) now surpassed that at Princeton and Harvard, making observers wonder how high the cost of a private school education would go.[10]

Was $40,000 a year, and soon more than that, if history was any judge, a fair price for what a student received? (It was close to $50,000 at boarding schools.) That was a lot of cash, by any measure, but with things like a high teacher-to-student ratio, learning specialists, and great arts programs, parents who could afford it felt it was money well spent. Good teachers deserved to be paid well (and get health insurance) and building and equipment got old, making it understandable why tuitions were so high. (Tuition generally covered about 80 percent of educating a child, explaining why schools spent so much time and energy on fundraising.) Then there were all the amenities and classes that were unlikely to be found in the local public school; the Trinity School had three theaters, six art studios, two tennis courts, a pool, and a diving pool, while five sections of Mandarin were taught at Poly Prep, Zen Dance at Dalton, and Roman Travel Writing at Columbia Grammar.[11]

THE PUBLIC SCHOOL ADVANTAGE

While certainly intriguing, such exotic offerings were side dishes to the main course: the college search process. Elite independents in Manhattan and elsewhere usually began in eleventh grade, not wanting to put more pressure on students by starting earlier. At Leman Manhattan Preparatory School, however, a for-profit school, ninth graders began the process, and that was the plan for another for-profit opening in the fall of 2012 called Avenues: The World School. Students at Leman (the city's first international boarding school) actually began earlier, as seventh and eighth graders were invited to visit college campuses on a spring trip. Should the academic experience be strictly about planning for college admission, as administrators of the new for-profits believed, or instead offer excellent learning opportunities that allow students to develop as individuals, as traditional nonprofits held?[12]

Whether college-focused or otherwise, the appearance of new private schools in New York City offered a diverse set of choices to traditional schools and their over-the-top admission standards. In addition to the unfortunately named World Class Learning Academy, there was the even odder Blue School—a creative nursery and elementary school founded by the three members of the theater troupe Blue Man Group. There were a lot of potential customers for such schools, but breaking into the market was easier said than done. Most of the new schools were taking an international approach to their curriculum, seeing that as a meaningful point of difference and the best preparation for the emerging "global economy."[13]

If there was any common denominator among the nation's private schools at this time in their history, it was a search for new revenue streams as money drove more decision-making. As tuition surpassed levels that many American families could afford, more independents looked overseas as a lucrative market to tap. Asia was now the focus, with about forty-three thousand students from China, South Korea, India, Japan, Taiwan, and Vietnam attending American private high schools, according to the Department of Homeland Security (up from twenty-seven thousand in 2008). Many foreigners, especially Asians, considered a degree from an American university to be an avenue to success, and that graduating from one of the nation's private schools offered the best chance of getting into a good university. Asian families were charged full tuition, providing a boost to independents' budgets strained from offering more financial aid to American students.[14]

Chinese students represented about half of foreign pupils enrolled in American private schools. For decades, Chinese students had come to the United States for higher education, but now they were arriving at a younger age, trickling down from college to high school to middle school. An industry had sprung up specializing in recruiting Chinese students and finding host families in the States, a windfall for private schools whose enrollments had dipped in the Great Recession. There were thirteen Chinese students at Chase Collegiate in Waterbury, Connecticut, for example; most of them were surprised and delighted by the more open form of American education after having to memorize facts in schools in their home country.[15] Cape Cod Academy in Barnstable, Massachusetts, was also recruiting Chinese students from wealthier families in part to bring more of an international character to the school but, more importantly, to generate revenue that could be used for financial aid.[16]

A recent survey by the National Association of Independent Schools showed how important financial aid was to American families who sent a child to private school. Eighty-seven percent of those polled said that financial assistance was "extremely important," with another 10 percent saying it was "very important" in making it possible for their children to get an independent education. Forty-four percent reported that the financial aid they received in the 2012–2013 academic year covered more than half of the school's tuition. Financial assistance played an even more significant role among African American and Latino families; 60 percent of African

Americans and 58 percent of Latinos stated that financial aid took care of more than half of their tuition.[17]

Not surprisingly, financial aid was especially important for families with annual household incomes under $50,000, according to the NAIS survey. Sixty percent of families earning less than $25,000 a year and 69 percent of those with annual incomes between $25,000 and $49,999 reported that the assistance they received covered more than half of their children's tuition. Interestingly, the amount of financial aid awarded varied quite a bit. Fifty-three percent of the assistance ranged between $5,000 to $20,000, with 23 percent given grants between $5,000 and $9,999, 17 percent $10,000 to $14,999, and 13 percent $15,000 to $19,999.[18]

It had been widely reported that financial aid had substantially increased in recent years (largely due to the subprime mortgage kerfuffle) and the National Association of Independent Schools study bore that out. In 2006, 37 percent of families had received $10,000 or more in financial aid, while 50 percent of them had in 2012. In addition, just 3 percent of families reported receiving $25,000 or more in 2006, just one-fourth of the 12 percent in 2012. Most significant, however, was the finding that 71 percent of parents stated that it likely wouldn't be possible for their children to attend private school if they weren't awarded financial aid. (Seventy-seven percent of African American families and 80 percent of Latino families expressed that sentiment.) Very surprisingly, financial aid played a major role in the ability of families with high incomes to send their children to a private school. Just 16 percent of families with annual household incomes of $150,000 or more said that they would be "extremely likely" or "very likely" to commit to independent education for their children without financial aid, an unexpected finding.[19]

Seeing the need, several schools were offering an alternative kind of financial aid that better fit parents' wide range of income levels. An "indexed tuition plan," as it was commonly referred to, was basically "pay-what-you-wish," an approach that made it possible for some families to afford independent education who otherwise could not. The Duke School in Durham, North Carolina, was one school offering the plan, finding that it better led to socioeconomic diversity than the standard flat fee/financial aid model. While the amount of tuition to be paid could end up being the same, parents appeared to be more amenable to the indexing concept and were thus more likely to apply to schools that offered it. The indexed tuition plan bypassed the uncomfortable period of waiting to hear if financial aid would be awarded, better enabling parents to make the best educational choice for their child.[20]

A private school was likely to be that choice if money was no object. In 2012, when Gallup asked a representative sample of Americans whether private or public schools were better, 75 percent replied that private schools offered a "good to excellent" education while 37 percent said the same for public schools. As the title of their 2013 book *The Public School Advantage: Why Public Schools Outperform Private Schools* made clear, Christopher Lubienski and Sarah Lubienski argued that perception and reality were quite different. Students' learning in public schools was equal to or better than that at private schools, they found in their research, and practices such as teacher licensing and teacher-led reforms of instructional methods and curricula contributed to public school achievement.[21]

Independent education remained in considerable demand, however, even as the Lubienskis' book received considerable attention in the media. The nation's public schools did not receive a vote of confidence when it was announced that Arne Duncan and his wife Karen planned to send their children to the University of Chicago Laboratory Schools. The decision was newsworthy in that Arne Duncan happened to be the United States Secretary of Education, making him another prominent official to forgo public education. To be fair, Karen Duncan taught at the school, giving the couple a 50 percent discount on tuition, and the Duncans had sent their children to public school when they lived in the Washington, DC, area.[22]

GOOD OLD-FASHIONED COMPETITION

Justifying the choice of private over public, even for the Secretary of Education or President of the United States, typically boiled down to a single word: fit. Even critics had a tough time arguing against parents who had selected a particular private school based on it being the best fit for their individual child. Wouldn't any parent, knowing the importance of education in a young person's life, do the same? Fortunately, there was a startling variety of types of independent schools to choose from, including those for "gifted and talented" or special-needs students or children who just didn't feel comfortable in a traditional classroom environment. There were classical, traditional, progressive, creative, experiential, expeditionary, exceptional, and "differentiated" learning experiences to be had, a survey of private schools revealed, and even known brands such as Montessori and Waldorf.[23]

Despite such an amazing array, the packaging was less important than the product inside, which was almost always said to be the same. Private schools, regardless of whatever bucket into which they were sorted, provided what Michael Greenberg and Colleen Krueger described as "a quality, individualized education to children of families who want more from what their current or neighborhood school can offer." Delaware-based education consultants Independent School Management found there to be three main criteria in the choice of any school: a safe, caring community; positive academic outcomes; and clear guiding values, mission, and leadership. Free from state-determined curricula and a testing orientation, private schools were ideally equipped to deliver those three criteria, advocates argued, a sentiment to which many parents heartily agreed.[24]

A glaring weakness of private schools, however, was their lack of diversity compared to public schools. "Students in the nation's private schools are disproportionately—and in some states overwhelmingly—white," wrote Emma Brown in the *Washington Post* in 2016 after reviewing a study from the Southern Education Foundation. For decades now, private schools have made considerable efforts to diversify their student bodies, but much de facto segregation remained, particularly in the South and the West. Private schools were more likely than public schools to be virtually all-white, defined as a school where 90 percent or more of students were white. Forty-three percent of the nation's private school students attended virtually all-white schools versus 27 percent of public school students. The largest differential was in Mississippi where, in 2012, white students represented 51 percent of all school-aged students but 87 percent of private school students. The average spread on a national basis that year was about 15 percent.[25]

Administrators of nonprivate schools, meanwhile, decided to give independents a bit of their own medicine to showcase their own strengths. It was customary for private schools to market themselves to attract students but now some public and charter schools had begun to do so for the very same reason. In the Atlanta area, for example, North Springs Charter High School, Norcross High, and a few other public high schools held open houses in fall 2016, primarily aimed at students attending nearby private schools. There was no financial gain to be had, as the schools were free, but having more exceptionally bright students could raise a high school's academic standing. Administrators presented the open houses as an opportunity to share information about their schools rather than recruit students, but it was clear that the goal was to reel in a few top scholars. "It's just good ol' fashioned competition," said Steve Dolinger, president of the Georgia Partnership for Excellence in Education, with public schools boasting of not just free tuition but more Advanced Placement courses and better technology.[26]

A different kind of competition among schools was taking place in New York City. For-profits like Avenues popped up in recent years, offering an alternative to the elite and expensive private schools where applications far exceeded admission slots. Technology-based AltSchool opened its doors in 2015, while the Portfolio School and BASIS Independent Schools offered lower tuitions. The very British-sounding Wetherby-Pembridge School was just that, but now in Manhattan as well as London, and WeWork announced that it was starting a school called WeGrow (where parents and children could have lunch together). Education consultants discouraged parents from applying to such for-profits, thinking their lack of history made their future uncertain, but the schools seemed to be filling a niche.[27]

The emergence of for-profits was part of a broader reconfiguring of the nation's educational landscape. Enrollment in private schools was declining on a national basis, incentivizing some to lower tuition to stay competitive with the increasing number of options parents could choose from (including online education and homeschooling). For grades preK–12, including parochial schools, enrollment fell by 14 percent (to 6.3 million in 2016 from 7.3 million in 2006), according to data from the US Census Bureau. Private schools' loss was a gain for public schools and charter schools (public schools that commit to achieving specified educational objectives and are exempt from significant state or local regulations related to operation and management). By 2017, more than a dozen states were offering school voucher programs and tax-credit scholarship programs, but those benefits were not enough to make up for private school losses.[28]

Revelations of sexual abuse at a long list of private schools did not help their cause. Choate, Horace Mann, St. George's in Rhode Island, Deerfield Academy, Fessenden School in Massachusetts, and Hotchkiss were just a handful of elite independents to face allegations of sexual misconduct in the previous twenty-five years. (The *Boston Globe* reported instances of such at no less than 110 private schools, and that was just in New England.) The image of the schools was tarnished but not seriously damaged, as admissions and fundraising figures had not dropped. Some schools had to pay out large settlements, however, and others lost key staff members.[29]

Because many of the country's most prestigious private schools suffered no long-term damage from such serious and disheartening charges illustrated the enduring strength of their brands. Other factors could impact private schools' bottom lines, however. Birth rates were dropping in the United States, reducing the pool of candidates in a more dramatic way than for public schools, as just 10 percent or so of American students attended private schools. The situation for K–12 independents was much like that of small liberal arts colleges, which were also finding it difficult to fill seats due to demographics and costs. Both kinds of institutions were amplifying their fundraising and marketing efforts, the challenge being how to demonstrate they represented a good value vis-à-vis larger, more affordable public and state-funded schools. "Rebranding" was a word often heard in the offices of private schools, with much discussion dedicated to identifying a compelling point of difference in the very competitive academic marketplace.[30]

One of the public high schools' main selling points was their array of Advanced Placement (AP) courses, which often offered college credit. From a college admissions standpoint, high school seniors having AP courses (equivalent to university-level curricula) on their transcripts helped to level the playing field with those of students graduating from top private schools. Many private schools, including Exeter, Dalton, Fieldston, Sidwell Friends, Horace Mann, St. Albans, and Choate had dropped AP courses, thinking they made teachers "teach to the test." Without the AP hanging over their heads (and the pressure it put on students), teachers could explore material in greater depth and, if warranted, veer off in other directions, allowing what many agreed was a richer learning experience. Some notable independents such as St. Mark's and Hockaday in Dallas, Westminster in Atlanta, Pine Crest in Fort Lauderdale, and Cranbrook in Bloomfield Hills, Michigan, were, at least for the moment, holding onto AP courses, while Harvard-Westlake in Los Angeles was in the process of scaling them back.[31]

Private schools' pitch of having not to teach to the test was certainly compelling but then there was the matter of money. While some independents were simply lowering tuition to stay reasonably competitive, others were offering financial aid to families with high household incomes to keep them from moving their children to public or charter schools. Rather than call it "financial aid," which had negative connotations to a certain set, schools were referring to the assistance as "flexible" tuition. Like the indexed tuition plan, flexible tuition lessened the sticker shock that often came when parents saw the number attached to one year of education. Day school tuition had increased 41 percent between 2008 and 2018, reaching a median of $26,866, according to the NAIS. The numbers in New York City were, of course, much higher. At Trinity School, tuition and fees had hit about $55,000, a sum that prompted the school to offer financial assistance to families with incomes as high as $475,000.[32]

While that was an extreme example, nearly 10 percent of the roughly 123,000 families who requested financial assistance in the 2017–2018 academic year earned more than $250,000, the NAIS reported, with some of them having annual incomes quite a bit over $250,000. Again, schools were attempting to even out the "barbell effect," in which enrollment skewed toward low-income students on sizable scholarships and children of the wealthy who could pay full fare. The aid was, in other words, deemed necessary to ensure there was a sizable presence of students from middle-class and upper-middle-class families, although an income of a quarter-million dollars certainly seemed more than middle class.[33]

A VERY EXPENSIVE CONSUMER PRODUCT

Alongside issues of socioeconomic class, those of race continued to shape the contours of American private schools. The killing of George Floyd in Minneapolis and the acceleration of the Black Lives Matter movement appeared to have a direct effect on independents, both in terms of acknowledging past inequities and determining how to move forward. In New York City, private schools made concerted efforts to become more inclusive, mostly through financial aid. At many of the schools, however, fewer than 10 percent of students identified themselves as African American, a clear sign that institutional racism remained embedded in their culture. Black alumni from the Brearley, Chapin, and Spence Schools said as much on Instagram, documenting a pattern of discrimination. At Chapin, actions were being taken to diversify staff, alter curricula to more fully recognize contributions made by African Americans, and put in place new inclusion programs for faculty on new reporting systems for students.[34]

Alumni from several Connecticut institutions including Loomis Chaffee, Suffield Academy, Pomfret School, Westminster School, and the Taft School were also sharing their experiences on Instagram (as well as Snapchat and X, formerly Twitter) as a means to expose racism at the nation's elite prep schools and demand change. Data showed that the nation's private schools were overwhelmingly white, but such stories brought to life the experiences of being a student of color at the institutions. Regular microaggressions, unfair discipline, and expectations of lower academic performance were routine. "Taken together, the testimonies reveal the degree to which systemic racism is felt within these elite campuses," observed Daniela Altimari of the *Hartford Courant*.[35]

Social media dedicated to "being Black" at prep schools spread like wildfire in the summer of 2020. Pages soon appeared for the Potomac School in McLean, Virginia, Georgetown Day School, and Sidwell Friends, where the Obama children were currently students. "They show that even at schools with plenty of resources and thoughtful mission statements, educational equity is not yet a reality for many students of color," wrote Theresa Vargas of the *Washington Post* after reading some of the personal stories. While the events had taken place in the past (most of it recent), they still seemed to haunt the graduates of the institutions, and one had to question whether the culture had changed to any significant degree despite mission statements like Potomac's "to foster a diverse, inclusive learning community where all voices and viewpoints are valued."[36]

While private schools faced what was perhaps the most virulent criticism ever directed toward them, the COVID-19 pandemic put even that on hold. As for public schools, the pandemic turned things upside down for private schools, although the latter often had greater resources to keep students learning. Some independents were setting up new videoconference cameras, pitching tents, and installing Plexiglas shields, spending six figures in the process. Others, however, were struggling to survive as families moved out of larger cities and as schools were forced to invest in safety measures and new technologies.[37] Independents had more say about when students could return to classrooms, but some parents were threatening not to pay tuition for virtual education, saying that that was not what they agreed to when signing their contracts.[38]

Students eventually returned to classrooms, and there was no loss in enrollments at independents despite parents' dissatisfaction with the switch to remote learning. Private school enrollment rose slightly in the 2021–2022 school year—about 1.7 percent—even with the early loss of some international students because of COVID-19. Charter schools and homeschooling grew at a higher rate during and after the pandemic, with parents more open to alternative forms of education, especially as voucher programs spread to additional states.[39]

Attempts to level the field of education through voucher programs were being foiled, however, despite the best-laid plans. In certain states, families with higher incomes could use taxpayer money to pay for private school tuition, not what had been intended. More families than what had been forecasted were taking advantage of the subsidies, draining state budgets. Supporters of vouchers had proposed them in terms of "school choice" and as a means for students in low-performing schools to get a better education, but it wasn't working out exactly as envisioned.[40]

It's safe to say that the problematic voucher program and the COVID-19 pandemic each served to further expose the inequities in access to education in the United States. Already reeling from the allegations of sexual abuse and racist policies and practices, private schools were vulnerable to attacks, and critics didn't hold back. Caitlin Flanagan's 2021 article in *Atlantic*, "Private Schools are Indefensible," was the most vituperative condemnation of independents; the piece took the century-old claim that private schools were antidemocratic institutions to a whole new level. "The gulf between how rich kids and poor kids are educated in America is obscene," she wrote, vividly pointing out the vast differential in resources along the spectrum of private and public. Flanagan took special aim at Dalton, which had an archaeologist on staff, a teaching kitchen, and a rooftop greenhouse (and paid its head $700,000 a year). Exeter had a $1.3 billion endowment and Andover was raising $400 million in its current capital campaign, she also mentioned, a literal embarrassment of riches.[41]

To be clear, Flanagan's target was limited to the most exclusive of the nation's 1,600 independent schools, as it was those that "passed on the values of our ruling class" by sending a large percentage of their graduates to Ivy League colleges. It was true that these elite institutions blessed a certain number of students with financial aid, but this was more to "salve their consciences" than anything else. Assertions of equity and inclusiveness were ridiculous, Flanagan charged, labeling the schools simply as "a very expensive consumer product for the rich."[42]

Not surprisingly, Flanagan was lambasted by the conservative right (writing for the *National Review*, Graham Hillard deemed her article a channeling of her "inner Marxist").[43] Criticism of private schools was coming from all sides, however. Parents in New York were complaining about "woke" curricula that had become obsessively focused on race and identity, alleging that teachers were making white children feel bad about being white.[44] Another group of parents in New England were similarly unhappy with what their children were learning (after taking a peek into their remote classrooms during the pandemic). Teaching critical race theory— the intellectual movement grounded in the idea that racism is embedded into the nation's fundamental structures—was a particularly sensitive issue that parents objected to.[45]

Framed as an extension of the culture wars and fueled by social media, the protests over curricula were making private schools resemble combat zones. "Battles over ideology have long existed in higher education, but the arrival of this charged debate at the secondary level has left people at both ends of the spectrum shell-shocked," observed Nicole Laporte in *Town and Country*.[46] Parents were divided politically at many schools, and their sense of community—a precious thing for any institution or organization—was shaken. Heads of schools, including those at Dalton and Middlesex in Massachusetts, were resigning in the wake of the conflict. "Diversity" had been a presence in private schools in one form or another for a half-century, but it had never been such a source of divisiveness.[47]

Ginia Bellafante, who had earlier described elite private schools as experiencing "an existential moment," soon added an "identity crisis" to their psychic woes.[48] Race and class were at the center of the struggle, as institutions of privilege confronted the nation's indisputable social and economic divisions, both past and present. At the same time, however, admission to a top private school, even for kindergarten, remained as desirable as ever, illustrating the extreme contradictions built into independent education. The future of American private schools was uncertain, but there was little doubt that our century-long love-hate relationship with them would continue.

NOTES

INTRODUCTION

1. David Resnick, "Film Images of Private Schools," *Journal of Educational Thought (JET)* (April 2000): 76, 78. The 1990 *Metropolitan* is the definitive film about Manhattan prep culture, but the characters have since graduated from their private schools.

2. Ernest Barrett Chamberlain, *Our Independent Schools: The Private School in American Education* (New York: American Book Company, 1944).

3. E. G. West, *Non-Public School Aid: The Law, Economics, and Politics of American Education* (Lexington, MA: D.C. Heath, 1976).

4. Thomas Vitullo-Martin, "Federal Policies and Private Schools," *Proceedings of the Academy of Political Science* (1978): 124.

5. Mark Walsh, "Public Versus Private," *Education Week*, October 20, 1999; James W. Fraser, *Between Church and State: Religion and Education in a Multicultural America* (Baltimore: Johns Hopkins University Press, 1999).

6. Lloyd P. Jorgenson, *The State and the Non-Public School, 1825–1925* (Columbia: University of Missouri Press, 1987). See also Robert N. Gross, *Public Versus Private: The Early History of School Choice in America* (New York: Oxford University Press, 2018) and Dick M. Carpenter and Krista Kafer, "A History of Private School Choice," *Peabody Journal of Education* (2012): 336–50.

7. Susan D. Rose, *Keeping Them Out of the Hands of Satan: Evangelical Schooling in America* (New York: Routledge, 1988).

8. Luis Benveniste, Martin Carnoy, and Richard Rothstein, *All Else Equal: Are Public and Private Schools Different?* (New York: RoutledgeFalmer, 2003).

9. Ruben Gaztambide-Fernandez, *The Best of the Best: Becoming Elite at an American Boarding School* (Cambridge, MA: Harvard University Press, 2009).

10. Francie Latour, "Private School Confidential," *Boston Globe*, September 20, 2009, K.1; Ruben Gaztambide-Fernandez, *The Best of the Best: Becoming Elite at an American Boarding School* (Cambridge, MA: Harvard University Press, 2009).

11. Christopher A. Lubienski and Theule Lubienski, *The Public School Advantage: Why Public Schools Outperform Private Schools* (Chicago: University of Chicago Press, 2013).

12. Michelle Purdy, *Transforming the Elite: Black Students and the Desegregation of Private Schools* (Chapel Hill: University of North Carolina Press, 2018). See also Stefan Bradley, *Upending the Ivory Tower: Civil Rights, Black Power, and the Ivy League* (New York: New York University Press, 2018).

13. For a deep dive into the early private schools in a particular part of the country, see, for example, Martha Gallaudet Waring, "Savannah's Earliest Private Schools 1733 to 1800," *Georgia Historical Quarterly* (December 1930): 324–34; L. Minerva Turnbull, "Private Schools in Norfolk, 1800–1860," *William and Mary College Quarterly Historical Magazine* (October 1931): 277–301; Robert Francis Seybolt, "The Private Schools of Seventeenth-Century Boston," *New England Quarterly* (September 1935): 418–24.

14. George A. Boyce, "Is the Private School Fulfilling Its Function?" *School Review* (May 1929): 347, 361.

15. Donald W. Rogers, "Private Schools in American Life," *Journal of Higher Education* (December 1944): 473. See Abraham Flexner, *The American College: A Criticism* (New York: Century Company, 1908).

16. Boyce, "Is the Private School Fulfilling Its Function?"

17. David V. Hicks, "The Strange Fate of the American Boarding School," *American Scholar* (Autumn 1996): 523–35.

18. Hicks, "The Strange Fate of the American Boarding School."

19. Boyce, "Is the Private School Fulfilling Its Function?"

20. Patricia M. Lines, "The New Private Schools and Their Historic Purpose," *Phi Delta Kappan* (January 1986): 374.

21. Lindsey Gruson, "Private Schools for Blacks," *New York Times*, October 21, 1986, C.1.

22. D. Joseph T. Durham, "America's 'Other' Private Schools," *Crisis* (January/February 2000): 68. See Worth Kamill Hayes, *Schools of Our Own: Chicago's Golden Age of Black Private Education* (Chicago: University of Chicago Press, 2019).

CHAPTER 1

1. "Teachers in Private Schools," *Christian Science Monitor*, January 20, 1920, 12.

2. "End of Private Schools Sought," *Christian Science Monitor*, March 23, 1920, 2.

3. Frank S. Hackett, "Shall Private Schools Continue?" *New York Herald Tribune*, August 29, 1920, C6.

4. Hackett, "Shall Private Schools Continue?"

5. Frank S. Hackett, "Private Schools for Children of Unusual Intelligence," *New York Herald Tribune*, September 5, 1920, C6.

6. Frank S. Hackett, "The Country School under Private Auspices," *New York Herald Tribune*, September 12, 1920, C6.

7. Hackett, "The Country School under Private Auspices."

8. Hackett, "The Country School under Private Auspices."

9. Hackett, "The Country School under Private Auspices."

10. Hackett, "The Country School under Private Auspices."

11. Hackett, "The Country School under Private Auspices."

12. Hackett, "The Country School under Private Auspices."

13. Walter Lafeber and Richard Polenberg, *The American Century: A History of the United States since the 1890s* (New York: Wiley, 1975), 97. For a full discussion of Wilson's political agenda, see Lloyd E. Ambrosius, *Wilsonian Statecraft: Theory and Practice of Liberal Internationalism during World War I* (Wilmington, DE: SR Books, 1991).

14. Lafeber and Polenberg, *The American Century*, 101.

15. Lafeber and Polenberg, *The American Century*, 102.

16. "End of Private Schools Sought."

17. "Contest over School Measure," *Christian Science Monitor*, June 29, 1920, 4.

18. "Law to Eliminate Private Schools Issue in Michigan," *Christian Science Monitor*, June 20, 1922, 11.

19. "Oregon Voters Rally to Plan Eliminating Private Schools," *Christian Science Monitor*, June 24, 1922, 5.

20. Walter S. Hinchman, "Private Schools—Their Distinctive Merits," *Independent*, August 19, 1922, 76.

21. Eloise R. Tremain, "The Appeal of Private Schools to Parents," *Red Book Magazine*, October 1922, 6.

22. M. Mercer Kendig, "The Boon of the Private School," *Red Book Magazine*, October 1922, 12.

23. Angelo Patri, "The Private School," *Red Book Magazine*, June 1923, 6.

24. "New President of N.E.A. Challenges School Enemies," *Christian Science Monitor*, July 6, 1923, 7.

25. "The President of Vassar College Indicates the Advantages of Our Democratic Private Schools," *Red Book Magazine*, August 1923, 6.

26. S. P. Capen, "The Private School's Contribution—Nonconformity, Progress," *Red Book Magazine*, October 1923, 6.

27. Norman Fenton and Lowry S. Howard, "The Challenge of the Private School," *Journal of Educational Research* (January 1924): 22–28.

28. Fenton and Howard, "The Challenge of the Private School."

29. I. N. Edwards, "Review," *Elementary School Journal* (March 1925): 549.

30. Carter V. Good, "Review: State Legislation and Judicial Opinions Affecting Private Schools," *School Review* (April 1925): 316–17.

31. "Children Driven to Private School," *Christian Science Monitor*, January 1, 1921, 4.

32. "Massachusetts Private Schools Safe from Serum," *Christian Science Monitor*, March 16, 1923, 3.

33. "Private School Standards Set," *Christian Science Monitor*, November 21, 1925, 4.

34. "Private School Development Assured by Property Division," *Christian Science Monitor*, May 6, 1926, 11.

35. "Advertisement: Americanism of the Private School," *Red Book Magazine*, September 1926, 159.

36. "Advertisement: Americanism of the Private School."

37. "Democracy and the Private School," *Christian Science Monitor*, November 21, 1927, 16.

38. "Democracy and the Private School."

39. William E. Chancellor, "Why Private Schools Thrive," *Journal of Education* (June 18, 1928): 724.

40. Chancellor, "Why Private Schools Thrive."

41. Mary Yost, "Modern Education and the Private School," *Red Book Magazine*, December 1928, 6.

42. Chancellor, "Why Private Schools Thrive."

43. Marie Thienes, "What School for Your Boy or Girl," *Parents Magazine*, August 1929, 20.

44. "Private School Salaries Show Wide Variances," *Christian Science Monitor*, April 8, 1929, 5.

45. Chancellor, "Why Private Schools Thrive."

46. *The Education of the Modern Boy: A Symposium by Six Private School Masters* (Boston: Houghton Mifflin, 1928).

47. *The Education of the Modern Boy*.

48. George A. Boyce, "Is the Private School Fulfilling Its Function?" *School Review* (May 1929): 347–62.

49. His Mother, "John's Adventures in Education," *North American Review* (September 1929): 331–37; "In Defense of Private Schools," *North American Review* (December 1929): 755–60.

CHAPTER 2

1. "Private School Denies Charges of Snob Output," *Christian Science Monitor*, April 29, 1930, 8.

2. Porter Sargent, *A Handbook for Private School Teachers* (Boston: Porter Sargent, 1930).

3. Sargent, *A Handbook for Private School Teachers*.

4. Henry Suzzallo, "The Romance of Private Schools," *Red Book Magazine*, July 1930, 6.

5. "Private Schools Reported Unaffected by Depression," *New York Herald Tribune*, November 5, 1930, 22.

6. "Private Schools Inferior, Boyce Survey Reveals," *New York Herald Tribune*, November 9, 1930, 22.

7. "Course in Doing for Others," *Christian Science Monitor*, May 26, 1931, 16.

8. "Course in Doing for Others."

9. Margaret E. Wells, PhD, "Private Schools Relegate 'Fads' in New Methods," *New York Herald Tribune*, September 13, 1931, A6.

10. Eugene Randolph Smith, "A Pioneering Private School," *Journal of Education* (October 5, 1931): 169–70.

11. "Private Schools Decide to Press On," *Christian Science Monitor*, April 12, 1932, 8.

12. Morton Snyder, "Modern Trends in Education: How Private Schools Are Meeting the Economic Crisis," *New York Herald Tribune*, August 21, 1932, A7.

13. Snyder, "Modern Trends in Education."

14. Snyder, "Modern Trends in Education."

15. "Tuition Cut-Rate Plans," *Christian Science Monitor*, June 3, 1933, 4.

16. "Tuition Cut-Rate Plans."

17. "15,000 Private Schools Declared in Need of Aid," *New York Herald Tribune*, March 6, 1933, 14.

18. "Mrs. Roosevelt Advises Girls to Help Others," *New York Herald Tribune*, April 19, 1934, 9.

19. "Mrs. Roosevelt Advises Girls to Help Others."

20. Millicent J. Taylor, "A Brief for Private Schools," *Christian Science Monitor*, February 12, 1935, 8.

21. "Private School Gains Taken to Show Rise in Trade Prospects," *Christian Science Monitor*, August 7, 1935, 7.

22. A Mother of Four, "Choose the Right School for Your Child," *Parents Magazine*, August 1933, 24.

23. A Mother of Four, "Choose the Right School for Your Child."

24. "Why Private School?" *Parents Magazine*, August 1935, 20.

25. Nina Warren Wilhelm, "What Private School Did for Our Boys," *Parents Magazine*, August 1936, 24.

26. "Enrollment Increases in Private Schools," *Christian Science Monitor*, November 7, 1936, 4.

27. "Fuess Criticizes Training in U.S. Private Schools," *New York Herald Tribune*, March 13, 1937, 13.

28. Frances Frisbie O'Donnell, "The School Shapes the Child," *Parents Magazine*, July 1937, 27.

29. Myra Reed Richardson, "What School for a Daughter?" *Parents Magazine*, May 1938, 30.

30. Marian Castle, "What Good Are Finishing Schools?" *Forum and Century*, January 1938, 34.

31. Castle, "What Good Are Finishing Schools?"

32. Castle, "What Good Are Finishing Schools?"

33. Sven Nilson, "Finishing Schools: A Defense," *Forum and Century*, April 1938, 250.

34. "What School for a Daughter?"

35. "What School for a Daughter?"

36. Mary Elizabeth O'Conner, "Are Private Schools So Superior?" *Journal of Education* (October 1937): 321.

37. O'Conner, "Are Private Schools So Superior?"

38. Richard J. Gabel, *Public Funds for Church and Private Schools* (Washington, DC: Catholic University of America, 1937).

39. Floyd W. Allport, "A New Perspective on Schools," *Parents Magazine*, August 1938, 27.

40. "A New Perspective on Schools."

41. "71 Per Cent of Private Schools Anticipate Full Enrollments," *New York Herald Tribune*, September 4, 1938, A7.

42. Marjorie Shuler, "U.S. Aid to Private Schools Opposed by N.E.A. Official," *Christian Science Monitor*, February 25, 1939, 1.

43. "Baptists Oppose Federal Aid for Private Schools," *Christian Science Monitor*, May 20, 1939, 15.

44. "Nation's Private Schools Show Rise in Enrollment," *New York Herald Tribune*, March 19, 1939, A7.

45. Helen Maynard, "Private School Was Our Answer," *Parents Magazine*, May 1939, 31.

46. Mary Thurman Martin, "Questions to Ask of a School," *Parents Magazine*, August 1939, 29.

47. Martin, "Questions to Ask of a School."

48. Millicent Taylor, "Through Loved, Familiar Gates Back to One's Old School," *Christian Science Monitor*, July 22, 1939, 4.

CHAPTER 3

1. Hiram Haydn, "Satire Turns to Burlesque," *New York Herald Tribune*, April 3, 1949, D4; John Horne Burns, *Lucifer with a Book* (New York: Harper and Brothers, 1949). For a more contemporary fictional take on private schools, see Curtis Sittenfeld's *Prep: A Novel* (New York: Random House, 2005).

2. Haydn, "Satire Turns to Burlesque"; Burns, *Lucifer with a Book*.

3. Eugene Randolph Smith, "In the Midst of American Free Education Private Schools Flourish and Serve," *Christian Science Monitor*, April 13, 1940, 9.

4. Smith, "In the Midst of American Free Education Private Schools Flourish and Serve."

5. Smith, "In the Midst of American Free Education Private Schools Flourish and Serve."

6. John de Quedville Briggs, "The Non-Public School in a Democracy," *American Scholar* (Autumn 1941): 428–32.

7. William Oliver Stevens, "Why Boarding School?" *Parents Magazine*, June 1940, 32.

8. Edward Cooke Willcox, "What Parents Should Ask of a School," *Parents Magazine*, July 1941, 24.

9. Stevens, "Why Boarding School?"

10. "Private Schools Seen Heading to State Control," *New York Herald Tribune*, February 9, 1941, 34.

11. "Private Schools Warned of Government Control," *New York Herald Tribune*, April 18, 1941, 34.

12. "Young Women to Assist in U.S.O. Fund Drive," *New York Herald Tribune*, June 8, 1941, D2.

13. "Children's Art on Sale," *New York Herald Tribune*, November 19, 1941, 14.

14. "Million Pupils Quit Classes in 1st Alarm Here," *New York Herald Tribune*, December 10, 1941, 19.

15. Rudolph D. Lindquist, "Can Schools Pass the Test?" *Parents Magazine*, June 1942, 36.

16. Lindquist, "Can Schools Pass the Test?"

17. "Manhattan Has Big Variety of Private Schools," *New York Herald Tribune*, September 6, 1942, C2.

18. "Manhattan Has Big Variety of Private Schools."

19. Charles L. Stevens, "The Private School and the War," *Christian Science Monitor*, January 16, 1943, 9.

20. Harvey S. Reed, "A Private School Changes Its Ideas and Its Curriculum," *Clearing House*, February 1943, 356.

21. James I. Wendell, "Private Schools Facing Issue of Survival in War," *New York Herald Tribune*, February 7, 1943, A7.

22. Wendell, "Private Schools Facing Issue of Survival in War."

23. Laurence G. Leavitt and Dorothy H. Leavitt, "What the Right School Can Give Them," *Parents Magazine*, June 1943, 32.

24. "Private Problems," *Time*, July 12, 1943.

25. "Private Schools Well Filled," *Christian Science Monitor*, December 18, 1943, 14.

26. "Many Officers among Private School Alumni," *New York Herald Tribune*, April 23, 1944, A5.

27. Kimmis Hendrick, "A Private School Measuring Rod," *Christian Science Monitor*, September 2, 1944, 10.

28. "Schools for Boys," *Fortune*, May 1944, 165–66; Donald W. Rogers, "Private Schools in America Life," *Journal of Higher Education* (December 1944): 472–75.

29. Homer F. Barnes, "Should I Send My Children to Boarding School?" *Parents Magazine*, June 1945, 28.

30. "Discipline in Private Schools," *Christian Science Monitor*, August 4, 1945, 11.

31. Millicent Taylor, "Through the Editor's Window: Today's Challenge to the Private Schools," *Christian Science Monitor*, November 23, 1946, 18.

32. "U.S. Aid for Private Schools Draws Broad Opposition," *Christian Science Monitor*, April 24, 1947, 10.

33. Charlotte Adams, "I Sent My Child to Private School," *Parents Magazine*, June 1947, 38.

34. Millicent Taylor, "Through the Editor's Window: Budgeting Those Private-School Bills," *Christian Science Monitor*, August 9, 1947, 9.

35. Henry F. Pringle and Katherine Pringle, "America's Oldest Private School," *Saturday Evening Post*, September 27, 1947.

36. Pringle and Pringle, "America's Oldest Private School."

37. Pringle and Pringle, "America's Oldest Private School."

38. Pringle and Pringle, "America's Oldest Private School." Because they were not "subject to public control," private schools could legally discriminate against African Americans or any other group, even if the schools received aid from the city or state. See "Recent Cases," *Harvard Law Review* (November 1948): 126.

39. Dorothy Dunbar Bromley, "P.E.A. Fires Opening Salvo in Drive to Improve Schools," *New York Herald Tribune*, December 21, 1947, A5.

40. Bromley, "P.E.A. Fires Opening Salvo in Drive to Improve Schools."

41. Millicent Taylor, "Through the Editor's Window: Private Schools Acting Together," *Christian Science Monitor*, February 21, 1948, 10.

42. Taylor, "Through the Editor's Window."

43. Crosby Hodgman, "Private Schools Finding Mutual Benefits in Sharing Their Plants with Community," *Christian Science Monitor*, April 17, 1948, 11.

44. Dorothy Greener, "Trend of Independent Schools toward Active Community Cooperation," *Christian Science Monitor*, June 12, 1948, 11.

45. "Education Officials Oppose U.S. Aid to Private Schools," *Christian Science Monitor*, March 1, 1949, 16.

46. Julie R. Forman, "Small Private School Seen as Guarding Abilities of the Unusual Child," *Christian Science Monitor*, October 29, 1949, 14.

CHAPTER 4

1. Dorothy Kahn Jaffe, "Private School Trend Aired," *Christian Science Monitor*, October 13, 1959, 3.

2. Jaffe, "Private School Trend Aired."

3. "House Unit Rejects Private School Aid," *Christian Science Monitor*, March 7, 1950, 3.

4. John P. Marquand Jr., "Frank Talk about Private Schools," *Hearst's International*, August 1950, 16.

5. Marquand Jr., "Frank Talk about Private Schools."

6. Marquand Jr., "Frank Talk about Private Schools."

7. Fred M. Hechinger, "The Private School's Role," *New York Herald Tribune*, May 20, 1951, A6; Allan V. Heeley, *Why the Private School?* (New York: Harper & Brothers, 1951).

8. Hechinger, "The Private School's Role," A6; Heeley, *Why the Private School?*

9. Lloyd Neidlinger, "A Splendid Treatise," *Journal of Higher Education* (December 1952): 501; Heeley, *Why the Private School?*

10. Millicent J. Taylor, "700 Private Schools, U.S.A.," *Christian Science Monitor*, September 8, 1951, 13; James E. Bunting, *Private Independent Schools: The American Private Schools for Boys and Girls*, 4th ed. (Wallingford, CT: James E. Bunting, 1951).

11. Taylor, "700 Private Schools, U.S.A."

12. "Functions of Independent Secondary Education in the United States," *School and Society*, September 8, 1951, 145.

13. "Private School Held Equally 'American,'" *New York Herald Tribune*, April 17, 1952, 14.

14. Larry Sims, "Private-School 'Uneasiness' Is Laid to Probes," *New York Herald Tribune*, March 8, 1953, 26.

15. Sims, "Private-School 'Uneasiness' Is Laid to Probes."

16. Sims, "Private-School 'Uneasiness' Is Laid to Probes."

17. Henry Lesesne, "South Acts as School Segregation Issue Rushes to Climax," *Christian Science Monitor*, April 27, 1953, 11.

18. C. Gerald Fraser, "A Private School Solving Problems of Education," *New York Amsterdam News*, February 6, 1954, 15.

19. Hans Maeder, "How One Private School Teaches 'Equality' as a Positive Way of Life," *Christian Science Monitor*, October 9, 1954, 11.

20. "Duke University Law Professor Warns Dixie States on 'Private School Plan," *Atlanta Daily World*, November 18, 1954, 1.

21. Fraser, "A Private School Solving Problems of Education."

22. M. D. Cartwright, "Private School Encounter," *New York Amsterdam News*, February 12, 1955, 18.

23. Cartwright, "Private School Encounter."

24. Cartwright, "Private School Encounter."

25. Michael Marsh, "Private Schools Show Big Enrollment Gain," *New York Herald Tribune*, February 27, 1955, A2.

26. Ellen Geer Sangster, "Choosing a Private School," *Parents Magazine*, June 1955, 109.

27. Fred M. Hechinger, "The 'Independents' in America Education," *New York Herald Tribune*, May 20, 1956, A5.

28. Hechinger, "The 'Independents' in America Education."

29. Hechinger, "The 'Independents' in America Education."

30. Hechinger, "The 'Independents' in America Education."

31. Bicknell Eubanks, "Enrollments Soars in Dixie Private Schools," *Christian Science Monitor*, October 17, 1956, 3.

32. "Groton's Intention," *Time*, February 25, 1957.

33. "Groton's Intention."

34. "Groton's Intention."

35. Terry Ferrer, "Private-School Pay Plight Called Grim," *New York Herald Tribune*, October 16, 1957, 15.

36. David Lawrence, "Private Schools May Face Next Test in 'Integration,'" *New York Herald Tribune*, November 13, 1957, 27.

37. Lawrence, "Private Schools May Face Next Test in 'Integration,'" in Arthur S. Miller, *Racial Discrimination and Private Education: A Legal Analysis* (Chapel Hill: University of North Carolina, 1957).

38. "Nixon's Daughters at Private School," *Norfolk New Journal and Guide*, September 20, 1958, 1.

39. David Lawrence, "Gain for Private Schools Seen in Integration Issue," *New York Herald Tribune*, October 2, 1958, 21.

40. "High Court Kills Private School Plan," *Pittsburgh Courier*, October 4, 1958, 1.

41. "Open New Private School for Little Rock Whites," *Chicago Defender*, October 28, 1958, 2.

42. Al Kuettner, "Dixie Private School Pupils Face Rating Loss," *Chicago Defender*, November 15, 1958, 20.

43. Terry Ferrer, "Prep School Guide Has 1,800 Listings," *New York Herald Tribune*, November 13, 1958, 15; Clarence E. Lovejoy, *Lovejoy's Prep School Guide* (New York: Harper and Brothers, 1958).

44. Ferrer, "Prep School Guide Has 1,800 Listings"; Lovejoy, *Lovejoy's Prep School Guide*.

45. "Private Schools Show Record Enrollment," *New York Herald Tribune*, December 30, 1958, 6.

46. "Private Schools Full," *Christian Science Monitor*, February 21, 1959, 12.

47. "Private Schools Report Progress," *Christian Science Monitor*, April 25, 1959, 14.

48. James J. Morisseau, "Private Schools Face Crisis, Too," *New York Herald Tribune*, August 16, 1959, A3.

49. Dorothy Kahn Jaffe, "Private School Goal: Improved Quarters," *Christian Science Monitor*, October 26, 1959, 10.

50. Jaffe, "Private School Goal: Improved Quarters."

51. Rudolf Flesch, *Why Johnny Can't Read—And What You Could Do about It* (New York: Harper Bros., 1955).

52. Flesch, *Why Johnny Can't Read—And What You Could Do about It*.

53. James J. Morisseau, "Private Schools Face Crisis, Too," *New York Herald Tribune*, August 16, 1959, A3.

CHAPTER 5

1. Mary Kelly, "Private School Ideals Stressed," *Christian Science Monitor*, March 9, 1960, 16.

2. Kelly, "Private School Ideals Stressed."

3. Terry Ferrer, "Calls Private School Backers 'Subversive,'" *New York Herald Tribune*, July 1, 1960, 15.

4. "Private Schools Face 'Full House,'" *Christian Science Monitor*, September 10, 1960, 11.

5. "Times Articles to Study Boom in Private Schools," *Los Angeles Times*, February 18, 1961, B1.

6. Mary Lou Loper, "Do They Offer Snob Appeal or an Improved Curriculum?" *Los Angeles Times*, February 19, 1961, H1.

7. Harlan Trott, "Lodge: U.S. Aid to Private Schools," *Christian Science Monitor*, October 12, 1960, 14.

8. "Catholic Heat," *Time*, March 10, 1961.

9. Terry Ferrer, "Dr. Taylor Opposes Private School Aid," *New York Herald Tribune*, March 24, 1961, 21.

10. "Aid Seen Spur to Segregation," *New York Herald Tribune*, April 3, 1961, 8.

11. "Private School Aid Opposed by A.D.L.," *New York Herald Tribune*, April 3, 1961, 8.

12. "Fifty Million Students," *Time*, September 15, 1961.

13. Terry Ferrer, "Girls' Private Schools Not Path to Big Seven," *New York Herald Tribune*, November 12, 1961, A4.

14. James V. Moffatt, "How to Get Your Child into Private School," *Parents Magazine*, December 1961, 56.

15. James E. Bunting and Mansfield Lyon, *Private Independent Schools* (Wallingford, CT: James E. Bunting and Mansfield Lyon, 1962).

16. Millicent Taylor, "The Private School Pattern," *Christian Science Monitor*, June 30, 1962, 7.

17. "U.S. Private School—G.B. Public School," September 29, 1962, 7.

18. "Booklet to Aid in Private School Admission Issued," *Atlanta Daily World*, November 4, 1962, A1.

19. Joseph Michalak, "For East Harlem Co-op: Exclusive Private School," *New York Herald Tribune*, November 26, 1962, 6.

20. "Washington Area Private School Integrated, Too," *Atlanta Daily World*, December 15, 1963, A6.

21. "Washington Area Private School Integrated, Too."

22. "Gifts Aid Private Schools," *Christian Science Monitor*, December 28, 1963, 5.

23. "Gifts Aid Private Schools."

24. "Private Schools on Boom Due to Social Conditions," *Washington Post*, November 28, 1963, A3.

25. "In the Teacher's Room," *Christian Science Monitor*, August 21, 1965, 4.

26. "100 Boys Get Opportunity to Attend Private School," *New York Amsterdam News*, August 28, 1965, 35.

27. "100 Boys Get Opportunity to Attend Private School."

28. Josephine Ripley, "Most Private Schools in Washington Integrated," *Christian Science Monitor*, October 28, 1966, 5.

29. Donald Barr, "Should Your Child Go to a Private School?" *Parents Magazine*, September 1966, 74.

30. Barr, "Should Your Child Go to a Private School?"

31. Susan Filson, "Enrollment in Private Schools Tripled Since 1955," *Washington Post*, September 13, 1966, C1.

32. Filson, "Enrollment in Private Schools Tripled Since 1955."

33. "New Hope for Harlem's Bright Youth," *Ebony*, May 1967, 27.

34. "New Hope for Harlem's Bright Youth."

35. "New Hope for Harlem's Bright Youth."

36. "New Hope for Harlem's Bright Youth."

37. "More and More Students Go to Private Schools," *Hartford Courant*, September 1967, 16.

38. "N.Y. Private Schools Flooded with Requests Due to Strike," *Christian Science Monitor*, December 5, 1968, 22.

39. "N.Y. Private Schools Flooded with Requests Due to Strike."

40. Carolyn F. Ruffin, "Private Schools Lend Hand in Community," *Christian Science Monitor*, May 24, 1969, 13.

41. Ruffin, "Private Schools Lend Hand in Community."

42. "South's Private Schools Grow," *Christian Science Monitor*, May 24, 1969, 13.

43. Jerry DeLaughter, "Desegregation Ruling Chafes Officials," *Christian Science Monitor*, November 1, 1969, 10.

44. "The Last Refuge," *Time*, November 14, 1969.

45. Leon W. Lindsay, "Private Schools Boom in Dixie, but Quality Varies," *Christian Science Monitor*, December 30, 1969, 12.

46. Lindsay, "Private Schools Boom in Dixie, but Quality Varies."

47. Lindsay, "Private Schools Boom in Dixie, but Quality Varies."

48. Yvonne V. Chabrier, "Blacks in Private Schools," *Washington Post*, April 20, 1969, 251.

49. Chabrier, "Blacks in Private Schools."

50. "'Parochaid' Disputed," *Christian Science Monitor*, December 12, 1969, 5.

51. "'Parochaid' Disputed."

52. "Private Schools Would End 'Mediocrity,' Cashman Says," *Hartford Courant*, December 6, 1969, 8D.

53. "Private Schools Would End 'Mediocrity,' Cashman Says."

CHAPTER 6

1. Karen Branan, "Westledge—An Exciting New Concept in Education," *Parents Magazine*, February 1970, 64–65.

2. Branan, "Westledge—An Exciting New Concept in Education."

3. "Boarding-School Blues," *Time*, September 7, 1970.

4. "Boarding-School Blues."

5. "Boarding-School Blues."

6. "Boarding-School Blues."

7. Charles E. Johnson Jr. and Larry E. Suter, "Private Schools: Enrollment Trends and Student Characteristics," *Education*, February 1971, 237.

8. President Nixon's "Message on Educational Reform to the Congress of the United States," March 3, 1970.

9. Johnson Jr. and Suter, "Private Schools: Enrollment Trends and Student Characteristics."

10. Charles T. Clotfelter, "School Desegregation, 'Tipping,' and Private School Enrollment," *Journal of Human Resources* (Winter 1976): 29.

11. Dr. Benjamin E. Mays, "White Private Schools," *Chicago Daily Defender*, August 1, 1970, 8.

12. Dr. Benjamin Mays, "White Private Schools in Dixie Mushrooming," *Chicago Daily Defender*, November 28, 1970, 8.

13. Mays, "White Private Schools."

14. "Klan Sponsoring Private Schools," *Norfolk Journal and Guide*, August 14, 1971, 2.

15. "Nixon vs. Private Schools," *Chicago Daily Defender*, July 15, 1970, 15.

16. Otto F. Krauschaar, "Private Schools and the Public Interest," *Current History* (August 1972): 68–72; See also Krauschaar's *American Nonpublic Schools: Patterns of Diversity* (Baltimore: Johns Hopkins University Press, 1972).

17. "Youth Compares His Public, Private School Experiences," *Philadelphia Tribune*, September 14, 1971, 7.

18. Grace and Fred M. Hechinger, "Private Schools: The Current Crisis," *Harper's Bazaar*, September 1972, 92–93.

19. Hechinger, "Private Schools: The Current Crisis."

20. Hechinger, "Private Schools: The Current Crisis."

21. "Economic Pinch Causes Private Schools Merger," *New York Amsterdam News*, January 15, 1972, B5.

22. G. R. Bowers, "The Future—Brighter in Education," *Vital Speeches of the Day*, January 15, 1974, 221.

23. "No Private Segregation," *Time*, August 13, 1973, 49.

24. "Challenging Exclusion," *Time*, June 21, 1975.

25. "Segregated Academies," *Time*, December 15, 1975.

26. "Segregated Academies."

27. Carol A. Morton, "The Prep School: An Alternative," *Ebony*, October 1975, 102.

28. Morton, "The Prep School: An Alternative."

29. Morton, "The Prep School: An Alternative."

30. Thomas J. Flygare, "The Supreme Court Ruling on Exclusion by Private Schools," *Phi Delta Kappan* (November 1976): 279–80.

31. Flygare, "The Supreme Court Ruling on Exclusion by Private Schools."

32. Cynthia Parson, "Private Schools: Serving, Thriving," *Christian Science Monitor*, February 24, 1975, 16.

33. Parson, "Private Schools."

34. Janet Lynch, "Is Your Child a Failure at Four?" *Harper's Bazaar*, October 1976, 118–19.

35. Lynch, "Is Your Child a Failure at Four?"

36. Lynch, "Is Your Child a Failure at Four?"

37. Hilary Cosell, "Is It True What They Say about Private Schools?" *Seventeen*, October 1977, 138.

38. Cosell, "Is It True What They Say about Private Schools?"

39. Cosell, "Is It True What They Say about Private Schools?"

40. Cosell, "Is It True What They Say about Private Schools?"

41. Cosell, "Is It True What They Say about Private Schools?"

42. Cosell, "Is It True What They Say about Private Schools?"

43. Bartley B. Nourse Jr., "Students Exploring Alternative Life-Styles," *Phi Delta Kappan* (February 1979): 448.

44. James W. Peterson, "What's It Like in a Private School?" *Phi Delta Kappan* (September 1979): 22–23.

45. Peterson, "What's It Like in a Private School?"

46. Peterson, "What's It Like in a Private School?"

47. Peterson, "What's It Like in a Private School?"

48. Peterson, "What's It Like in a Private School?"

49. Peterson, "What's It Like in a Private School?"

50. Peterson, "What's It Like in a Private School?"

51. Peterson, "What's It Like in a Private School?"

CHAPTER 7

1. M. Stanton Evans, "The Private School Boom," *National Review*, May 16, 1980, 602.

2. Evans, "The Private School Boom."

3. Dena Kleiman, "City's Private Schools Start a New Year Stressing the Old Values," *New York Times*, September 15, 1980, B1.

4. "Big Crunch for Kindergartens," *Time*, September 29, 1980, 78.

5. Gene I. Maeroff, "Private Schools Look to Bright Future," *New York Times*, January 4, 1981, EDUC1.

6. "Private Schools, Public Duty," *New York Times*, April 10, 1981, A30.

7. "Can Public Learn from Private?" *Time*, April 20, 1981, 50.

8. Julia Malone, "Drive Begins for Tuition Tax Credit," *Christian Science Monitor*, June 8, 1981, 3.

9. Donna Joy Newman, "Legions Marching Off to the Private Schools," *Chicago Tribune*, February 20, 1980, B1.

10. "How to Pick a Private School," *Time*, July 20, 1981, 57.

11. Mary Lou Loper, "Private Schools Mix Boys, Girls," *Los Angeles Times*, August 13, 1981, 1.

12. Loper, "Private Schools Mix Boys, Girls."

13. John A. Bikales, "The Single-Sex Private School in Today's Changing Society," *Boston Globe*, February 20, 1981, 46.

14. Dan Kaercher, "Would Your Youngster Be Better Off in a Private School?" *Better Homes and Gardens*, August 1981, 23–24.

15. John T. Guthrie, "Traits of Private Schools," *Journal of Reading* (November 1981): 188–91.

16. Margot Slade, "Independent Schools: Private Schools No Longer for Private Wealth," *New York Times*, November 14, 1982, A27.

17. Slade, "Independent Schools."

18. Priscilla Van Tassel, "Private Schools Bucking Economic Tide," *New York Times*, November 21, 1982, NJ1.

19. Phyllis Coons, "Survey: Students Go to Private Schools to Find Greater Academic Challenge," *Boston Globe*, March 6, 1983, A109.

20. Bonnie Schreiter, *The ABC's of Starting a Private School* (Palo Alto, CA: R&E Research Associates, 1982).

21. Marilyn Stassen-McLaughlin, "Why I Teach in a Private School," *English Journal* (April 1984): 18.

22. Bill Barnhart and Sally Saville Hodge, "These Educators See Progress, Profit in Private Schools," *Chicago Tribune*, January 4, 1984, B1.

23. Susan Heller Anderson, "Youngsters and Parents Shop for Private Schools," *New York Times*, October 26, 1984, A22.

24. Anderson, "Youngsters and Parents Shop for Private Schools."

25. Michael deCourcy Hinds, "Private Schools: The First Steps," *New York Times*, November 14, 1984, C1.

26. Maureen Dowd, "'Trauma Week' Begins for Parents Seeking a Private School for Tots," *New York Times*, February 11, 1985, B1.

27. Dowd, "'Trauma Week' Begins for Parents Seeking a Private School for Tots."

28. Dowd, "'Trauma Week' Begins for Parents Seeking a Private School for Tots."

29. Dowd, "'Trauma Week' Begins for Parents Seeking a Private School for Tots."

30. Dowd, "'Trauma Week' Begins for Parents Seeking a Private School for Tots."

31. Sam Roberts, "Racial Barriers: Private Schools Confront Reality," *New York Times*, June 15, 1987, B1.

32. Dowd, "'Trauma Week' Begins for Parents Seeking a Private School for Tots."

33. "U.S. Sees Private School Enrollment Surge in 80's," *New York Times*, December 21, 1984, A15.

34. Gene I. Maeroff, "Private School Enrollment Takes Off," *New York Times*, February 3, 1985, E6.

35. Beth Sherman, "Asian-Americans Turn to Private Schools," *New York Times*, January 5, 1986, EW63.

36. Lindsey Gruson, "Private Schools for Blacks," *New York Times*, October 21, 1986, C1.

37. Dr. Leonard Krivy, "Fed Up with Public, Blacks Turning to Private Schools," *Philadelphia Tribune*, November 28, 1986, 11A.

38. Roberts, "Racial Barriers."

39. Roberts, "Racial Barriers."

40. Deirdre Carmody, "Private Schools Look to High-Powered Marketing," *New York Times*, March 2, 1988, B7.

41. Michele Seipp, "Uniformity Gets a Touch of Personality," *Los Angeles Times*, November 13, 1986, H28; Jonathan Gathorne-Hardy noted in his *The Old School Tie: The Phenomenon of the English Public School* (New York: Viking, 1977).

42. Seipp, "Uniformity Gets a Touch of Personality."

43. Seipp, "Uniformity Gets a Touch of Personality."

44. *Private Schools of the United States* (Shelton, CT: Council for American Private Education (CAPE) Schools, 1988).

45. Porter Sargent, *The Handbook of Private Schools* (Boston: Porter Sargent, 1988).

46. Diana T. Slaughter and Deborah J. Johnson, eds., *Visible Now: Blacks in Private Schools* (Westport, CT: Greenwood Press, 1988).

47. Carmody, "Private Schools Look to High-Powered Marketing."

48. Stacey Okun, "Private Schools' Thin Edge," *New York Times*, April 10, 1988, 756.

49. Barbara Bronson Gray, "Checking Out," *Los Angeles Times*, May 4, 1989, VY_B12.

50. Andree Brooks, "For Private Schools, Popularity Brings Catch-22," *New York Times*, November 30, 1988, B14.

51. Brooks, "For Private Schools, Popularity Brings Catch-22."

52. "Private Schools Seeking Allies Beyond Parents," *New York Times*, March 22, 1989, B6.

53. "Private Schools Seeking Allies Beyond Parents."

54. "Most Private Schools Encourage Parents to Get Involved," *Chicago Tribune*, December 3, 1989, N3.

CHAPTER 8

1. Christy Appleby, "Private School Weighs Giving Out Condoms," *Hartford Courant*, January 11, 1992, B4C.

2. Priscilla Van Tassel, "Enrollment Slips at Many Private Schools," *New York Times*, January 21, 1990, NJ1.

3. Andrew L. Yarrow, "Slump Not Exclusive, Private Schools Find," *New York Times*, February 18, 1991, 25.

4. Robert A. Frahm, "Prestigious Private Schools No Longer Immune to Recession," *Hartford Courant*, September 8, 1992, A1A.

5. Stephanie Griffith, "Recession Pinches Private Schools," *Washington Post*, June 23, 1991, C1.

6. Barbara Bronson Gray, "Tests Provide No Map in Hunt for Private Schools," *Los Angeles Times*, February 15, 1990, VYE13A.

7. Marjorie Coeyman, "Is Private School Necessarily Better?" *Christian Science Monitor*, July 27, 1990, 13.

8. Edwin Salazar, "Students' Choosing Private Schools May Skew SAT," *Hartford Courant*, September 21, 1991, G3E.

9. Chris Sheridan, "Private Schools Learn Lesson in Marketing," *Hartford Courant*, October 21, 1991, C1.

10. Jon Marcus, "Private Schools Drawing More Pupils Despite Cost," *Baltimore Sun*, December 27, 1991, 3A.

11. "Private School: Costly but It Could Be Worth It," *Philadelphia Tribune*, August 18, 1992, 5A.

12. Susan Griffith, "Is It Public or Private School?" *Cleveland Call & Post*, February 6, 1992, 3C.

13. Jean Merl, "Are Private Schools Better?" *Los Angeles Times*, March 29, 1992, A1A.

14. George E. Conway, "School Choice: A Private School Perspective," *Phi Delta Kappan* (March 1992): 561.

15. "The Benefits of an 'Unreal' World," *Baltimore Sun*, September 13, 1992, SM5.

16. "The Benefits of an 'Unreal' World."

17. Janet Cawley, "Clintons' Daughter Will Attend Posh Private School," *Chicago Tribune*, January 6, 1993, D3.

18. Steve Daley, "Decision to Send Chelsea to Private School Becomes Part of Public Debate," *Chicago Tribune*, January 10, 1993, C4.

19. "Chelsea Joins Private School," *Chicago Tribune*, January 12, 1993, F3.

20. Karen Carrillo, "Group Stresses Need for Cultural Training in U.S. Private Schools," *New York Amsterdam News*, April 10, 1993, 37.

21. Stephen Buckley, "Private Schools Reaching for the Rainbow," *Washington Post*, May 2, 1993, B1.

22. Buckley, "Private Schools Reaching for the Rainbow."

23. Beth Shuster, "Bad News about Scores Means a Windfall for Private Schools," *Los Angeles Times*, March 14, 1994, A1.

24. Carol Chasting, "Girls' Private Schools Put Pupils on Even Terms," *Los Angeles Times*, July 10, 1994, EVB16.

25. Susan Jaques, "Private Schools: An Oasis in Education," *Los Angeles Times*, January 11, 1995, E3.

26. David Holmstrom, "Private Schools Check Their Moral Compasses," *Christian Science Monitor*, March 7, 1995, 14.

27. Valerie Strauss, "Private Schools Learn to Think Diversity," *Washington Post*, May 30, 1995, B1.

28. Marilyn McCraven and Mary Maushard, "Diversity at Private Schools Is Expanding," *Baltimore Sun*, December 2, 1996, 1B.

29. Kathy Seal, "Private Schools Join to Recruit Minorities," *Los Angeles Times*, June 12, 1995, VYB8.

30. Valerie Strauss, "A Study in Sacrifice," *Washington Post*, February 18, 1996, B1.

31. John Rosemond, "Choice between Public, Private School Isn't Easy," *Hartford Courant*, July 2, 1995, H5.

32. Rosemond, "Choice between Public, Private School Isn't Easy."

33. Robin Stansbury, "Private Schools Require Students to Do Community Service," *Hartford Courant*, November 23, 1995, AA78.

34. David V. Hicks, "The Strange Fate of the American Boarding School," *American Scholar* (Autumn 1996): 523–35.

35. Hicks, "The Strange Fate of the American Boarding School."

36. Kathleen Day, "When the Choice Isn't Elementary," *Washington Post*, December 12, 1996, D1.

37. Peter W. Cookson Jr., "New Kid on the Block? A Closer Look at America's Private Schools," *Brookings Review* (Winter 1997): 22.

38. Cookson Jr., "New Kid on the Block? A Closer Look at America's Private Schools."

39. Cookson Jr., "New Kid on the Block? A Closer Look at America's Private Schools."

40. Valerie Strauss, "Popularity Puts Squeeze on Private Schools," *Washington Post*, April 10, 1997, D1.

41. Mary Maushard, "Private Schools Expanding Quickly," *Baltimore Sun*, September 28, 1998, 4B.

42. Valerie Strauss, "The Private School Boom," *Washington Post*, September 24, 1998, DC4.

43. Mary Maushard, "Going Once, Going Twice: Schools Sold on Auctions," *Baltimore Sun*, November 20, 1998, 4B.

44. Kate Folmar, "Pricey Private Schools Thrive as a Class Apart," *Los Angeles Times*, April 20, 1997, VCB1.

45. Lee Lawrence, "The Pros and Cons of Public vs. Private Schools," *Christian Science Monitor*, April 28, 1997, 12; Arthur Powell, *Lessons of Privilege: The American Prep School Tradition* (Cambridge, MA: Harvard University Press, 1980).

46. Valerie Strauss, "Private Schools Make Parents Apply Themselves," *Washington Post*, February 22, 1998, B1.

47. Kate Folmar and Martha Groves, "Multiple Choices," *Los Angeles Times*, May 19, 1999, OCB2.

48. Karen Alexander, "Private Schools Succeed with Holistic Approaches," *Los Angeles Times*, June 16, 1999, OCB2.

49. Susan Saulny, "Private Schools Have Changed with the Times," *Washington Post*, August 25, 1999, 16.

50. Lucille Renwick and Efrain Hernandez Jr., "Exclusive—and Inclusive," *Los Angeles Times*, September 2, 1997, VCA3.

51. Randall C. Archibold, "Minority Growth Slips at Top Private Schools," *New York Times*, December 20, 1999, A1.

CHAPTER 9

1. "N.Y. Girls Give Needy a Prom Dress to Remember," *Los Angeles Times*, April 23, 2002, A.13.

2. Mary Ann Zehr, "NCES Study Finds Greater Success in College by Private School Grads," *Education Week*, June 12, 2002.

3. Chris Hedges, "Fund-Raising Takes Toll on Private School Heads," *New York Times*, January 26, 2000, B8.

4. Kathleen Megan, "Private School Squeeze: Competition to Get in Is Increasingly Tough," *Hartford Courant*, April 5, 2000, D1.

5. Richard Urban, "Perks That Pay: Cheap Air Fares, Private School Tuition among Benefits People Will Work For," *Hartford Courant*, April 24, 2000, E1.

6. "Public and Private School Differences," *Education Digest*, April 2000, 55.

7. Christine B. Whelan and Liz Seymour, "New Teachers Hard to Snare: Private Schools Scramble for Hires," *Washington Post*, August 27, 2000, VO1.

8. Kathy McCabe, "Private Schools a Magnet to Many: Area's Academies Experiencing Huge Growth," *Boston Globe*, September 24, 2000, 1.

9. Amanda Paulson, "More Knock at the Door of Private Schools," *Christian Science Monitor*, May 8, 2001, 18.

10. Massie Ritsch, "Private School Tuition Up, but Demand Is Still Strong," *Los Angeles Times*, September 12, 2001, B1.

11. Samatha Henig, "How the Other Half Matriculates: From SAT Tutoring to Club Opportunities, Private Schools Pave the Way to College," *Washington Post*, December 10, 2001, C.10.

12. Massie Ritsch, "Entrance Exam Pressure at Age 11," *Los Angeles Times*, December 31, 2001, B.1.

13. Yilu Zhao, "Despite Uncertain Times, Parents See Private School as a Necessity," *New York Times*, January 10, 2002, B1.

14. "Crime Stats Reveal Private Schools Safer," *Human Events*, April 26, 2004, 30.

15. Sandy Coleman, "Private Schools Buffing Up Contest for Top Students Spurs Amenity-Building Boom," *Boston Globe*, February 11, 2002, A.1.

16. Cindy Rodriguez, "Minority Students Tread Path to Private Schools," *Boston Globe*, February 16, 2002, B.1.

17. Mary Ann Zehr, "NCES Study Finds Greater Success in College by Private School Grads," *Education Week*, June 12, 2002.

18. Mary Ann Zehr, "Studies Cite Segregation in Private Schools," *Education Week*, June 12, 2002.

19. Robert W. Fairlie, "Private Schools and 'Latino Flight' from Black School-children," *Demography* (November 2002): 655.

20. Valerie Strauss, "Private Schools' Shift Was Slow, Painful for First Enrolled Blacks," *Washington Post*, May 17, 2004, B.01.

21. Samuel G. Freedman, "Increasingly, African-Americans Take Flight to Private Schools," *New York Times*, May 19, 2004, B11.

22. Jane Gross, "Tuition Hits $26,000, and in Private School New York, That's Just for Kindergarten," *New York Times*, March 10, 2004, B8.

23. June Kronholz, "Extracurricular Business: Private Schools Short of Funds Turn to Entrepreneurialism," *Wall Street Journal*, January 26, 2005, B.1.

24. Kronholz, "Extracurricular Business."

25. Kronholz, "Extracurricular Business."

26. Don O'Briant, "Private Schools: Prestige for a Price," *Atlanta Journal-Constitution*, September 30, 2003, E.13.

27. Patti Ghezzi, "Mailboxes and Admission Anxiety," *Atlanta Journal-Constitution*, April 6, 2003, C.1.

28. Jean Merl, "Through Thick and Thin: Families Brace for the March Arrival of the Envelopes Carrying the Admissions Decisions of Selective Private Schools," *Los Angeles Times*, March 27, 2005, B.1.

29. Suein Hwang, "Private School Admissions: The New Math," *Wall Street Journal*, August 25, 2005, D.1.

30. Anne Marie Chaker, "Tuitions Rise Sharply at Private Schools," *Wall Street Journal*, March 29, 2006, D.1.

31. Valerie Strauss, "$26,000 Cost Pushes Up Barriers to Area Private Schools," *Washington Post*, April 2, 2006, A.01.

32. Strauss, "$26,000 Cost Pushes Up Barriers to Area Private Schools."

33. Alison Lobron, "I'm Unqualified to Teach Your Kids; Or Am I?" *Boston Globe*, May 7, 2006, BGM.16.

34. Mary Ann Zehr, "Public Schools Fare Well against Private Schools in Study," *Education Week*, July 26, 2006.

35. Nancy Keates, "Opting Out of Private School," *Wall Street Journal*, September 15, 2006, W.1.

36. Keates, "Opting Out of Private School."

37. Keates, "Opting Out of Private School."

38. Pamela Toutant, "Unreal World," *Washington Post*, November 4, 2007, WMAG15.

39. Carla Rivera, "Appealing to the Highest Common Denominator," *Los Angeles Times*, November 19, 2007, A.1.

40. Carla Rivera, "Private Schools Getting Their 'Appeals' Out," *Los Angeles Times*, November 2, 2007, B.1.

41. Daniel de Vise, "Slump Squeezes Enrollment at Private Schools," *Washington Post*, August 14, 2008, A.1.

42. Cassandra A. Fortin, "Private Schools Feeling Economic Slowdown," *Baltimore Sun*, August 31, 2008, G.3.

43. Carla Rivera, "Private Schools Are Feeling the Pinch," *Los Angeles Times*, November 10, 2008, B1.

44. Clarence Page, "Obama's Private School Shopping Goes Public," *Chicago Tribune*, November 16, 2008, 4-A.

45. Richard Leiby, "Obama Girls Will Go to Sidwell Friends," *Washington Post*, November 22, 2008, C1.

46. Winnie Hu and Alison Leigh Cowan, "We're Doing Fine in Downturn, City's Private Schools Reassure Parents," *New York Times*, November 29, 2008, A19.

47. Carla Rivera, "California Private Schools Reevaluate Tuition Practices in Troubling Economy," *Los Angeles Times*, December 21, 2008, B1.

48. Mary Pilon, "Private Schools Feel the Pinch Amid Recession," *Wall Street Journal*, January 27, 2009, D1.

49. Carla Rivera, "Economy Tests Private Schools' Fundraising," *Los Angeles Times*, March 23, 2009, A.3.

50. Helen A. Colson, ed., *Philanthropy at Independent Schools* (Washington, DC: National Association of Independent Schools, 2009).

51. Michael Birnbaum, "Tackling a Tough Assignment," *Los Angeles Times*, September 21, 2009, B.2.

52. Kelly Liyakasa, "Private Schools Adapt to Lean Times," *Westchester County Business Journal*, September 29, 2009, 25.

53. Grace E. Merritt, "Private Schools Prospering," *Hartford Courant*, November 12, 2009, A.1.

CHAPTER 10

1. Sonali Kohli, "Early Learning: Boot Camp for Kids," *Los Angeles Times*, August 16, 2016, B1.

2. Sonali Kohli, "A Different Type of (Rug-)Rat Race," *Los Angeles Times*, March 21, 2016, B.2.

3. Kohli, "A Different Type of (Rug-)Rat Race."

4. Christine Lennon, "Why Makes the Rich Beg?" *Town and Country*, March 2013, 98.

5. Shelly Banjo, "Kindergarten D-Day Arrives," *Wall Street Journal*, December 12, 2011, A19.

6. Sophia Hollander, "Parents Take Gamble for Top School Spots," *Wall Street Journal*, April 30, 2012, A17.

7. Jenny Anderson, "A Test Parents Fear and Loathe Loses Luster in Private Schools," *New York Times*, May 7, 2010, A1.

8. D. Aileen Dodd, "Getting Prepped for College," *Atlanta Journal-Constitution*, February 24, 2011, D1.

9. Jenny Anderson, "Push for A's at Private Schools Is Keeping Costly Tutors Busy," *New York Times*, June 8, 2011, A1.

10. Sophia Hollander, "Private School Tuition Bill Tops $40,000," *Wall Street Journal*, June 20, 2011, A.17.

11. Jenny Anderson and Rachel Ohm, "Bracing for $40,000 at City Private Schools," *New York Times*, January 29, 2012, LI1.

12. Jenny Anderson, "A New Breed of Private Schools, College Hunt Starts in 9th Grade or Even Sooner," *New York Times*, March 7, 2012, A23.

13. Miriam Kreinin Souccar, "Private Schools Boom," *Crain's New York Business*, February 21, 2011, 1.

14. Joel Millman, "Private Schools' Foreign Aid," *Wall Street Journal*, January 23, 2013, A.3.

15. Miriam Jordan, "Schools Draw More Chinese," *Wall Street Journal*, December 18, 2015, A.3.

16. Daniel Gross, "Seeking Admission to Top Colleges, Chinese Students Flock to U.S. Private Schools," *Washington Post*, August 23, 2016.

17. Amada Torres, "Financing a Private School Education," *Independent School*, January 2014, 16.

18. Torres, "Financing a Private School Education."

19. Torres, "Financing a Private School Education."

20. Paul Sullivan, "At Private Schools, Another Way to Say Financial Aid," *New York Times*, February 22, 2014, B5.

21. Gene V. Glass, "Myth: Private Schools Are Better," *School Administrator*, August 2014; Christopher and Sarah Lubienski, *The Public School Advantage: Why Public Schools Outperform Private Schools* (Chicago: University of Chicago Press, 2013).

22. Shontee Pant, "US Secretary of Education Will Send His Kids to Private Schools," *Christian Science Monitor*, July 10, 2015.

23. Michael Greenberg and Colleen Krueger, "Private Schools Serve Parents Seeking Best Fit for Children," *BizWest*, January 8–14, 2016, 15.

24. Greenberg and Krueger, "Private Schools Serve Parents Seeking Best Fit for Children."

25. Emma Brown, "The Overwhelming Whiteness of U.S. Private Schools, in Six Maps and Charts," *Washington Post*, March 29, 2016.

26. Eric Stirgus, "Private School Students Courted by Public Systems," *Atlanta Journal-Constitution*, November 9, 2016, A.15.

27. Kate Taylor, "Making Private Schools High-Tech, Personalized and Profitable," *New York Times*, November 21, 2017, A.22.

28. Tawnell D. Hobbs, "Private Schools Pursue Enrollment," *Wall Street Journal*, December 30, 2017, A.3.

29. Elizabeth A. Harris and Katherine Q. Seelye, "Choate Rosemary Hall, a Very Private School, Publicly Catalogs Its Sins," *New York Times*, February 15, 2017, A16.

30. Rachel Abbey McCafferty, "Schools of Thought," *Crain's Cleveland Business*, June 18, 2018, 11.

31. Caitlin Macy, "AP Tests Are Still One of the Great American Equalizers," *Wall Street Journal*, February 23, 2019, C.4.

32. Leslie Brody, "High-Income Families Get Tuition Breaks," *Wall Street Journal*, March 2, 2020, A.10A.

33. Brody, "High-Income Families Get Tuition Breaks."

34. Leslie Brody, "Private Schools Pledge to Fight Racial Bias Within," *Wall Street Journal*, June 15, 2020, A.12B.

35. Daniela Altimari, "Black Students, Alumni Reveal Racism at Private Schools," *Hartford Courant*, June 28, 2020, A.1.

36. Theresa Vargas, "Will Private Schools Hear Their Black Students?" *Washington Post*, July 2, 2020, B.1.

37. Leslie Brody, "Private Schools Face Mixed Prospects," *Wall Street Journal*, August 17, 2020, A.6.

38. Mark Trumbull, "Pay Tuition in a Pandemic?" *Christian Science Monitor*, August 28, 2020.

39. Nirvi Shah, "Private, Charter, Homeschooling Grew after Pandemic, but Most Kids Attend Public Schools," *USA Today*, December 9, 2023.

40. Geofff Mulvihill, "Parents Like Private School Vouchers So Much That Demand Is Exceeding Budgets in Some States," *APnews.com*, October 25, 2023.

41. Caitlin Flanagan, "Private Schools Are Indefensible," *Atlantic*, April 2021.

42. Flanagan, "Private Schools are Indefensible."

43. Graham Hillard, "Private Schools Will Not Save Us," *National Review*, May 3, 2021.

44. Ginia Bellafante, "Private Schools Brought in Diversity Consultants. Outrage Ensued," *New York Times*, April 24, 2021.

45. Jenna Russell, "Parents Push for 'Diversity of Thought,'" *Boston Globe*, July 12, 2021, A.1.

46. Nicole Laporte, "What's Next for Private Schools?" *Town and Country*, September 2021, 48.

47. Matthew C. Edmunds, "Elite Private Schools Find Themselves Caught between Two Sets of Parents," *Washington Post*, December 1, 2021.

48. Ginia Bellafante, "The Identity Crisis in Elite Private Schools Comes Full Circle," *New York Times*, September 18, 2022, MB.3.

BIBLIOGRAPHY

Ambrosius, Lloyd E. *Wilsonian Statecraft: Theory and Practice of Liberal Interna-tionalism During World War I*. Wilmington, DE: SR Books, 1991.

Benveniste, Luis, Martin Carnoy, and Richard Rothstein. *All Else Equal: Are Public and Private Schools Different?* New York: RoutledgeFalmer, 2003.

Bradley, Stefan. *Upending the Ivory Tower: Civil Rights, Black Power, and the Ivy League*. New York: New York University Press, 2018.

Bunting, James E. *Private Independent Schools: The American Private Schools for Boys and Girls*, 4th ed. Wallingford, CT: James E. Bunting, 1951.

Bunting, James E., and Mansfield Lyon. *Private Independent Schools*. Wallingford, CT: James E. Bunting and Mansfield Lyon, 1962.

Burns, John Horne. *Lucifer with a Book*. New York: Harper and Brothers, 1949.

Chamberlain, Ernest Barrett. *Our Independent Schools: The Private School in American Education*. New York: American Book Company, 1944.

Colson, Helen A. ed. *Philanthropy at Independent Schools*. Washington, DC: National Association of Independent Schools, 2009.

The Education of the Modern Boy: A Symposium by Six Private School Masters. Boston: Houghton, Mifflin, 1928.

Flesch, Rudolf. *Why Johnny Can't Read—And What You Could Do about It*. New York: Harper and Brothers, 1955.

Flexner, Abraham. *The American College: A Criticism*. New York: Century Company, 1908.

Fraser, James W. *Between Church and State: Religion and Education in a Multicultural America*. Baltimore: Johns Hopkins University Press, 1999.

Gabel, Richard J. *Public Funds for Church and Private Schools*. Washington, DC: Catholic University of America, 1937.

Gathorne-Hardy, Jonathan. *The Old School Tie: The Phenomenon of the English Public School*. New York: Viking, 1977.

Gaztambide-Fernandez, Ruben. *The Best of the Best: Becoming Elite at an American Boarding School*. Cambridge, MA: Harvard University Press, 2009.

Gross, Robert N. *Public Versus Private: The Early History of School Choice in America*. New York: Oxford University Press, 2018.

Heeley, Allan V. *Why the Private School?* New York: Harper and Brothers, 1951.

Jorgenson, Lloyd P. *The State and the Non-Public School, 1825–1925*. Columbia: University of Missouri Press, 1987.

Krauschaar, Otto F. *American Nonpublic Schools: Patterns of Diversity*. Baltimore: Johns Hopkins University Press, 1972.

Lafeber, Walter, and Richard Polenberg. *The American Century: A History of the United States Since the 1890s*. New York: Wiley, 1975.

Lovejoy, Clarence E. *Lovejoy's Prep School Guide*. New York: Harper and Brothers, 1958.

Lubienski, Christopher A., and Theule Lubienski. *The Public School Advantage: Why Public Schools Outperform Public Schools*. Chicago: University of Chicago Press, 2013.

McLachlan, James. *American Boarding Schools: A Historical Study*. New York: Scribner's, 1970.

Miller, Arthur S. *Racial Discrimination and Private Education: A Legal Analysis*. Chapel Hill: University of North Carolina, 1957.

Powell, Arthur. *Lessons of Privilege: The American Prep School Tradition*. Cambridge, MA: Harvard University Press, 1980.

Private Schools of the United States. Shelton, CT: Council for American Private Education (CAPE) Schools, 1988.

Purdy, Michelle. *Transforming the Elite: Black Students and the Desegregation of Private Schools*. University of North Carolina Press, 2018.

Ravitch, Diane. *Slaying Goliath: The Passionate Resistance to Privatization and the Fight to Save America's Public Schools*. New York: Knopf, 2020.

Rose, Susan D. *Keeping Them Out of the Hands of Satan: Evangelical Schooling in America*. New York: Routledge, 1988.

Sargent, Porter. *A Handbook for Private School Teachers*. Boston: Porter Sargent, 1930.

———. *The Handbook of Private Schools*. Boston: Porter Sargent, 1988.

Schreiter, Bonnie. *The ABC's of Starting a Private School*. Palo Alto, CA: R&E Research Associates, 1982.

Sittenfeld, Curtis. *Prep: A Novel*. New York: Random House, 2005.

Slaughter, Diana T., and Deborah J. Johnson, eds. *Visible Now: Blacks in Private Schools*. Westport, CT: Greenwood Press, 1988.

West, E.G. *Non-Public School Aid: The Law, Economics, and Politics of American Education*. Lexington, MA: D.C. Heath & Company, 1976.

Wexler, Natalie. *The Knowledge Gap: The Hidden Cause of America's Broken Education System—and— How to Fix It*. New York: Avery, 2019.

INDEX

founding, 45; as leading advocate for private schools, 52; 1983 survey, 102; 1977 survey, 92; as one of more than a dozen private school associations, 108; and Yeomans, 75

National Education Association (NEA), 8, 29, 46, 66, 85

Native Americans, 106

New Deal, 28, 29

Nixon, Richard, 60, 67, 83, 85, 87, 118, 141

novels, 33–34, 91

nuns, 6

Obama, Barack, 141

Obama, Malia, 141, 156

Obama, Michelle, 141

Obama, Sasha, 141, 156

patriotism, 6, 53, 77

public (community or social) service: and boarding schools, 5; at Dalton, 70; exclusivity, 139; Fuess on, 25, 42; Garver on, 12; Greener on, 46; Hackett on, 3; Hechinger on, 57; in the 1990s, 122; Operation Prom Dress, 129; at the Scudder School, 19–20; at the Society of Friends schools, 76; and during World War II, 34

Reagan, Ronald, 99

Roosevelt, Eleanor, 23, 25

Roosevelt, Franklin Delano, 3, 58

Roosevelt, Teddy, 3, 62, 118, 141

scholarships: awarding of, 75; and "barbell effect," 136, 156; at boarding schools, 34; Boyce on, 15; data in *Private Independent Schools*, 52; and diversity initiatives, 70, 71, 83; as down, 86; and exclusivity, 139; Fraser on, 55; in *Finding Forrester*, x; at Groton, 58; growing pressure to offer, 61; Heeley on, 51; and Independent Schools Talent Search Program, 74; lack of, 114; at Miss Porter's, 131; as more prevalent than in past, 57; at Mount Hermon, 88; and National Negro

Student Fund, 72; at Oakwood School, 142; and teachers, 23; and tuition, 43; and voucher programs, 154

segregation: in Arkansas, 60; and *Brown v. Board of Education*, 54–55, 59–60, 67; de facto, 153; and federal aid, 67–68; and the Federal Civil Rights Act of 1866, 87; in Georgia, 77–78; and Groton, 58; integration of public schools, 70, 73, 107, 120; and 1964 Civil Rights Act, 76; and 1966 Coleman Report, 99; in private schools, 134; in the South before 1920, xvi; and Southern Christian schools, 84–85; and the Supreme Court, 60, 76, 88–89; White Citizens Council, 76–77

"Seven Sisters," 68, 69

standardized tests: and admission officers, 69–70; as centerpiece of educational reform, 114–15, 119; ERB, 147–48; ISEE, 120; and No Child Left Behind, 137; in private schools, 125–26, 155; SAT, 115, 117, 148; as state-directed, 93–94, 153; test preparation, 132

suburbs: and desegregation, 58; housing discrimination, 73; Lovejoy on, 61; and minority families, 126; older, 110; and private schools, 62, 116; as prosperous, 52; and public schools, 82–84; and urban decline, 45, 61

Supreme Court, xii, 54, 59–60, 67–68, 76, 78, 87–89

tax-exemption, 85, 87, 102

tutors: and Academic Achievers, 145; versus consultants, 123; as early form of homeschooling, xiv, 11; and Elmwood Franklin School, 135; as fill-in for parents, 111; and Flesch, 62; and ISEE, 120; at Riverdale Country Day, 148; and Roosevelt (Eleanor), 23; and SAT, 148; and Shady Hill School, 76; and teacher moonlighting, 109; and University School, 76

uniforms, 35, 91, 92, 108

urbanization, 4, 5, 61

ABOUT THE AUTHOR

Lawrence R. Samuel, who is based in both Miami and New York City, is an independent scholar and the author of many books including *Literacy in America: A Cultural History of the Past Century* (Rowman & Littlefield, 2024) and *The American Teacher: A History* (Rowman & Littlefield, 2024). He holds a PhD in American Studies and an MA in English from the University of Minnesota and was a Smithsonian Institution Fellow.